FOOD, FOODWAYS AND FOODSCAPES

Culture, Community and Consumption
in Post-Colonial Singapore

World Scientific Series on Singapore's 50 Years of Nation-Building

---

For more information about this series, go to http://www.worldscientific.com/page/sg50

World Scientific Series on
Singapore's 50 Years of Nation-Building

FOOD, FOODWAYS AND FOODSCAPES

Culture, Community and Consumption
in Post-Colonial Singapore

Editors

Lily Kong

Singapore Management University

Vineeta Sinha

National University of Singapore

World Scientific

NEW JERSEY · LONDON · SINGAPORE · BEIJING · SHANGHAI · HONG KONG · TAIPEI · CHENNAI · TOKYO

Published by

World Scientific Publishing Co. Pte. Ltd.

5 Toh Tuck Link, Singapore 596224

USA office: 27 Warren Street, Suite 401-402, Hackensack, NJ 07601

UK office: 57 Shelton Street, Covent Garden, London WC2H 9HE

Library of Congress Cataloging-in-Publication Data
Food, foodways and foodscapes : culture, community and consumption in post-colonial Singapore / edited by
Lily Kong & Vineeta Sinha (NUS, Singapore).
    pages cm
  Includes bibliographical references and index.
  ISBN 978-9814641210 (hardcover : alk. paper) -- ISBN 978-9814641227 (pbk. : alk. paper)
  1. Food habits--Singapore. 2. Food--Social aspects--Singapore. 3. Singapore--Social life and customs.
I. Kong, Lily, editor. II. Sinha, Vineeta, editor.
  GT2853.S56F66 2015
  394.1'2095957--dc23
                                        2015024788

British Library Cataloguing-in-Publication Data
A catalogue record for this book is available from the British Library.

Typeset by Stallion Press
Email: enquiries@stallionpress.com

Contents

About the Editors

Lily Kong is Lee Kong Chian Professor of Social Sciences at the Singapore Management University where she is also Provost. Her recent books include *Arts, Culture and the Making of Global Cities: Creating New Urban Landscapes in Asia* (2015); *Religion and Place: Landscape, Politics and Piety* (2012); and *Conserving the Past, Creating the Future: Urban Heritage in Singapore* (2011).

Vineeta Sinha is Professor at the Department of Sociology at the National University of Singapore. She is concurrently the Head, Department of Sociology and the South Asian Studies Programme at NUS. Her books include: *A New God in the Diaspora? Muneeswaran Worship in Contemporary Singapore* (2005), *Religion and Commodification: Merchandising Diasporic Hinduism* (2010) and *Religion State Encounters in Hindu Domains: From the Straits Settlements to Singapore* (2011).

List of Contributors

CHUA Beng Huat, PhD
Provost Chair Professor, Department of Sociology, Faculty of Arts and Social Sciences and Research Leader, Asia Research Institute, National University of Singapore

Jean DURUZ, PhD
Adjunct Senior Research Fellow, Hawke Research Institute, University of South Australia

Lily KONG, PhD
Lee Kong Chian Professor of Social Sciences, Singapore Management University

LAI Ah Eng, PhD
Adjunct Senior Fellow, University Scholars Programme (USP), National University of Singapore

Kelvin E.Y. LOW, PhD
Assistant Professor, Department of Sociology, Faculty of Arts and Social Sciences, National University of Singapore

Harvey NEO, PhD
Assistant Professor, Department of Geography, Faculty of Arts and Social Sciences, National University of Singapore

Vineeta SINHA, PhD
Professor, Department of Sociology, Faculty of Arts and Social Sciences, National University of Singapore

TAN Xiang Ru, Amy, MSocSc
Research Assistant, Research Division, Faculty of Arts and Social Sciences, National University of Singapore

Adeline TAY, PhD
Assistant Lecturer, Centre for Geography and Environmental Science, Monash University, Australia

Introduction

Theorising Contemporary Foodscapes: Conceptual and Empirical Insights from Singapore

Lily Kong and Vineeta Sinha

FOOD AS ANALYTICAL LENS

Far from being only material for consumption and nourishment, food is significant in many other respects. The social, scientific and historical study of food has explored the social and cultural aspects of food; political, economic and environmental issues in food production, distribution and consumption; changes in foodways and foodscapes; and the impact of foods on human health and nutrition. "Food studies" is a relatively young but an exciting and dynamic field of study that already boasts a rich body of scholarship. A long list of contributions can be cited to support this reading of the field as both imaginative and flourishing, with evidence of innovative empirical, cross-cultural and theoretical work. As a field of study, food studies has brought together scholars from a range of different disciplinary traditions. While firmly grounded analytically and methodologically in history, sociology, anthropology, geography, tourism and heritage studies, just to mention a few, students of food also engage the analytical and ethnographic contributions of these and other related disciplines to theorise the field of food. An interdisciplinary perspective and a comparative bent characterise the creative work that is being done in the field of food studies today.

1

Scholars have taken seriously the counsel offered by Bell and Valentine to "think through food" (1997: 3), recognising that food is "a highly condensed social fact" and a "marvellously plastic kind of collective representation" (Appadurai 1981: 494). According to Lind and Barham (2004),

> food provides a powerful lens through which to trace and illustrate the interconnectedness between material and symbolic exchanges around the world that are commonly associated with globalisation.

Food, as analytical "lens", enables society, culture, economy and polity to be scrutinised and theorised. Indeed, scholarship in this field has already transcended the idea that food is just "about sustenance", noting that it is instead packed with social, cultural, symbolic and political resonance. Unpacking this density is a challenging endeavour and engages the energies of food scholars globally. The chapters in this book demonstrate in concrete social, political, spatial, economic and cultural terms what it means to use food as a lens, both conceptually and empirically.

FROM PRODUCTION TO CONSUMPTION: DISRUPTING THE BINARY, UNSETTLING THE LINEAR NARRATIVE

Much of the research in this field of study has focused on articulating food systems/foodways as linkages between the processes of food production, distribution, preparation and consumption. Researchers have drawn attention to the fact that, in today's context, we are embedded in a highly specialised, industrial system of large-scale food production, which has increasingly and inevitably been globalised and delocalised, while remaining largely concealed and invisible to urban consumers. At the same time, the networks of food distribution are similarly international and global, but they also have important local dimensions. Invariably, there has come to be a strong reliance on mediating parties — a variety of other food experts (food processors, food packers, wholesalers, retailers, food regulators etc.). Consequently, the contemporary food system is marked by a vast distance between producers and consumers.

Despite this alienation, food studies scholars have observed critical inter-connections and intersections between and across these processes, cautioning against the assumption of a rigid "production/consumption" binary or divide. For example, the globalisation of food and its impact on food production and consumption are closely interconnected. Ayres and Bosia (2011) remind us how communities are turning to local food sources and embracing food sovereignty in an effort to counter food globalisation and commodification. In this sense, consumption is responding (negatively) to production trends. Consumers are seeking more control over where and from whom they buy their food, motivated by the desire to preserve traditional ways of life and food production, and standards of food quality. As a result, production practices are shifting in response to consumer demands. This fact is not new. What is perhaps different at this historical juncture is the specific manner in which consumer demands are transforming production practices. Whereas the shift has hitherto been towards massification and large-scale industrialisation, an emergent reversal is observable. In this regard, Whatmore and Thorne (2004) note the critiques that have been levelled against the partial and uneven processes of globalisation and examine the emergence of fair trade networks as methods of resistance aimed at enabling consumers to purchase foods from, and thus support small-scale farmers. Other scholars have likewise outlined ethical, political and social positions on the globalisation of food, and oppositional strategies that have been adopted (Pottinger 2013; Parrott *et al.* 2002; Baker 2004). These studies demonstrate how production, distribution and consumption are integrally related and the study of one is incomplete without an eye cast on the other as well. In many ways, there is a need for clarifying concepts and frameworks that enable us to examine not just production and consumption in their own rights but also the integral connections between the two.

PRODUCTION AND ITS LIMITS AS ANALYTICAL FRAME

The act of producing food is no longer the only, or even the primary, determinant of food consumption. As an example, for urban consumers, availability of a wide-raging choice of foods is not tied to seasonal variations. Rather, access to food is determined by its availability as a commodity in markets and then by financial means. It is thus insufficient to analyse food production processes, patterns and problems in our quest to understand societal or individual access to food. This supports the call to see production, distribution and consumption as integrally connected.

Yet, despite the caution against a rigid production/consumption binary, contemporary food systems have simultaneously become increasingly defined by the disjuncture between food production and food consumption processes.

Within a system of global capital, food has become commercialised, with the concomitant commodification of embedded practices, processes and labour. The development of contemporary food technologies has also led to a complex and troubled relationship between food and industrial modernity. Just understanding these complex production processes, the commodification and commercialisation of food, the global production networks that characterise food production and distribution, and the political economy of food production already occupy scholars' attention abundantly. Such work exemplifies one major body of research that deserves to remain firmly on the agenda.

CONSUMPTION AND ITS EMBEDDED MEANINGS AND PRACTICES

At the same time, a great deal of research in food studies registers a shifting emphasis to scrutinising food consumption practices. Further, scholars have taken enthusiastically to theorising consumption in societies where there is no food scarcity but the norm of abundance of food and food choices. How individuals relate to food practices (like eating and cooking), what meanings are assigned to them, how food is both medium and outcome in the construction of identities, are themes that have engaged food scholars. The essays in this volume address these issues in the main, and we therefore devote significant attention here in elaborating on extant scholarship in order to frame the Singapore narratives that follow in subsequent chapters.

Studies of food consumption have naturally inspired a focus on eating as a social practice. For food scholars, eating and cooking are far from a natural, banal, routine and mundane human activity. In fact, Susanne (2003: 3) notes that cooking has come to be viewed as "...sexy-and-fun" through recent TV shows and cookbooks such as those by Britain's Nigella Lawson and Jamie Oliver, perhaps better known as the "Naked Chef". She also notes how celebrity chef Anthony Bourdain has managed to generate excitement and fascination towards food through his written memoir *Kitchen Confidential* and TV shows that portray food as "death-defying adventure"; shows which essentially explore food stories, that is, narratives about the different foods that are eaten by people in different places. People have therefore come to regard food and cooking as something beyond the mundane with the potential to be highly interesting. Scholars have thus argued that humans relate to food in complex, social and culturally coded ways, setting for themselves the task of devising methodologies and conceptual apparatus to decipher and unpack these complexities. Students of everyday life have made a call for approaching the domain of food, an everyday, taken-for-granted world as an object of scholarly scrutiny. Articulating human relationships to multiple and layered dimensions of food requires precisely problematising those aspects of our interactions with food that remain implicit and condensed. This would mean mapping the field of everyday food-related practices and directing scholarly attention to what have been called "commonplace consumption practices including food shopping, drinking, eating" (Bell and Valentine 1997: 3). But it is as important to ask what constitute these commonplace 'consumption practices' in particular societal contexts. The essays in this volume offer responses to this question through a scrutiny of Singapore's foodways and foodscapes.

Scholars have noted that consumption is a dominant social practice in the present, often using the term "consumerism" to denote its excesses. Some have described the contemporary consumer as being on a "consumption treadmill" (Robinson 2006), caught in a vicious cycle of "overwork and overconsumption." These discussions have highlighted and explored points of contact between the processes of commodification, consumption and the overwhelming dominance of consumerist tendencies in contemporary societies. Questions have also been raised about effects of such social practices, and responses often framed in highly moralistic terms. In an edited volume, *Commodifying Everything* (2003), Strasser asks if there are limits to commodification and if everything is necessarily and inevitably commoditised ultimately. Philip Sampson notes that the "…culture of consumption is quite undiscriminating and everything becomes a consumer item, including meaning, truth and knowledge" (cited in Lyon 2000: 80).

How consumption should be interpreted has been a dominant strain in the literature. From the 1980s onwards, the following ideas have emerged: that it is limiting to view consumption as hedonistic self-indulgence and narcissism or to read consumers as passive recipients of market forces over which they have no control. In contrast, a more positive assessment of consumption has been read into Michel de Certeau's (1984) writings in the notice of its emancipatory potential and also as a form of resistance and subjectivation. But with respect to reading food through the lens of consumption, Warde notes:

> Food is thus a corrective to understandings of consumption which exaggerate identity-enhancing and status-symbolic aspects. However, because it is a complex field, its overall significance for theories of consumption is difficult to establish (1997: 180–181).

Warde adds that fears that consumption might become a terrain of egotistical and anomic decisions seem unfounded" (1997: 189). The chapters in this volume suggest that consumption in the food domain can be theorised using notions of identity formation and construction of subjectivities; that individuals use foods, cuisines, and a finely calibrated sense of taste to communicate and express a sense of the self.

Warde asks the important question: What would the features of an adequate theory of consumption vis-à-vis food be (1997: 204)? He cautions that it would be reductionist to see this simply as shopping or purchasing commodities in a marketplace, arguing that "much work is involved in adapting commodities for use" (*Ibid.*) through investment of labour, skills, aesthetics and capacities. The alternative formulations suggest that consumption could be an imaginative and creative process, involving the participation of active agents — the consumers — who appropriate goods and commodities for their own specific, meaningful purposes. Avoiding economistic conceptions of consumption, I concur with Hefner (1998: 25) that

> Consumption, then, is not the economist's inscrutable act of shapeless desire. On the contrary, consumption is implicated in identity and is socially communicative as well as technical or material.

This allows us to disconnect the idea of the inevitability of linking the functional utility of things from the process of consumption, and to approach the latter using a different conceptual terminology and motivation. In what follows, we offer some insights into these different conceptual terminologies and motivations that are apparent in the growing literature. At times, these conceptual categories lend themselves better to analysis of food consumption, but at other times, it is apparent that the binary of production/consumption is difficult to sustain and the conceptual lenses work well in explicating both production and consumption meanings and practices.

SOCIALITIES AND SUBJECTIVITIES

One of the productive lenses through which to examine food consumption is through the conceptual categories of socialities and subjectivities. Today, a significant proportion of the work on food studies focuses on the socialities of food, examining how food fulfils a social role and brings communities closer together (or divides them). Bell and Valentine (1997) provide a synthesising analysis of the social and cultural meanings of food consumption in their book *Consuming Geographies*. They note the role of "food as social glue", citing Hunt and Satterlee's (1986) work which describes how food-centred events like barbeques and street parties draw communities together, and how food can strengthen a community's sense of identity (Brown and Mussell 1984; Bell and Valentine 1997: p. 15). Food is also an integral element of traditional festivals such as Christmas and Chinese New Year, during which families and friends come together to celebrate, feast (Montanari 2006: 129) and prepare special dishes imbued with meaning. Eating together signifies inclusion and belonging, and it builds a collective identity for the group. As culinary historian Massimo Montanari states, "on all social levels sharing a table is the first sign of membership in a group" (Montanari 2006: 94). At the level of the family, food, in the form of family meals, is important in maintaining the family as a social unit and socialising children (Bell and Valentine 1997). In Bell and Valentine's book, Charles and Kerr (1988: 17) argue that family meals are vital to "the social reproduction of the family" and that food practices help instil a family's ideals and values throughout its social structure. Similarly, Fischler (1986) observes that food practices at the dinner table are an opportunity for children to acquire social graces and manners, and learn how to behave in an appropriate manner.

The link between food and social belonging and community is related to food and identity and hence subjectivities. Atkins and Bowler (2001: 273–274) write that foodways are an expression of a group's identity, with group affiliation often based on ethnicity, religion or social class. Ethnic migrant communities, for example, have their distinctive cuisines and eating practices which members continue to adhere to even after settling in a host country. These foods serve as a source of pride among migrant members and allow them to identify with a shared culture and heritage. Similarly, Johnston and Longhurst (2011) have examined the relationship between food, identity and belonging among migrant groups in New Zealand. They found that the sharing of food not only strengthened ties within a particular migrant ethnic group, but was also effective in establishing friendships *between* different ethnic groups. Cooking and eating together in one another's homes enables migrants to acquire "social capital" (Wise 2005: 182) in the form of trust, reciprocity and security, and to understand the culture, customs and history of other people (Johnston and Longhurst 2011: 329). However, just as food can be used for inclusion, so can it be used to exclude. Indeed, food is "one way in which boundaries get drawn, and insiders and outsiders distinguished"

(Bell and Valentine 1997: 62). Johnston and Longhurst (2011: 328), for instance, noticed that migrants inadvertently made distinctions between their ethnic cuisines and the food of others, using food as a marker to differentiate their own ethnic communities from other groups. Researchers have noted that food is used to denote social class and that social differentiation affects what people consume (Bordieu 1984; Atkins and Bowler 2001: 9). As geographer Derek Shanahan observes, food is a "social and cultural marker" and, together with food practices such as formal dining etiquette, can be used to signify class superiority or inferiority (Shanahan 2002: 7). Historian Jacques Le Goff (1980) wrote that, even in the Middle Ages, food was used by the upper classes of society to show off their superiority through the consumption of gourmet foods.

Several chapters in this book address the issue of socialities and subjectivities of food consumption. Low, for example, examines how memory is mediated by sensory experiences of food tastes and smells and how these recollections work to build community and solidarity (or not). Tan, on the other hand, studies food blogging and imaging, and these new discursive sites form the basis of a new food cyber-community and new subjectivities.

SPATIALITIES

Another productive lens for the analysis of food (this time, both production and consumption), is through the conceptual category of spatialities, most often but not exclusively used by geographers. "We are where we eat", Bell and Valentine (1997) declare. Cities, as they point out, are where many different sites of food consumption are concentrated. Sites of consumption that evolved from earlier forms like taverns and inns, today range from restaurants, coffee houses and cafés to fast food outlets, takeaway kiosks and coffee-and-doughnut drive-throughs. Each space has its own character and associated practices, from formal *haute cuisine* restaurants to casual pubs. New spatialities have developed, such as Internet or cybercafes which are an extension of café culture and meet the needs of modern consumers (Bell and Valentine 1997: 122–143). Traditional spaces evolve into emergent landscapes of eating with different characteristics, and the changing spatialities are both cause and effect of changing food habits. This is the subject of several chapters in this volume (see Duruz, Lai, Chua and Tay).

Another interesting food-related spatiality that has developed is home restaurants, as described by CJ Lim (2014), professor of urbanism and architecture. Home restaurants involve going to a stranger's house where they provide a home-cooked meal and one dines with other strangers. The novelty is in enabling people who enjoy cooking to share their culinary skills, and to meet and socialise with like-minded people. Like a restaurant, a person is served and must pay for the meal. But it is like a dinner party in the sense that the space or site is an individual's home, the meal is prepared by the host, and guests can mingle and interact (Lim 2014: 94). Other authors have examined more everyday spatialities of food consumption in the home, such as the kitchen and dining table, noting the gendered and class meanings attached to these spaces (Freidberg 2003: 5). Montanari (2006), for example, observes how different gender roles are played out at the dining table; in rural societies especially, men are seated at the dining table and served by women whose priority is to wait upon the men. Other authors add that in domestic kitchens, the gendered division of labour in the preparation of food remains largely traditional, with women still bearing most of the responsibility for cooking (Warde and Hetherington 1994; England and Farkas 1986). As for class meanings in such spatialities, an example is how the seating arrangement of people at a dining table in medieval and Renaissance times was based on strict norms that served to reflect the status and position of guests in the social hierarchy (Montanari 2006: 95–96). These studies are a stimulus to Sinha's analysis in this volume, where she examines the confining spatiality and temporality of daily home cooking, commonly performed by women and viewed with a sense of mundane tedium, as opposed to episodic cooking which is entertainment and recreation, often the playground for men. In relation to the latter, she adds to the analysis contributed by scholars interested in the role and power of the media, in particular, those studying TV shows featuring celebrity chefs who encourage creative food practices by experimenting with foods, reinventing culinary traditions, and elevating cooking and the presentation of food to an art or performance (Cook *et al.* 2013: 346; Bardhi *et al.* 2010; Lindenfeld 2007). Such shows, together with reality cooking competitions, portray cooking and food preparation as recreation, entertainment and art, and thus pleasurable.

MEMORIES, HERITAGES AND TRADITIONS

With modernisation and globalisation, traditional food customs have evolved over time. In some cases, they have been reinvented (and food spaces redeveloped) to fit contemporary needs and circumstances. This is true both of production spaces and practices as of consumption places and performances. That tastes and spaces transform has evoked individual and collective memories, leading sometimes to heritage-making and reinvention of traditions.

In chronicling the growth and development of Singapore's hawker centres, Kong's (2007) social history documents traditions and heritages and explains the forces of change (such as globalisation, migration, growing affluence, public policy, conceptions of modernity) that transferred itinerant hawkers to modern, hygienic, purpose-built buildings. The loss of traditional foods (a subject that Chua and Tay also deal with in this volume) that has come with the spatial relocation has been accompanied by nostalgic recollections and new national pastimes involving performative hunts for an original hawker, a last remaining presence of a long lost food, and so forth.

Similar studies in other contexts demonstrate common threads of globalisation and its effects. For example, other authors have explored how the conventional way of procuring food through small grocery stores in the UK, Europe, US and Canada has been transformed with the dominance of big chain supermarkets (Winson 1993; Wrigley *et al.* 2002; Gottlieb 2001; Kennison 2001; Desjardins 2010: 89). Before the rise of supermarkets, people would usually go to specialty shops in the neighbourhood — such as the butcher, bakery, greengrocer — or small family-run convenience stores, sometimes known as "mom and pop" stores, to purchase foodstuffs and daily necessities. Shop owners or staff would attend to customers personally and fulfil their orders. Customers tended to make small-volume but high-frequency food purchases, visiting such stores often and interacting with shop owners and other customers. Procuring food via these channels and in this manner therefore involved a strong social element, as noted by geographer Sophia Skordili. She describes small grocery shops as "an integral element of the neighbourhoods, places of meeting and socialising, part of the glue that binds communities together" (Skordili 2013: 134; Bennison *et al.* 2010). However, the rapid expansion of corporate supermarkets from the 1940s onwards changed this customary way of procuring food (Desjardins 2010). Consumers increasingly turned to large supermarkets, drawn by low prices and the convenience of the availability of a vast variety of foodstuffs in one location. Desjardins (2010: 91) notes that the intense competition has put many small-scale, family-run food stores out of business. The triumph of the supermarket over local stores (Symons 1993) has changed the food retail market and peoples' experience of procuring foodstuffs. Social interaction at supermarkets is minimal as self-service is practised; customers help themselves to goods from the supermarket aisles and check out at the cashier point. Modern self-scanning machines at some outlets have even eliminated any interaction with the cashiers. Conventional practices such as the "village" model of visiting homely neighbourhood stores thus seems to be fading into the past. Jean Duruz (2002) writes that the supermarket contrasts with the "remembered/imagined 'village' of home-grown products, regional foods and recipes and convivial social relations". Purchasing food in this remembered 'village' enabled consumers to access fresh produce in its most natural form, or foodstuffs whose preparation and packaging reflected its traditional or artisanal origins, but this is now being replaced by mass-produced supermarket food products (Duruz 2002: 376, 381).

Even traditional customs related to food production are being practised in reinvented ways. In Japan, rice is usually cultivated by farmers in paddy fields located in villages or rural areas. Lim (2014) notes how this rural tradition is being practised in the city and has undergone some modernisation. He describes an ongoing project in which an indoor rice paddy field has been created in Tokyo's business district of Otemachi. The "farmers" tending to this paddy field are office workers who are encouraged to cultivate the rice during their lunch breaks. Members of the public and passers-by can also participate in rice cultivation at this indoor paddy field. The re-creation of this practice in an urban setting is meant to motivate people to reconnect with their horticultural roots, generate interest in farming and ensure that agricultural skills are not lost in an age of increasing reliance on machines. It also aims to enable urban folk in Japan to experience paddy fields in their immediate environment, instead of remaining disconnected from this traditional custom. Bringing this traditional practice into a modern urban setting has involved implementing certain changes to the practice. For example, while traditional rice farming relies on natural sunlight, indoor rice cultivation involves simulated light sources using lamps (Lim 2014: 94–95).

Insofar as some of these studies are written with both an interested lay public and an academic audience in mind, the prose is as much evocative as it is documentary and analytical. In this regard, academic practice itself is engaged not only in theory building but also in memory-making, heritage-creation and tradition reinvention. In this regard, Neo's and Kong's chapters in this volume (Neo on pig farming and Kong on the globalisation of foods in and out of Singapore), while focusing primarily on the economics, politics and governance of food production, are also evocative in reminding readers of long-gone pig farming days and communities, as well as the threat of demise of local favourites with globalisation.

THE GEOGRAPHIES CLOSEST IN

Food scholars also devote attention to exploring food on the scale closest in, that is, in relation to the body, where relationships between food and the body are examined. At one level, the sensory experience of food and the memories evoked can only be experienced at the level of the body. For example, Cook *et al.* (2011) focus on the feelings that food-body relationships elicit. They write that food is connected with memories, past experiences, moods, as well as ideas, sounds, visions, beliefs and worries, "all of which combine to become material — to become bodily, physical sensations". Hayes-Conroy and Martin (2010) and Mann *et al.* (2011) similarly draw attention to the visceral feelings and reactions produced through bodily engagement with food when people touch, taste, see, smell or consume foods (Cook *et al.* 2013: 344–345). Food occupies a key role in memories of home and remembering the past, an observation which Bell and Valentine support with several examples (Bell and Valentine 1997: 65–66). They highlight sociologist David Morgan's argument that food "represents a particularly strong form of anchorage in the past" (Morgan 1996: 166), and Lupton's study in which participants used food as a way to express nostalgia for their home country, symbolise home and recall their childhood (Lupton 1994). Low's chapter in this volume continues this line of analysis and demonstrates how memory of Singapore foods is mediated by sensory experiences of taste and smell of foods.

Research at this scale of analysis also examines how the bodily practice of eating is influenced by religion and culture, and how bodily boundaries are controlled by abstaining from certain foods (Bell and Valentine 1997: 24). Grigg (1995: 348–349) and Atkins and Bowler (2001: 303) study how food taboos are often linked to religion, describing how Jews and Muslims refrain from eating pork and Hindus from beef as their religions declare these foods "unclean" or impure. Cultural preferences also explain why people in different countries avoid or favour certain foods. While this leads to abundant research opportunities in both food production and consumption, we have left topics such production and distribution of halal foods, and the limits placed on consumption by food taboos to other researchers.

Similarly, we have not ventured to address questions regarding food and health in this volume, though food scares throughout the 20th century make food safety an urgent issue. As numerous scholars have highlighted, diseases like "mad cow disease" (BSE), "bird flu" (avian influenza), salmonella in eggs, dioxin contamination and beef hormones have heightened consumer anxiety over food safety (Donald 2010: 119; Jackson 2011; 2010; Atkins and Bowler 2001: 201, 209). Genetically modified (GM) foods have also raised fears of adverse health and environmental impacts (Winter 2004: 668–669; Atkins and Bowler 2001: 230), as well as calls for greater government regulation. Such food panics have contributed to directing more attention towards alternative food networks (AFNs) and enhancing food security. Consumers are turning away from the conventional corporate agrifood industry to alternative food sources that supply healthy organic food produced in an environmentally and ethically responsible way, and/or locally produced foods (Parrott *et al.* 2002: 242; Whatmore and Thorne 2004; Pottinger 2013; Jackson *et al.* 2009; Ayres and Bosia 2011; Baker 2004). Countries are seeking greater food security to ensure people have access to safe, sustainable and nutritious foods that provide good health, with authors further pointing out that such access should be equitable by ensuring the poor are not overlooked (Battersby 2012; Slack and Myers 2014; Smith *et al.* 2000; Cloke 2013). More recently, health concerns have centred on the global obesity epidemic. Obesity is increasing in the Western world and countries beyond (Pollan 2012; Skordili 2013), and it has been linked to the growth of the fast food industry (Fraser and Edwards 2010; Fraser *et al.* 2010). Equally troubling is the rise of eating disorders — mainly anorexia nervosa (self-starvation) and bulimia nervosa (binge eating and purging) — which adversely affect the health of sufferers (Atkins and Bowler 2001: 304–306). Lim (2014) and Fox and Smith (2011) discuss how documentary filmmakers, writers, TV chefs and celebrity health campaigners have used the media to encourage healthy and ethical eating habits. Jamie Oliver's popular TV series "School Dinners" increased awareness of better nutrition and motivated parents to demand heathier food options in local schools. Documentary films like "Super Size Me" and "Fast Food Nation" dissuaded people from indulging in fast food (Lim 2014: 79). Finally, new research in food science has drawn attention to "functional foods" — "foods that are modified so that they deliver health benefits beyond providing typical nutrition" (Holm 2003: 533). Functional foods have been used to promote healthy ageing by protecting the elderly against chronic diseases (Ferrari 2004).

SINGAPORE FOOD NARRATIVES

The preceding discussion foregrounds theoretical perspectives and empirical analyses from a variety of disciplinary studies addressing themes and issues that the chapters in this volume pick up in the context of Singapore. Despite the centrality of food in the lives of Singaporeans, food and food practices have not frequently been approached by scholars as appropriate arenas for intellectual engagement. There has been some pioneering social science and historical work here (Chua and Rajah 2001; Duruz 2011; Duruz and Khoo 2015; Kong 2007; Kratoska 1998; Wong 2009) but by and large Singapore's food domain remains under-researched and under-theorised. Consequently, Singapore's foodscape has also been invisible from scholarly, cross-cultural global discussions. Thus one important contribution of this volume is to fill the important empirical gaps in making visible the complexities of Singapore's foodscape — ethnographically. Another intention is to abstract conceptual, analytical and theoretical insights from the complex material presented and critically engage the broader field of food studies.

The book begins with **Chua Beng Huat's** chapter — a photo essay about street foods in Singapore. This is a biographical narrative piece by a renowned Singaporean sociologist and presents the changing food street scene in the neighbourhood of Bukit Ho Swee, where the author lived with his family up to young adulthood. Chua reflects on the socio-historical dynamics of the years through which street foods were available before the advent of hawker centres and food courts. Relying on his personal memories and experiences, Chua recalls the specific food dishes that were sold by mobile hawkers and mobile food stalls through the 1960s and 1970s. The visuals that accompany the text bring to life the author's reminiscences graphically, and as discussed above, the redolent narrative ensures that this academic's intervention contributes not only to conceptual thinking about the empirical changes, but in memory making and heritage creation.

Adeline Tay's chapter similarly does this dual work of academic analysis and personal recollection of times past. In particular, she draws attention to snacks as "the material integuments of our history, identity, and culture". Her evocative prose at once brings us back to our childhood visits to the *mama* shop, the *kacang putih* seller and the golden biscuit tins, even while she theorises snacking in terms of the spatiality and temporality of the activity. In bringing us to the places and spaces in which snacks are served or sold, she reminds us how the nature and type of snacks have changed over the years. In analysing the ways in which snacking forms part of the rhythm of everyday lives, she points out that snacking is about "interjecting time as it is about making interjections in time". In the end, just as snacking engenders emotions and evokes memories, so too does her prose.

Kelvin Low's chapter similarly addresses the intersection of food and memories, this time through taste and embodied individual recollections. He argues: "By tasting memories, food serves as an intermediary towards such formation and maintenance of one's sense of self, as well as the social ties that anchor one's identity and personhood both in the past and in the present-day context". The intriguing idea of "tasting memories" foregrounds the sensory lens as a conceptual tool and also surfaces the visceral, organic, affective dimension of the eating experience, often dismissed as not cerebral or structural enough for academic scrutiny. He asks important questions about how memory is mediated by sensory experiences of taste and smell of foods; how these recollections also work or not to build community and solidarity. He grounds these inquiries empirically through a focus on cookbooks, oral histories, and popular history books and biographies.

From memories, heritages and traditions, the chapters then turn to the spaces and places of food production and consumption in Singapore, addressing their evolution (and even demise) over time. **Harvey Neo's** chapter begins from the point of food production in post-independence Singapore, highlighting the current complete absence of pig farms and examining their demise as a consequence of the chequered road taken by regulators. As part of the modernist and developmentalist agenda of the post-independence state, pig farms came to be seen as polluting and undeserving of scarce land. Despite official actions encouraging the modernisation and technologisation of pig farms, eventually, these directions were not sufficient to persuade the authorities to permit pig farming in Singapore. The phasing out of pig farming represented not only the loss of livelihoods but the disappearance of a way of life and the reshaping of community and family relations. As Singapore celebrates its 50th year of independence, the country has announced plans for another diminishing of agricultural space, as farms in one of the last remnants of agriculture in Lim Chu Kang face relocation, reduced leases and smaller plot sizes. Reflecting on the future of agriculture in Singapore, Harvey concludes that, moving ahead, sites of agricultural production are best conceived as spaces of/for nature and community, providing opportunities for education, recreation, eco-tourism and heritage conservation, and at most, playing minor supplementary (even symbolic) roles in the production of food.

From rural pig farms, we move to urban spaces. **Lai Ah Eng's** chapter tells the story of the local coffee shop. She argues that "the coffee shop may be viewed as a quintessential feature of Singapore everyday life and public culture". She unpacks this institution by revealing the foods, peoples and communities and the various practices that connect them. She argues for the "cultural evolution of the coffee shop as a site of Singaporean ethnicities and Singaporean multiculturalism that is derived from the continuous inputs and interactions of generations of immigrants, entrepreneurs and customers". She maps how this entity has not only been commercialised and commodified but enters the discursive frames of heritage and tourism, facing new economic and political challenges in the process.

Jean Duruz's chapter takes us to a specific suburban neighbourhood in the eastern part of Singapore, Katong — familiar to Singaporeans as home to a staggering range of local foods of high quality but also continuously evolving. Conceptually, Duruz addresses "through the analysis of gentrification of 'mixed' neighbourhoods, complex intersections of culinary memories, nostalgia, commodification and cosmopolitanism, underwritten by relations of class and ethnicity". Using the motif of "retro" as past, she queries the importance that its remembering has for a contemporary sense of identity. She finds some instrumental value in invocation of "retro" but holds that it is "more than a marketing exercise: it has multiple meanings and analytic uses". The chapter maps empirically these multiple nuances of "retro"and how this constructs culinary nostalgia for taste and commensality. This is achieved through a focus on popular sources, such as interviews, ethnographic observations, cookbooks, website reviews and food blogs.

From places and spaces, we move to two chapters that examine food practices — the practice of cooking, and the practices of food blogging and food imaging. **Vineeta Sinha's** chapter focuses on the social practice of cooking in Singapore, noting the disconnect between "eating and cooking". Mapping the island's current culinary landscape, she contemplates the future for cooking skills in Singapore. Her chapter seeks to document Singaporeans relationship to the practice of "cooking": What meanings does "cooking" connote? Who is cooking and why? What is the interest in cooking? What kind of cooking is popular? What is the status of cooking? She argues that Singaporeans are increasingly registering preference for occasional, event-related, episodic cooking as a recreational activity. In this logic, cooking is viewed as "play", a sensory experience, a hobby and as entertainment and pleasurable. In contrast, Singaporeans are less enthused about "everyday cooking" defined as a set of routinised, laborious, tedious, time-consuming activities which must be undertaken on a daily basis. The shift towards "cooking" as an activity of choice, as art form/creative endeavour in contrast to "cooking" as an imposition (and obligatory), as "work" (and drudgery) is apparent.

Next, **Amy Tan's** chapter provides an example of a new kind of "consumption practice": food imaging and food blogging. She holds that "food and eating has never been less banausic and more provocative in contemporary Singapore." Acknowledging that even though the food scene has been defined as "intoxicating" for foodies, "the dawn of the Information Age" has offered exciting new opportunities taking the attraction and appeal to new heights. In her words, "This phenomenon marks a significant juncture in the socio-foodscape of Singapore as novel practices and worldviews constructed/appropriated around food and eating are normalised in everyday life." Some of the new practices she documents include food photography and imaging and how these "immortalise each dining experience, and with increased connectivity facilitated by social media and smartphone technology". She also includes food blogs and food critics in her discussion, fast emerging as a new discursive site, "dialectically and profoundly altering most Singaporeans' personal relationship with food".

The final chapter takes the analysis to a different scale. Whereas earlier chapters focus on the micro-scale of the body and individual memory, and the local scale of home, community and city, **Lily Kong's** chapter addresses changing foodscapes and foodways with global flows. Specifically, she examines the globalisation of food in Singapore and the globalisation of Singapore food, drawing out their implications for Singapore's future foodways and foodscapes. She traces the increasingly diversified foods in Singapore as foreign foods enter the country and examines the factors that have enabled this globalisation of food in Singapore. She argues that the defensiveness against globalising forces, of which resistance to "other" foods is an articulation in many other places, is not apparent in Singapore. She also traces the converse globalisation of Singapore food, meaning the spread of Singapore foods to other parts of the world, and the enabling factors. The chapter concludes with an examination of the dynamic nature of foodways and cuisines, and discusses the future of Singapore foods in a globalised world.

Taken together, the chapters range over time and space — from the early days of post-colonialism and post-independence to contemporary times, from the spatial scale of the body and its sensory experiences to the home, community spaces to global sites. They have dealt with production and consumption, spatialities and socialities, memories, heritages and traditions. Through food, we provide in this volume a window to understanding Singapore society, culture, economy, politics and governance. Food matters.

REFERENCES

Appadurai A (1981) Gastro-politics in Hindu South Asia. *American Ethnologist* **8**: 494–511.

Atkins PJ and Bowler IR (2001) *Food in Society: Economy, Culture, Geography*. London: Arnold.

Ayres J and Bosia MJ (2011) Beyond global summitry: food sovereignty as localized resistance to globalization. *Globalizations* **8**(1): 47–63.

Baker LE (2004) Tending cultural landscapes and food citizenship in Toronto's community gardens. *Geographical Review* **94**: 305–325.

Bardhi F, Ostberg J and Bengtsson A (2010) Negotiating cultural boundaries: food, travel and consumer identities. *Consumption Markets and Culture* **13**(2): 133–157.

Battersby J (2012) Beyond the food desert: finding ways to speak about urban food security in South Africa. *Geografiska Annaler: Series B, Human Geography* **94**(2): 141–159.

Bell D and Valentine G (1997) *Consuming Geographies: We Are Where We Eat*. New York: Routledge.

Bennison D, Warnaby G and Pal J (2010) Local shopping in the UK: towards a synthesis of business and place. *International Journal of Retail and Distribution Management* **8**(11–12): 846–864.

Bordieu P (1984) Distinctions: a social critique of the judgement of taste. London: Routledge and Kegan Paul.

Brown L and Mussell K (1984) Introduction. In: L Brown and K Mussell (eds.) *Ethnic and Regional Foodways in the United States: The Performance of Group Identity*. Knoxville: University of Tennessee Press, pp. 3–15.

Charles N and Kerr M (1988) *Women, Food and Families*. Manchester: Manchester University Press.

Chua BH and Rajah A (2001) Hybridity, ethnicity and food in Singapore. In: D Wu and CB Tan (eds.) *Changing Chinese Foodways in Asia*. Hong Kong: Chinese University Press, pp. 161–200.

Cloke J (2013) Empires of waste and the food security meme. *Geography Compass* **7**: 622–636.

Cook I, Hobson K, Hallett IV L, Guthman J, Murphy A, Hulme A, Sheller M, Crewe L, Nally D, Roe E, Mather C, Kingsbury P, Slocum R, Imai S, Duruz J, Philo C, Buller H, Goodman M, Hayes-Conroy A, Hayes-Conroy J, Tucker L, Blake M, Le Heron R, Putnam H, Maye D and Henderson H (2011) Geographies of food: afters. *Progress in Human Geography* **35**(1): 104–120.

Cook IJ, Jackson P, Hayes-Conroy A, Abrahamsson S, Sandover R, Sheller M, Henderson H, Hallett IV L, Imai S, Maye D and Hill A (2013) Food's cultural geographies: texture, creativity and public. In: N Johnson, R Schein and J

Winders (eds.) *The Wiley-Blackwell Companion to Cultural Geography*. Oxford: Wiley-Blackwell, pp. 343–354.

De Certeau M (1984) *The Practice of Everyday Life*, S Rendall (trans.) Berkeley: University of California Press.

Desjardins E (2010) The urban food desert: spatial inequality or opportunity for change? In: A Blay-Palmer (ed.) *Imagining Sustainable Food Systems: Theory and Practice*. Surrey, England: Ashgate, pp. 87–111.

Donald B (2010) Food systems planning and sustainable cities and regions: the role of the firm in sustainable food capitalism. In: A Blay-Palmer (ed.) *Imagining Sustainable Food Systems*. Surrey, England: Ashgate, pp. 115–134.

Duruz J (2011) Tastes of hybrid belonging: following the laksa trail in Katong, Singapore. *Continuum* **25**(5): pp. 605–618.

Duruz J (2002) Re-writing the village: geographies of food and belonging in Clovelly, Australia. *Cultural Geographies* **9**(4): 373–388.

Duruz J and Khoo GC (2015) *Eating Together: Food, Space and Identity in Malaysia and Singapore*. Lanham Ml: Rowman and Littlefield.

England P and Farkas G (1986) *Employment, Households and Gender: A Social Economic and Demographic View*. Hawthorne, NY: Aldine de Gruyter.

Ferrari CKB (2004) Functional foods, herbs and nutraceuticals: towards biochemical mechanisms of healthy aging. *Biogerontology* **5**: 275–289.

Fischler C (1986) Learned versus "spontaneous" dietetics: French mothers' views of what children should eat. *Social Science Information* **25**: 945–965.

Fox R and Smith G (2011) Sinner ladies and the gospel of good taste: geographies of food, class and care. *Health and Place* **17**: 403–412.

Fraser LK and Edwards KL (2010) The association between the geography of fast food outlets and childhood obesity rates in Leeds, UK. *Health and Place* **16**(6): 1124–1128.

Fraser LK, Edwards KL, Cade J and Clarke GP (2010) The geography of fast food outlets. *International Journal of Environmental Research and Public Health* **7**: 2290–2308.

Freidberg S (2003) Editorial: Not all sweetness and light: new cultural geographies of food. *Social and Cultural Geography* **4**(1): 3–6.

Gottlieb R (2001) *Environmentalism Unbound: Exploring New Pathways for Change*. Cambridge, MA: The MIT Press.

Grigg D (1995) The geography of food consumption: a review. *Progress in Human Geography* **19**: 338–354.

Hayes-Conroy A and Martin DG (2010) Mobilising bodies: visceral identification in the slow food movement. *Transactions of the Institute of British Geographers* **35**: 269–281.

Hefner RW (ed.) (1998) *Market Cultures; Society and Morality in the New Asian Capitalisms*. Boulder: Westview Press.

Holm L (2003) Food health policies and ethnics: lay perspectives on functional foods. *Journal of Agricultural and Environmental Ethics* **16**: 531–544.

Hunt G and Satterlee S (1986) Cohesion and division: drinking in an English village. *Man,* **21**: 521–537.

Jackson P (2011) Families and food: beyond the "cultural turn"? *Social Geography* **6**: 63–71.

Jackson P, Ward N and Russell P (2009) Moral economies of food and geographies of responsibility. *Transactions of the Institute of British Geographers* **34**: 12–24.

Johnston L and Longhurst R (2011) Embodied geographies of food, belonging and hope in multicultural Hamilton, Aotearoa New Zealand. *Geoforum* **43**(2): 325–331.

Kennison R (2001) World on a platter: consuming geographies and the place of food in society. *Body and Society* 7(1): 121–125.

Kong L (2007) *Singapore hawker centres: people, places, food.* Singapore: National Environment Agency.

Kratoska P (ed.) (1998) *Food Supplies and the Japanese Occupation of Southeast Asia.* New York: Palgrave Macmillan.

Le Goff J (1980) *Time, Work and Culture in the Middle Ages.* Chicago: University of Chicago Press.

Lim CJ (2014) *Food City.* New York: Routledge.

Lind D and Barham E (2004) The social life of the tortilla: food, cultural politics, and contested commodification. *Agriculture and Human Values* 21(1): 47–60.

Lindenfeld L (2007) Visiting the Mexican American family: tortilla soup as culinary tourism. *Communication and Critical/Cultural Studies* 4(3): 303–320.

Lupton D (1994) Food, memory and meaning: the symbolic and social nature of food events. *Sociological Review* **42**(4): 665–685.

Lyon D (2000) *Jesus in Disneyland; Religion in Post-modern Times.* Oxford: Polity Press in association with Blackwell Publishers Ltd.

Mann AM, Annemarie MM, Satalkar P, Savirani A, Selim N, Sur M and Yates-Doerr E (2011) Mixing methods, tasting fingers: notes on an ethnographic experiment. *Journal of Ethnographic Theory* 1(1), 221–243.

Montanari M (2006) *Food is Culture.* New York: Columbia University Press.

Morgan DHJ (1996) *Family Connections.* Cambridge: Polity Press.

Parrott N, Wilson N and Murdoch J (2002) Spatializing quality: regional protection and the alternative geography of food. *European Urban and Regional Studies* **9**: 241–261.

Pollan M (2012) *In Defence of Food: The Myth of Nutrition and the Pleasures of Eating.* London: Penguin Books.

Pottinger L (2013) Ethical food consumption and the city. *Geography Compass* 7: 659–668.

Robinson T (2006) *Work, Leisure and the Environment; The Vicious Cycle of Overwork and Overconsumption.* Cheltenham, UK: Edward Elgar.

Shanahan D (2002) The geography of food. *Journal for the Study of Food and Society* **6**(1): 7–9.

Skordili S (2013) Economic crisis as a catalyst for food planning in Athens. *International Planning Studies* **18**(1): 129–141.

Slack T and Myers CA (2014) The great recession and the changing geography of food stamp receipt. *Population Research and Policy Review* **33**(1): 63–79.

Smith LC, El Obeid AE and Jensen HH (2000) The geography and causes of food insecurity in developing countries. *Agricultural Economics* **22**(2): 199–215.

Symons, M (1993) *The shared table: Ideas for Australian cuisine.* Canberra: AGPS Press.

Valentine G (1999) Eating in: home, consumption and identity. *The Sociological Review* **47**(3): 491–524.

Warde A (1997) *Consumption, Food and Taste.* London: Sage.

Warde A and Hetherington K (1994). English households and routine food practices: a research note. *Sociological Review* **42**: 758–778.

Whatmore S and Thorne L (2004) In: TJ Barnes, J Peck, E Sheppard and A Tickell (eds.) *Nourishing Networks: Alternative Geographies of Food, Reading Economic Geography.* Oxford, UK: Blackwell Publishing Ltd, pp. 235–247.

Winson A (1993) *The Intimate Commodity: Food and the Development of the Agro-Industrial Complex in Canada.* Toronto: Garamond Press.

Winter M (2004) Geographies of food: agro-food geographies — farming, food and politics. *Progress in Human Geography* **28**(5): 664–670.

Wise A (2005) Hope and belonging in a multicultural suburb. *Journal of Intercultural Studies* **26**(1–2): 171–186.

Wong HS (2009) *Wartime Kitchen: Food and Eating in Singapore, 1942-1950.* Singapore: Didier Millet Editions.

Wrigley N, Guy C and Lowe M (2002) Urban regeneration, social inclusion and large store development: the Seacroft development in context. *Urban Studies* **39**(11): 2029–2040.

Chapter 1

Taking the Street
Out of Street Food

Chua Beng Huat

INTRODUCTION

One of the consequences of the practically complete physical reconstruction
of Singapore since the People's Action Party came to power in 1959 was the
sprouting of "hawker centres". To clear the streets of clutter that impeded
traffic flow, which resulted in unproductive wasted time, itinerant hawkers
(whether on wheels or pedestrianised) were herded into purpose built hawker
centres. Historically in Singapore, "street foods" used to be available according
to routinised schedules and routes of the itinerant hawkers; consequently, the
rhythm of hawkers' movements structured the routines and cycles of social life
of the consumers. Now, hawkers and their fare are available simultaneously,
at one place and time with minimal scheduling; those which are in public
housing estates (tied to wet market facilities) serve predominantly breakfast
foods and stretch into lunch, with largely stable public housing residents as
clients. The less locality defined hawker centres can run from early in the
morning to the the wee hours of the night, with different hawkers opening
and closing their stalls at different times throughout the business day, and
with consumers drawn from everywhere, including tourists. In addition to the
spatial organisation, the production of street food has also undergone radical
changes. In the past, the food items were wholly produced by the hawkers
themselves, often in their own kitchen. Today many stalls, especially those in
food courts (which are not to be equated with hawker centres), are supplied

by industrially produced food and to add to insult to injury, the industrial food is cooked by migrant workers or new immigrants. For a discerning local consumer, there is a constant search for the artisanal, the "authentic" foods. Every Singaporean has his/her favorite hawker stall for a particular food and is willing to travel to different points across the island just for a particular hawker or food, thus reversing the travel pattern between hawkers and consumers. Now consumers go to hawkers rather than hawkers travelling to consumers, leading to "auto-tourism", i.e. Singaporeans touring Singapore. This chapter is essentially a biographical account of the experience of street food consumption (drawn from life in a Singapore neighbourhood) that was interrupted by the spatial and temporal transformation of street food into hawker food.

ROUTINE STREET FOOD

Broadly speaking, food can be divided into two major categories: daily food and occasional/occasioned food. Daily food might be available but need not be eaten every day; what makes a food item "daily" food is that it is not considered exceptional; it is unremarkable. Occasioned food is that which is tied to special occasions, which follow different cycles, such as weekly, monthly or annually; a typical example would be food consumed on religious or other ritualistic occasions. In Singapore's past, hawker foods were loosely similarly structured; nevertheless, this distinction has been "blurred" over time by the concurrent/ simultaneous availability of the foods in a hawker centre.

Bukit Ho Swee was a *kampong* (Malay for village, neighourhood) of houses with wood sidings and *atap* roofs, at the edge of the colonial city; it began where permanent housing built by the Singapore Improvement Trust (SIT), the colonial housing authority, stopped. Through the 1950s, the following hawker foods were available through the day in Bukit Ho Swee: *chai tow kuay*, trishaw noodles, *char beehoon*, peanut porridge and *mee jian kuey* were regular breakfast foods, for adults and children alike. They were sold typically in small quantities and rather inexpensive, never costing more than thirty cents. In the mornings, these hawkers would gather to sell their foods at the major intersection of the two main roads, Beo Crescent and Jalan Bukit Ho Swee, which constituted the "centre" of the kampong (see Figure 1). Breakfast was the only meal which was most commonly purchased from the hawkers; hence, business could be quite brisk. The lunch offering included *yong tau foo* — of which two different "types" were available: the Hakka and Teochew versions. The former worked around

Figure 1: Road side hawker selling food to children, 1963.

Source:
MINISTRY OF INFORMATION AND THE ARTS (MITA)
Unedited Description Supplied by Transferring Agency:
A ROAD-SIDE HAWKER SELLING FOOD TO THE CHILDREN

"tofu" as the basic ingredient and had limited offerings, while the latter included a wide variety of items with fish-paste as the main ingredient, including as filling for various vegetables, such as chilli and bitter gourd. Interestingly, the distinction appears to have survived till today.

Between lunch and dinner, one could savour *kok-kok mee*, so named because the hawker's assistant would announce their arrival in the late afternoon by beating a wooden stick on a piece of hand-held bamboo, to create a melodious, rhythmic sequence. This would be an itinerant hawker on wheels; a three-wheel leg-pedal cycle mounted with a custom-built platform that held a glass cupboard (for the ingredients) and a boiling cauldron (with compartments for

Figure 2: Hawker selling Laksa at Club Street, 1983.

Source:
NATIONAL ARCHIVES OF SINGAPORE
Unedited Description Supplied by Transferring Agency:
HAWKER SELLING LAKSA AT CLUB STREET

holding soup and boiling water) to cook the noodles. While the cart was parked at the street intersection, the assistant would walk through all the narrow lanes of the kampong with his "musical" instrument to register his presence and solicit business. A duck porridge hawker would arrive at around three in the afternoon and set down his stall at the intersection for the rest of the day until his food was completely sold by the evening. This stall consisted of two parts: a small platform for the braised ducks and an earthen pot of porridge set on top of a charcoal burner, one at each end of a wooden pole that was used to lift both items on the shoulder as the old man, with severe short-sightedness (judging by the thick and heavy lens of his round-rim spectacles) made his rounds. The *laksa* man would also make his brief appearance around this time (Figure 2). Few hawkers were present around dinner time. But, just before the kampong went to sleep, there would be the bird's nest soup man, again on foot, swinging the two constituent parts of his stall on a wooden pole; the hot soup in the back and cold ingredients in the front. The temporal regularity of the appearance of these itinerant hawkers suggested that each had his own daily distribution circuit, of which Bukit Ho Swee was just one stop. The circuits were unknown and of no concern to customers at each of these stops. However, the daily fixed sequence of their appearance marked/segmented the different times of the day for the residents of Bukit Ho Swee. This could have been either in anticipation of the hawkers" arrival so as to purchase the foods or remained in the background as a "seen-but-unnoticed" element in their perceptual horizon of a structured day. Apart from the hawkers who came daily to Bukit Ho Swee as part of their regular business routes, there were also the occasional ones who brought different foods. Of these, two are recalled as notable: one was *yua kuey*, a very dense steamed rice cake in a deep bowl (thus the Hokkien name) with very little other ingredients except some dried shrimps and slivers of Chinese mushroom with or without a thin layer of egg baked onto the top of the cake: the other was *mee the*, nothing more than rice flour fried with fragrant oil to which one simply added boiling water and stirred it to get a fragrant rich brown coloured gruel, to which eggs were sometimes added. The first of these two items has made a recent appearance in the Whampoa hawker centre as a "weekend special" in a *chwee kuey* store; the last time I had tried the latter item was in Taiwan and I had found it quite a "nonsensical" food as the basic ingredient was flour fried with onion-scented oil and when mixed and stirred with boiling water it turned into a heavy and indigestible glue. Any lingering "fondness" for it, carried over from kampong days, dissipated completely with this last experience.

In addition to these itinerant hawkers, there was the *kopitiam* at the centre of the kampong. With its very wide frontage, it rented space to a *wanton* noodle stall (Figure 3). Parked to the side of the *kopitiam* in the open space was the ice *kacang* stall. All these three were immobile. The *kopitiam* was the exclusive centre of sociality of the neighbourhood/village. This was where the unemployed and underemployed men "hung-out" all day, with or without buying any coffee; women were not to be seen in this establishment, except for a few known gamblers. Without much or any money, the men engaged in swapping stories, challenging the veracity of the more outrageous ones. As the central meeting place of the kampong society, the *kopitiam* was open all day from six in the morning till around ten at night, after the nightly, one-hour broadcast in Hokkien of a *wuxia* serial. The attached *wanton* stall began business before noon until shortly after dinner and, ice *kacang* was an afternoon "food", from late morning till before sunset.

The cost of the hawker food seemed to vary according to the time of day it was sold and consumed. Breakfast foods were the cheapest, with practically no meat included. For example, trishaw noodles had only yellow noodles boiled to mushy texture, a taste of dried shrimps in the stock and overcooked *chye sim*. Lunch food and mid-afternoon foods were slightly costlier, with meat included, in dishes like *wanton mee* and *yong tau foo*. Duck porridge would be the most expensive because duck was rarer relative to the greater ubiquity of chicken and pork. Bird's nest soup in the night was obviously a luxury; a small teaspoon full of bird's nest with boiling sweet soup of rock sugar in a tiny bowl could cost as much as a bowl of *wanton mee*. Not surprisingly, the volume of food sales varied correspondingly with their costs. Overall, the cost of any of these routine hawker foods never exceeded fifty cents. However, consumption was not as causal and commonplace as the prices might suggest. This was also reflected in the fact that in spite of the small quantum of food produced for sale (produced in homes with limited labour and few instruments not amounting to "technology") the itinerant hawkers had to travel through different individualised circuits for the better part of an entire day to sell their food. With few exceptions, the residents of Bukit Ho Swee were poor and being able to purchase hawker food was out of the ordinary rather than a routine event. Children seldom bought hawker food beyond breakfast. However, coming from the small-business family, who owned one of the two *kedai* at the centre of the kampong, I was a regular customer of all these hawkers, even though I was barely a teenager at the time. As always, consumption was a reflection of the relative financial standing of the consumers.

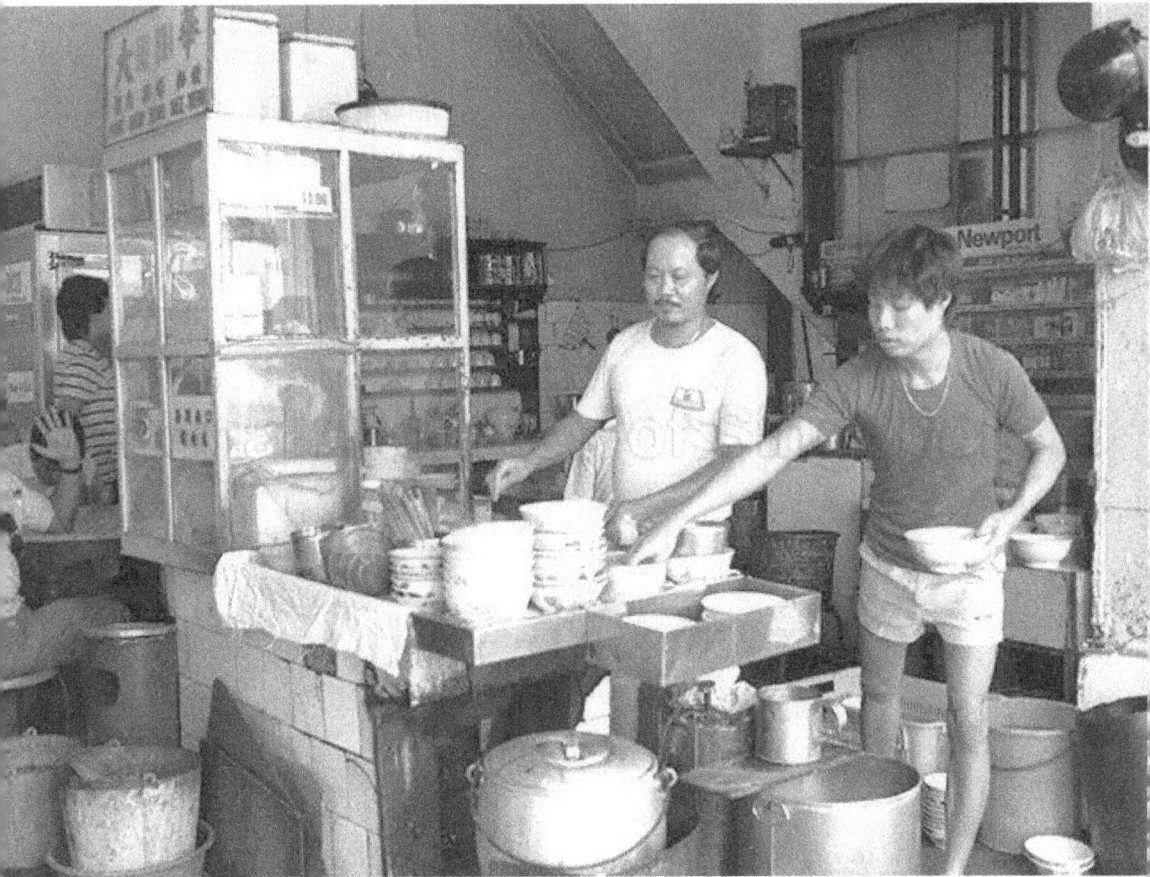

Figure 3: Noodle hawker stall in a coffee shop, Hill Street, 1980.

Source:
NATIONAL ARCHIVES OF SINGAPORE
Unedited Description Supplied by Transferring Agency:
NOODLE HAWKER STALL IN COFFEE-SHOP, HILL STREET (C1980)

Many of the hawker foods sold in Bukit Ho Swee were produced by hawkers who also resided in Bukit Ho Swee. These hawkers were known and generally addressed by their trade, such as the "man who sold Hakka *yong tau foo*" or the "*wanton mee* auntie". Only the name of the *kopitiam* owner — Zhong Peng — was known to the Bukit Ho Swee residents. On the other hand, interestingly, the names of the hawkers' children were known to all. Perhaps this was because they grew up in the kampong in contrast to their parents who had moved there from elsewhere. Not only was I a regular customer of all these hawkers, there were additional (what network sociologists call) "weak links" between some of them and myself. In immediate spatial terms, the *wanton mee*

Figure 4: Portable hawker stall, 1930s.

Source:
SINGAPORE PRESS HOLDINGS (SPH)
Unedited Description Supplied by Transferring Agency:
A HAWKER PEDDLING FOOD IN SINGAPORE STREET

sold in the *kopitiam* were made in our house; my family rented out a room to the Hokkchiu man, who produced the noodles for his stall here. He subsequently fell into serious debt and abandoned his wife, son and daughter. The mother and son continued running the stall but ceased to produce their own noodles and bought it from a supplier instead. Unfortunately his son, Ah Ti (亚俤), left a couple of years later too, leaving the mother and daughter, Ah Choon (亚春) to manage the work. Our immediate neighbour to the left also had a big house; one room was rented to the Hakka *yong tau foo* man, who had a teenage daughter, Kau Mui (九妹). Perhaps as a result of the physical stress of "lifting the stall" on his distribution rounds, he paid the price in acquiring heavy varicose veins on his legs (Figure 4). The daughter was quite self-aware that she was attractive in her tightly fitted *samfoo* ensemble; but nothing is known of her mother. A little further down the road from our house was the "*mee jian kuey* man" and his wife, but no children. My family supplied the flour that he used for his *kuey* and I often carried the fifty-pound bag of flour on my shoulder to his house. The Hakka *yong tau foo* was very popular; this hawker punctually began selling his food at around eleven in the morning and would return home, his stall emptied of food, within two to three hours of starting his business. It was thus an advantage to be his neighbour. The fragrance of the deep frying that wafted through the house told us that he was ready to start business and we were often the very first customers to purchase the food from his workplace/home, before he started on his route.

OCCASIONED FOODS

In Bukit Ho Swee, occasioned hawker foods followed specific timings. These were available and bought from itinerant hawkers who set up stalls for the duration of noisy Hokkien or Teochew *wayangs*, staged by local temples to celebrate their respective deities and commemorate the temples' founding. For each temple the street opera was an annual event, fixed by the Chinese lunar calendar. These temple celebrations were major annual events for the Bukit Ho Swee residents who were believers of Chinese folk religions; there were only a few Christian families in the entire settlement. The street operas were well attended by adults, especially the women who would bring their own stools and seat themselves near the front of the stage. In addition, even those who were not interested in the operas would come and mingle in the crowd and purchase small consumer items from itinerant traders and enjoy hawker fare. This could be called "window shopping at the mall" — for food — in kampong days.

During these events, itinerant hawkers would set up stalls on both sides of the road leading to the street opera. Each stall would be very brightly lit with several kerosene hurricane lamps. The entire length of the illuminated road to the *wayang* added significantly to the mood and ambience of a carnival and celebration. Foods were laid out on wide, long platforms. Customers would sit along its outer edge on low stools to consume freshly prepared food. Tables and chairs were also available by the side of the stalls. The same hawkers would turn up each year, suggesting that they also had a fixed "annual" circuit of travel, going from one temple festival to the next throughout the island of Singapore.

Among the occasioned hawker food was "cotton candy" — thin threads of pink cotton candy appeared magically from the sides of a spinning "home-made" metal drum, driven by the mechanical power of a bicycle wheel; the candy threads attached themselves, layer by layer, on the small stick held in the centre of the drum until a "substantial" puff stuck to the stick and handed to the customer. It remains a mystery to me, how the candy threads flew out from the metal drum — sustaining the mystique and enchantment of this childhood delicacy. Fresh cockles were part of the offerings of the *satay beehoon* stall. Cockles were a source of machismo among teenagers — the challenge being to eat them raw; a tooth-pick would be pierced at an open cockle to prevent it from closing up and the bloody soft flesh pried out and ostentatiously chewed. Those were the days when hepatitis and cockles were not "connected". Then there were the big-ticket items, sold in terms of dollars: *orh luark* (a thin fried layer of sweet potato starch mixed with eggs, garnished with a few fresh oysters and *hé pia* (a mixture of small deep fried food items, including deep fried fritters topped with small shrimps, hence the name *hé pia* (Hokkien for shrimp biscuit). For these, my father would either buy them personally or dispatch one of his sons to do so and bring it home as a treat for the family. When the two-day temple festival was over, the *wayang* troupes moved on to the next performance, and the itinerant hawkers followed, returning the next year, during the same dates on the Chinese ritual calendar.

The spatial and temporal rhythms of hawker foods and the organisation of social life in the *kampong* went up in smoke, literally, with the famous 1961 "Bukit Ho Swee Fire" (Figure 5 and Figure 6). The fire was the biggest "kampong fire" at the twilight of colonialism; more than 10,000 people lost their homes in one afternoon. It became historically marked not only as an event but it also symbolically registered the beginning of the HDB (Housing Development Board) era. The fire effectively cleared the "unhygienic urban slum" and on its site, within three years, emerged rows of public housing in a purportedly "healthy" environment. This bore evidence of the efficacy of self-government under the People's Action Party and signaled its commitment to the betterment of the material environment of the newly enfranchised citizens. After the fire, my family moved to several different locations on the island for a couple of years but finally, permanently lived in a public housing flat of the SIT era in Boon Tiong Road, within two hundred meters from where our Bukit Ho Swee home had stood. My mother was determined to return after the fire to Bukit Ho Swee where she had spent her entire life up until the tragic inferno that destroyed her home, amongst innumerable others.

Figure 5: Bukit Ho Swee fire, 1961.

Source:
MINISTRY OF INFORMATION AND THE ARTS (MITA)
Unedited Description Supplied by Transferring Agency:
BUKIT HO SWEE FIRE

Figure 6: Bukit Ho Swee fire, 1961.

Source:
MINISTRY OF INFORMATION AND THE ARTS (MITA)
Unedited Description Supplied by Transferring Agency:
BUKIT HO SWEE FIRE

HANGING OUT WITH HAWKER FOOD

In the SIT estate, there was no *kopitiam* as a magnet to bring together hawkers. Consequently, hawker foods for breakfast were no longer available; breakfast was either home-cooked or bought at school or at the workplace. This was the early 1960s and itinerant hawkers were still plying their trades. However, the only hawkers who wheeled around to the housing estate came in the afternoons and late at night; their offerings were clearly meant to be "snack" or "supper" foods. There were no familiar neighbours to hang out with and I spent my time with friends from school at some other location, away from home. This suited teenagers fine, then and as it does now. Two locations were memorable for me: Waterloo Street on Friday afternoons and Clifford Pier, any day after ten o'clock at night (Figure 7). For any Singaporean who lived through that time, Waterloo Street was remembered as having two or three large stalls selling Indian *rojak*. For secondary school students, that this location was close to the National Library, made the latter a convenient alibi for not going home

Figure 7: View of Clifford Pier 1950s.

Source:
ARTHUR B REICH

after school, especially on Friday afternoons. A big plate of *rojak* would be shared among a few friends before ambling off to the library. Going to Clifford Pier in the late nights was an uncommon practice for teenagers. During "A" level days, one of my school mates was old enough to have a driver's license and, more importantly, the use of the family car. The two of us, plus another classmate, who also had the freedom to be out late would drive to Clifford Pier and we would "idle" for a few hours. The food was always the same, *char kway teow* and coffee from the Indian stall. The concentration of street foods was a distance away in Shenton Way car park; after office hours, the itinerant hawkers would gather at the empty car park in symbiotic presence to attract customers. Clifford Pier was quiet, even isolated and the sea breeze and the dark night made it a "cool" place, literally and symbolically, which made food secondary. The place was more important than tastes on offer.

FROM STREET HAWKERS TO HAWKER CENTRES

The radical physical transformation of Singapore, so visually compelling, is a well-told story by every statutory authority that has participated in it. Within this process was the herding of itinerant hawkers and street food into "cooked food centres" in public housing estates and standalone "hawker centres", not tied to residential districts but serving, arguably the entire population and tourists. At cooked-food centres, a sense of neighbourhood developed due to the relatively stable clientele constituted by the residents in the housing estate. Standalone hawker centres, including those in public housing new town centres are "deterritorialised" spaces that admit all who constitute the "passing" and ever changing clientele drawn potentially from every point of the island and beyond. This reorganisation has removed the "street" out of street food as all hawkers are now stationary; correspondingly the streets have been cleared of "obstruction" by itinerant hawkers. This reorganisation has also relatedly transformed relations between hawkers, hawker foods and consumers.

The division of foods by meal time is still maintained to a significant extent, partly determined by spatial reorganisation: Cooked food centres in public housing estates are essentially breakfast businesses trailing off towards lunch, as their operating hours are tied to the fresh-produce market which operates in the mornings, as in the past. However, those in the public housing new town centres may stay open from morning till night, with some stalls operating exclusively in the morning to noontime and others from afternoon to late at night. The "heavier" items such as *orh luark* and *satay* are absent in the morning cooked food centres; they generally begin business from lunch, at the earliest, and stay in business until after dinner (Figure 8).

The distinction between "everyday" and "occasional" foods has largely disappeared in hawker fare. While some of the breakfast items might not be available throughout the day, many, if not most, of the food items are available simultaneously in standalone hawker centres. These include, for example, noodles of different kinds — fried, dry with gravy — in soup with *wanton* or fish balls or prawns — along with *satay, orh luark, yong tau foo*, little steamboats, and grilled

Figure 8: Itinerant satay seller, 1950.

Source: SINGAPORE CHINESE CLAN ASSOCIATIONS
Unedited Description Supplied by Transferring Agency:
ROADSIDE HAWKER

seafood. It is a cornucopia and smorgasbord that groups of consumers may share. With stationary emplacement, hawkers no longer gather during festivals in temples and neighbourhoods. The street operas continue to be staged but the actors are "playing" for/to invisible deities and wandering spirits of the dead during the annual "Hungry Ghost Festival", as living audiences have all but disappeared. Young Singaporeans schooled in English and Mandarin no longer understand the operas sung in Hokkien or Teochew. The street operas are just a cacophony of annoying noises, increasingly replaced by *getai* (Figure 9).

The behaviors of consumers have also undergone radical changes. With fifty years of economic development and, in spite of serious income inequalities, consumption of hawker food has become commonplace. Indeed, for many it has become a substitute for daily home-cooked meals, whether by choice or by circumstance. With stationary hawkers gathered in one location, now it is the consumers who travel to the hawkers rather than the other way around. Apart from low-income families with two working parents for whom purchasing daily meals from the local cooked food centre is a necessity, preference and "taste" have become a more critical factor in consumption of hawker foods. If one had to take the trouble to go to the food, consumer sovereignty to choose becomes a primary consideration. The result is a constant search for the "most" in hawker foods: the most authentic and the best of a particular category of food. It is commonplace for a whole family to travel to a particular hawker centre because of the chicken rice or *char kway teow* or even just Chinese *rojak*. With public housing estates that are largely cookie cutter replicas of each other, there is little reason for Singaporeans to travel from one housing estate to another, except possibly for hawker food. Hawker food has become the motivation for Singaporean auto-tourism.

There is also a proliferation of hawker food advice, from the *Makan Sutra* to short radio programmes, to television programmes in search of the "lost" famous hawker to internet blogs by self-proclaimed experts. Appearance in the broadcast media has become advertisement for particular hawkers, with write-ups and photographs prominently pasted on the glass cases that contain the ingredients to be cooked. Finally, with a shallow history and a poverty of impressive cultural monuments, such as temples, churches and other edifices that constitute the "national" heritage, generically hawker food has been elevated to "heritage" status (is it tangible or intangible?) — in the promotion of Singapore as a tourist destination. Obviously, hawker food is now highly fetishised. Unfortunately, the offerings have remained unchanged, lacking

Figure 9: Chinese stage opera during a Chinese temple festival, Queen Street, Singapore, 1962.

Source:
K F WONG
Unedited Description Supplied by Transferring Agency:
CHINESE STAGE OPERA DURING CHINESE TEMPLE FESTIVAL AT QUEEN STREET

innovation. Is it "tradition" or simply "stale"? This is compounded by the fact that despite the myth of Mercedes-driving hawkers, it remains a tough trade — long hours, hot and greasy — that attracts few young entrants. Foreign workers and new immigrants "passing" as "hawkers" only add to the lowering of quality of the food. In Penang, another place that has fetishised its hawker food, there is already public pressure to disallow non-native "Penangites" to be hawkers. Fortunately, such xenophobia has not reached Singapore's hawker sphere; the "authorities" are just trying to entice new entrants into the trade by sponsoring apprenticeships. However, regardless of the quality of food, cooked-food centres and hawker centres will not disappear as they are essential economic institutions which are central to the low-wage policies of Singapore: keeping food cost low through hawker centres keep wages low, the rent forfeited on the land that could generate greater revenue than these food centres is an avenue of subsidising capital which brings in foreign investments and keeps the national economy competitive.

Chapter 2

Singapore's "Snackscapes"

Adeline Tay

INTRODUCTION

Ting ting ting. Ting ting. With the precision of sculptor choosing at first instance an unhewn piece of rock, the *ting ting tang* uncle chisels away with rhythmic knocks on the wall of hardened, sticky sugar. It is sometime in the early 1990s, and I receive my fifty cents worth of candy, now tamed into separation by flour. A dusting will invariably land up on my school uniform, but school is out, and the sheer pleasure of masticating these irregular candies, letting their sweetness run the length of the inner check, far surpasses care of much otherwise. Properly timed, they should last the bus journey home.

The *Ting ting tang* uncle stood around an inconspicuous nook of the foyer just as one rounded the corner to descend into the MRT station. Counterpoised with the gleaming MRT tiles, he appeared anachronistic to time. I often wondered where he came from. Had he been stationed near the previous site of my school in days gone? Or had he always stood at this same spot, perhaps displaying intransigence to the MRT station that now usurped his place? There was also no particular regularity to his coming and going insofar as he was there when he was, frequent enough for his candy treat to form part of my going home routine. As he appeared in many ways to be of time past, his persistence into the future seemed tentative. There was always an impending feeling that there would come a time when he would no longer be there. And perhaps this was why I always bought from him.

This reflection thus begins my thinking about the ways in which snacks figure in the foodscape and landscape of Singapore. Pieced together with personal vignettes and observation, it aims to resonate with individual and collective experiences in regards to what it might mean "to snack" in Singapore. These experiences are not comprehensive, and can only be snapshots in time and space, providing particular insights as one cuts through the landscape with analytical lenses. But perhaps it is fair to say too that this approach aims to captures the spirit in which snacking occurs. For unlike a prescribed meal (breakfast, lunch, dinner) or a specific food group (carbohydrates, proteins), snacking appears to transcend dominant food demarcations. Wildly popular and diverse, snacks conjure a freewheeling, carefree attitude, a foil and complement to the strictures of everyday living. As this chapter will also argue, however, snacks are not just "lightweight" food entities but form an integral part of the food landscape of this nation-state. As much as they are desirable, they are also necessary. Snacks are the material integuments of our history, identity, and culture.

SNACKS IN SINGAPORE

What, in Singapore, is a snack? A logical starting point of naming and categorising snacks becomes a slightly tricky exercise, due to the types, varieties and possible debates about where the boundaries between snacks and non-snacks lie. I present here one such attempt at a typology.

A snack may be defined in the negative — it is not a main meal the way one conceives of breakfast, lunch and dinner. Often, it is what is consumed in the time in-between these meals, what is eaten, in other words, at other times. It is likely, therefore, that what one chooses to eat during teatime, or supper (the so-called late night snack), may be classified as a snack, though snacks themselves do not make those meals, at least not in the conventional sense: grazing is fast becoming a known (if not always accepted) practice, one way in which we might structure our meals. It is entirely possible, furthermore, that items consumed during main meals (for instance, a breakfast of *roti john*, a local version of French toast) could be appropriated and consumed at other times as snacks. Snacks, relative to what one may consider meals, may also be perceived to take up less time (though this is truer about their consumption than production). They may be procured quickly or "instantly" as they are often presented post-preparation. Because of this, they are presented as being amenable to be consumed "on the go". Overall, snacks make an important injunction about timing and time.

Snacks lend themselves to discussion about size and amount. They are not "full" but as aptly termed, snack or bite-sized. Similar to the original translation of *dim sum* (touch of heart), they are a "touch" of food, portrayed to fill a "hole" in the stomach. Importantly, snacks are often individually sized and portable, and they may arguably pass the test of being held (and consumed) with one hand. Often, a plastic bag will serve as a receptacle (for example, the local chain BreadTalk ensures that each item bought will be placed in individual bags on the assumption of their discrete consumption). Snacks may also be threaded through a skewer for ease and convenience.

A common categorisation sees snacks divided between savoury and sweet. While this at first instance may reflect distinctive flavour profiles, the reality is that many snacks exist on a continuum between these two categories. Nonetheless, this is a useful measure and may be applied in an intuitive manner, as one does when looking for something "sweet" or "salty". A sweet snack may be included under the broad umbrella term of confectionary. Desserts and sweet snacks are sometimes mutually constitutive, determined by contexts rather than actual food type. The savoury snack market is contrasted to this, being viewed as a more natural extension of the food industry. In 2009, the savoury snack market in Singapore had a market value of $172.1 million dollars (Rajaram 2014: 173). This, however, is not a stable category even in statistical count, having been subsumed in a most recent report to be classified as its locale: the "snack bar" as a food industry (Singstat 2012). In this context, the terms are more common in industry use than they are in everyday parlance.

Snacks can sometimes be considered "freshly made" or "manufactured". The former is envisioned as smaller scale, involving direct human labour and an open environment of display and contact with said snack; the latter is processed, industrially produced, has pre-packaging and likely a much longer shelf life. Obviously these terms are employed loosely and may be more a result of perceived rather than actual differences. Notwithstanding, they settle into patterns of agglomeration depending on makers/producers, sites of production, transport journeys (type and length), storage options, and a plethora of suppliers and retailers who are themselves swayed by market demands and persuasion as they are by historical trade relations and traditions. The presentation of them as states of "freshly made" and "manufactured" may also be understood as measures of their "liveliness" (Delind 2006) in an understanding that corresponds to how "natural" (lively) or transformed (less lively, more processed) they are.

Venturing to discuss the (main) ingredients of snacks results in an inexhaustible listing that will confront and confound even the most dedicated snack addict. One reason for this relates to the hybridity and borrowings of cultures that take place in the food arena (Chua and Rajah 2001; Duruz 2011). As much as there are similar (and overlapping) snacks and ingredients (*kueh tutu* and *putu piring,* both variations on steamed rice flour cakes, come to mind), the innovation, adaptation and interpretation have also meant an increased number of variations on similar snack themes. Observation, nonetheless, can be made on the following. Firstly, that many snacks have as a main ingredient a food type that can be deemed a staple. In this we might include particularly flour (rice, corn and wheat), whole rice (white, glutinous, black), and tapioca (cassava root starch). To this, one might require the addition of "filling", or the flavour by which the snack may be termed. This may include nuts (most commonly peanuts), sesame (black and white), beans (red and green variety), and yam. Popular snacks such as *min jiang kueh* (Chinese pancake) and *tau sar piah* (red bean cookie) are included here. The inclusion of sugar is key, and the usage of its white, palm or *gula melaka* (coconut palm) forms varies as each imparts a distinct sweetness. In many cases, the addition of coconut is vital, whether in its fresh (whole, grated, milk), canned (milk) or dried (grated) form. In fact, most *kuehs* (the Malay term for cakes) will include some form of coconut, and most will certainly be considered snacks. Coconut is also the one ingredient that muddies the distinction between a sweet and savoury snack. On the savoury end, one might find the use of vegetables, of which cooked radish appears to figure prominently. *Chwee kueh* (water rice cakes with radish topping), *shui jing bao* (crystal dumpling), *popiah* (fresh spring roll), carrot cake, and *kueh pie tee* (vegetable filled top hat shells) come to mind. If meat or seafood (shrimp, fish, cuttlefish) is used, it is usually diced, with only small amounts used. Often, their flavouring (natural, synthetic) is what is used to flavour snacks ranging from fish *keropok* (fried crackers) to *satay* fish sticks; in some instances, their dried forms are themselves flavoured to create snacks.

The preparation of snacks, similarly, spans an array of cooking techniques ranging from those carried out in industrial food settings, to those that may require steaming (*bao*), wok-frying (chestnuts), baking, and deep frying (*goreng pisang* — fried banana, *yu tiao* — fried dough stick) or, likely, a combination of cooking styles. For instance, a snack such as a curry puff requires a boiled egg, a wok-fried curry paste filling, and then a pastry outer layer that is most commonly finished with deep-frying in oil.

In the last few years at least, there has been a steady stream of writing and/or imagery that celebrates and pines for, in varying doses, the yesteryear. From write-ups in local newspapers to blogs and even Pinterest pages, one finds mention of snacks that were popular and/or readily available in varying eras (1970s, 1980s, 1990s) as one does references to childhood and "old school" treats. This more likely than not features a mixed bag of sweet and savoury offerings, each perhaps tagged with a reminiscence, a recreation of time past. At the same time, a country that prides its cosmopolitan nature would be keenly observant of new food trends. This relates too, and perhaps especially, to snacks as popular culture easily translates into these food entities. An ascendant Japanese popular culture that may have brought *Yami* yoghurt and *doriyaki* (Japanese pancake) gave way to Taiwanese street food (Taiwanese sausage, oyster *mee suah*) and drinks (surely bubble tea is a snack!), to now include Korean snacks (tornado potato, for instance). Alongside this, the popularity of treats such as cupcakes and donuts, in their various guises, have ebbed and flowed through the nation's snacking palate. Suffice to say then that "old school" or "new/trendy" snacks may have arrived at different times, with different lengths of staying power. However, this gamut of snacks is worthy of mention and may well form part of the snacking psyche of the nation. Esssentialising only some snacks — however iconic — at the expense of others only serves to narrow its food identity.

The wide array of snacks may be found in a range of places and spaces. Their portability, and ability to be consumed "on the go" lend flexibility to where one might be able to purchase snacks. Of particular note are the colloquially termed *mama* ("uncle" in the Tamil language) provision and minimart shops. A cross between a milk bar and a grocery shop, these are places where more often than not, snacks occupy central and prominent placement. Found in the void decks of HDB blocks, within housing estates, at major bus stops and interchanges, and along thoroughfares, they serve the local population and passers-by in what are sometimes considered interim spaces. Further to that, however, the places one might find snacks are not dissimilar to the location of food per se. Often a local coffee shop (see Lai 2010) will have, alongside its drinks store, an electronic steamer with requisite hot items such as *char siew bao* (roast pork bun), *chee cheong fun* (steamed rice rolls) and *lor mai gai* (leaf wrapped glutinous rice) ready to be served immediately. Furthermore, there are dedicated snack shops, ranging from old Chinese confectionaries to stalls in hawker centres, to updated eateries such as Hans, Polar café and Prima Deli, whose reputations have been built on local snacks.

Snacks may also appear in temporary spaces. One locale that comes to mind is the *pasar malam* (night market), a pop up bazaar that usually takes place in an open field adjacent to a housing development. For a period of three days to a week, one may be able to enjoy the snacks that are sold as one wanders around to take in the bustling atmosphere. Another way to consider snacks as occupying temporary spaces is in their appearances during festivities and celebrations, such as the New Year holidays celebrated by some in the Chinese, Malay and Indian populations where "goodies" in the form of cakes, biscuits and pastries are bought, exchanged and consumed in the rituals of visiting relatives and friends. Once "out of season", snacks that may be easily found in these spaces are much harder to procure.

Finally, one might consider how snacks, importantly, engender feeling and emotions. That is, snacks are sought, and consumed for reasons that cannot solely relate to practicality or the essential quality of filling the stomach. In popular media such as blogs, television programmes, and newspaper articles, snacks speak to a yearning and a desire. Sometimes familiar, sometimes a rediscovery, sometimes new fangled, snacks are portrayed as happiness in a titbit, a whimsical moment, a glee. They escape the strictures (and etiquette) that follow meals, and lighten the weighty issues surrounding food cultures. There is a measure of cheekiness in sneaking in a snack at unscheduled times in the day, as there may be unadulterated joy when a child is presented with one. Snacks are about moments interspersed in everyday living.

SNACKING

The previous section considered a typology (of sorts) of snacks in Singapore, taking into consideration ideas of time, size, flavour profile, processing, ingredients, method of preparation, chronology, places and temporary spaces, and feelings. However, snacks — notwithstanding their qualities and characteristics–are not discrete entities. As I have alluded to, snacks may be so termed when they are consumed at certain times and not others. Snacks are also defined in the contexts in which they are found. Here, the use of the term "snacking" is an important one that is at once inextricably tied to the snacks themselves as it is distinguished from them. By this it is meant that while snacks embody qualities that may well draw one "to snack", the act of snacking in itself may well include snacks, as well as allude to a wider orchestration of behaviours, rhythms, and habits. It may allude to a wider range of "doings" that take place.

So, snacking may be considered, first and foremost, as the act of consuming snacks. As mentioned, it is also the context in which this consumption takes place: the conditions under which snacking occur (for instance, if someone were on the run and could not stop for a sit-down meal), as well as the activities that may accompany snacks being consumed (watching a movie, chitchatting with friends). Snacking, in other words, extends beyond any individual person or act, taking into consideration the collection of people, places and spaces that create a provision for snacking and an environment for it to occur. This means that in tracing the trajectory of snacks in Singapore, one also needs to take into account the movement and changes in this provisioning and environment as one does in the snacks themselves.

Snacking as an activity also offers a succinct commentary on the issue of time. Habits and behaviours that induce snacking (or not) are part of the rhythms of everyday life, existing within, and alongside the other rhythms that ebb and flow through the day. In turn, the act of snacking also creates particular times in and of itself. While not unique to Singapore, it can be argued that time holds a particular sort of significance here. On the one hand, Singapore, as a model of efficiency, with time-squeezed and often hurried denizens, creates the conditions that make snacking a convenient, sought after, and perhaps even common eating practice. On the other hand, the attraction of snacks and snacking may signal a desire to break out of tightly managed routines, to slip, squeeze or intersperse between them "a little something" to chew and masticate on. Snacking is thus as much about interjecting time as it is about making interjections in time.

The following sections aim to illuminate parts of this snacking landscape — snackscape if you will — of Singapore. The first returns to the iconic snack stand, the *mama* shop, as a tribute to a place that is seared into the memories of children growing up. If one could speak about an education in snacks, this is where it begins, the formative years to a lifetime of understanding the role of snacks in Singapore. The second does not detract too far from this ethos, taking in a fast disappearing trade of the *kacang putih* seller. Here, not unlike the *ting ting tang* man I first recounted, a changing landscape charts the rise and fall of this trade. Attention will be paid also to its varied fortunes following a sequence of events in one defined leisure space, that of the cinema. Finally, this chapter takes a step towards a commentary on the history, to date, of Singapore's snacks and snacking practices through the tale of the humble biscuit. Hitherto not discussed, the biscuit is removed enough to allow one to consider snacks with fresh insight and observation. At the same time, the assertion is put forward that biscuits can indeed be considered the quintessential snack item in the modern nation-state.

THE *MAMA* SHOP

There are few places that hold as vivid a memory for me as the *mama* shop. It might seem strange but, for me, the force of this memory is not tied to a specific locale or shop. So while I may still recall the layout and assortment of snacks for a couple of places that I frequented more regularly, the overall memory is one in which collective fragments are neatly folded onto one another. The specificities did not matter as much, for upon entering the shop, I could

Figure 1: A typical suburban *mama* shop.

Source:
www.iisjong.com. With permission granted by Joey Ong.

always scan, detect and zoom in on what I was after, or at the very least, the type of snacks on which important decisions could then be made. The *mama* shops, by and large, performed a similar role (there was always a substitute to be had!) and provoked similar feelings in me.

When given space and time, attention forged in the present can bring about moments of recall of "pasts" that have occurred. Vignettes of childhood sociality are bundled up with the flavours and tastes that are as distinctive as the memories they hold to order. There were the days where "sour" dictated tubes of golden-foiled plum flavoured *Lin Mong* candy, the mini brown packets featuring a stern looking *Mo Far Kor* "Uncle". And when the extreme candy — Super Lemon — appeared, the stakes were upped. If you were in the know, then the battle was one of keeping the sweet in your mouth long enough (and with a nonchalant expression) till the sweetness took over; if this was a new thing, then the effect of tricking others elicited laughter towards the unsuspecting. On other days, snacks were decided on the actual flavour(ing) one might be after: chicken-flavoured chickadees, curry twisties, Calbee's BBQ potato chips or perhaps some Ken Ken salty/chilli cuttlefish to liven up the palate. To an extent, being an only child meant the snacks were often singularly consumed, though as one grew older, the concept of sharing gained its own currency in friendship and camaraderie. The sugar department, undoubtedly, was where you could get a bang for your buck. On a warm and humid day, a cold ice flavoured pole would go a long way. If one were feeling particularly poor, a choice of three candy pieces for ten cents would suffice.

The moments that were spent in *mama* shops were often unstructured, or what is sometimes referred to as "informal time" (Shove 2009). Visits to these shops may have started out as accompanying play/ground time, but as one grew older and went to kindergarten and then school, they often signalled the end of "formal" school time. Gradually, as time spent in school grew longer, the visits to these shops would have become shorter, but they were used more efficiently, and likely slipped between the strictures of school, homework, play, and social meetings more readily. This did not dampen the regularity of visits: in fact, it made the placements and availability of these shops even more essential.

Casting my glances back, I wonder why these memories have taken such a hold in the past, why my mind has readied itself to bring these as foremost thoughts into the present (Bergson 1988 (1896)). One of these relates to the *mama* shop and its links to a childhood that is culturally and historically specific (see Ariès 1962). This means that most who grew up in a particular era can relate to this scenario of visiting *mama* shops and procuring snacks, though the actual time frame, shop make-up and location may differ. The *mama* shop has become a collective memory (Halbwachs 1992) for many who have spent their childhoods in Singapore, a topic that invites easy conversations about joyful moments. Also, there is a sensory attunement to the palatal liveliness of snacks that appears to accompany these recollections. There is a sense that as one goes through the ever-quickening paces of life brought on by demands of work as they are by rushes of technology, it is the sensations of gustation and taste that have held out. As Virilio (1991) asserts, these sensations remain the only ones that have not been effectuated by technical means that create "an aesthetics of disappearance" in our modern world. While visual and sonar qualities may now move easily and quickly through our devices which may render their "live" presence obsolete (e.g. paper to read words, a piano to play music), those of gustation and taste still remain bound to their material presence — the actual snack item is one with its taste and flavour.

There is one more thing about the *mama* shop that anchors firmly in my mind. Rather than being a static entity, a discrete place of time past, the *mama* shop has grown as I have. When I was younger, I had unwittingly honed my budgeting skills (and learnt about opportunity costs) while figuring out the combination of items one could have with the spare change in the pocket. Concurrently, one also learnt temperance. The "excesses" of sugar or salt could be curtailed not just by finances but also by acts of obedience in listening to an adult reason on why a particular item was not a good choice, or how the timing for a snack was not an appropriate one. As one grew older, the risk hedging (or more likely, betting) on *tikum tikum* posters gave way to endeavours in procuring stationery for school emergencies. Now that I think about it, the *mama* shop has always had this malleable quality of providing for the life that surrounds the snacks: the skillsets to be acquired, associated things to be purchased, interaction with friends and neighbours, the memories that it created, the memories that it creates.

THE *KACANG PUTIH* SELLER

The snackscape of Singapore is steadied by the accessibility and availability of snacks across a range of spaces. It is also served by the collective and individual memories of things that, like the *mama* shop, may persist into the present day, or things that, as a nation progresses, may fade away. The snacks that are colloquially referred to as *kacang putih* (sugar-coated white peanuts) fall into this latter category. In name, they are, as is sometimes found with other local food, a synecdoche for the entire snack group (see Chua and Rajah 2001). So in addition to the mentioned peanuts, one might also find roasted peas, chickpeas and lentils, freshly steaming broad beans, *muruku* (crunchy flour snacks) and flavoured crackers, as well as a selection mix of some of these tossed together. With the exception of the steamed offerings, all the snacks would be neatly packed into circular plastic containers that would fill a (usually mobile) stand. To the side would be the intended receptacles of these snacks: multiple cones fashioned out of magazine or phone directory pages stacked high in an impressively towering and leaning structure. While many of these items would be considered staples of a *kacang putih* cart, there may be subtle differences and variation depending on the seller, traditionally an Indian (man) who has pre-prepared these snacks at home.

A couple of stories can be told to chart the changing fortunes of the *kacang putih*. The first one ties this snack-type to a particular locale, namely: the cinema. Already, this particular coupling lies somewhere in the middle of the snack's own biography (see Kopytoff 1986). By the time of this coupling

Figure 2: A *kacang putih* seller hawking his wares outside a shopping centre.

Source:
www.ghettosingapore.com. With permission granted by Johnny Chen.

in the early 1980s, it had left many street corners and places of gathering to concentrate on its stranglehold within cinema venues. This was at a time where cinemagoers stood in line at stall booths, and willing parties scanned a flickering computer screen for the best seats that were handwritten on perforated ticket stubs. From there, it was a natural progression to the *kacang putih* seller, where cones (usually multiple!) of snacks were chosen prior to entry into the theatre proper.

One reason, I suspect, that I remember this so vividly is that this coincides with a period where cinemas were standalones, presenting themselves as singular destination points. I have a clear recollection largely because if a particular destination was the cinema, the sole purpose was to watch a movie. Over time, however, this relationship with the cinema has changed. There have been interesting reasons for the change in these dynamics in Singapore (for an excellent commentary, see Ravenscroft *et al.* 2001). If one were to paint these trends broadly, a possible narrative follows. Firstly, the land pressures in Singapore have meant that the standalone spatial form of the cinema was no longer a viable option. Yet, to meet the demand of an increasing population, it was necessary to find ways of provisioning for the cinemagoer. This has had the twin effect of needing to provide for cinema options not just in the city centre but also in suburban locations, and a necessity to make efficient use of space (and time) where they could be found. The urban/suburban shopping mall, rising in popularity in the 1980s, met this need particularly effectively. It provided a space for the co-location of the cinema as well as served the demands of a population adjusting to the conveniences of finding their leisure needs fulfilled in a single place.

Unwittingly, this coupling of the cinema with the shopping mall had a detrimental effect on *kacang putih*. This was in part due to the changing form and configuration of the cinema itself. The single screen cinemas of Cathay, Lido and Odeon (to name just three) were replaced by a multi-screen Cineplex format brought in by a revamped Shaw Organisation, as well as international cinema outfits such as Golden Village and United Artists. The Cineplex tweaked to the challenges surrounding the wider film industry and its audiences. In addition, it brought with it a culture of American/Western snacks centred on the popcorn machine. Set behind a row of counters, this shiny machine worked tirelessly popping the corn kernels, giving an impression that warm, "fresh" popcorn was always ready at hand to be served. The choice was between sweet and salty, divided up in clear glass containers that were pressed up against the counter for maximum visual effect. While one could just order popcorn, the format was more akin to a fast food restaurant, featuring "combos" of (soft) drink and popcorn of varying sizes that could be purchased. The visual coherency of plush surroundings and settings not too dissimilar to the Hollywood red carpet left the *kacang putih* and its seller cold. It did not fit the schema to have a piecemeal, external seller that would appear incongruent with the branding of the Cineplex. As for the snacks themselves, it would be hard to say which precipitated their demise quicker: the dominating landscape of American movies that lent a smooth transition to the popcorn as choice snack, or the lack of visibility of the *kacang putih* that led to its slow fade from memory.

This is not to say that the actual snacks that the *kacang putih* seller proffered no longer exist. A second story here can be told that counters the narrative of the first one. *Kacang putih* has not disappeared altogether: one just needs to know where to look for it. If one made a trip to a shopping mall that happened to have a foyer food bazaar with a Singapore, heritage, or yesteryear theme, it would be possible to find *kacang putih*, or a similar "lost" snack (for instance, *popiah* candy or maltose on a stick) making a reappearance. There are many reasons why a particular snack is no longer made or why it has fallen out of favour. Similarly there are reasons why it has reappeared or is being recalled. Kopytoff (1986) discusses the formation of a "value class" for which items — in this case, snacks — that are not utterly singular or completely common may be placed. In this case, a "value class" of disappearing snacks is formed, arguably, on such a memory of them: a memory that holds shared experiences in the consumption of these snacks, but with distinguishing characteristics such that they are not like any other snacks being consumed at present. It is argued that when sufficient time has passed for these snacks to coalesce as a "value class", they are recalled into their own biographical model and brought back into being. The story that travels alongside this is that a forgotten snack worth its weight will eventually be remembered and reintroduced.

It is not clear if one story trumps the other. Disappearances and (re) appearances may be relative when spoken of at a particular place and time. What they often raise, however, is the spectre surrounding "authenticity". In the former story, one witnesses a dying trade that has been pushed out by the exigencies of the Cineplex or has, more broadly, succumbed to the changes in how leisure time is orchestrated. The place and time of the (real) *kacang putih* seller is no more. In the latter story, an optimism propels forgotten snacks back into popular consciousness. More often than not, in both cases, a lament underlies them. The snacks exist, insofar as their names and ingredients do, but the flavour that accompanies it, the sense of a particular time and place, has been lost. The phrase "it was different/nicer, last time" is oft-mentioned. While this may be true, it is also troubling. It is true in that it is important to remember and recall, and in so doing, illuminate and bring back snacks that have formed part of the identity of a nation. It is troubling in that focusing on *kacang putih* and charting its relative demise appears to eviscerate other storylines. How does one, for instance, make sense of the packaged nuts and crackers that have lived parallel biographical lives in supermarkets? Where are the places for the stories for the brands such as Camel and Tong Garden, the same brands of snacks that were sometimes smuggled into cinemas when the *kacang putih* seller was no longer to be found? Does it matter that a teenager going to the cinemas now might not know what *kacang putih* is? After all, who is to say that popcorn will not eventually go the way of the *kacang putih*, to be replaced by something newer, and then brought back when popcorn is reintroduced in its own value class further down the road?

Kacang putih, together with its trade and consumption within and outside of the cinema landscape, is constituted within particular discourses: the narratives and storylines portrayed here are a way of affixing it to a Singaporean landscape, attenuated and rejuvenated through time and space. It is also constituted as particular material forms. In this case, the *kacang putih* cones have ceded to the popcorn in the cinema, only to resurface in differentiated surroundings; alongside this, the ready packets of nuts and crackers found in supermarkets exist, not just for the cinema but for a variety of social settings too. Perhaps it is fair to say then that *kacang putih* assuredly has temporal and material resilience. But it may not be in the time, or form, of our choosing.

STORY OF SINGAPORE TOLD THROUGH BISCUITS

Snacks form an integral part of Singapore's food landscape. They are varied, and defy any attempt to encompass them in actuality: in ingredients, shapes, sizes, and forms; across cuisines, cultures, races, ages and gender. Even if one managed to pull together an anthology of snack items in Singapore, there will be specificities, discrepancies in recipes, preferences and tastes, and entanglements of feelings and emotions that cannot be captured in lists. And so it appears discordant to end on a note that tells, purportedly, the story of Singapore through the humble biscuit. But it is really the biscuit that is Singapore's snack *par excellence*.

There are two memories I reflect on which have brought me to this. The first one is circa 1983. As a child, I disliked going to the wet market. This was an age before I understood food provenance. The wet market was fishy and damp, and hard as I tried, my slippers would kick up gunk onto my shins. However, on the second storey, where it was neat and dry, nestled among tailors and seamstresses, buttons and zippers, was the biscuit shop. Or perhaps it was half a shop, so cramped full it was of golden, square-shaped tins sitting on metal shelving, and a simple stool on which the storekeeper whiled away time perusing the newspaper or chatting to a neighbouring stallholder. In these tins, one may have found biscuit gems with icing sugar tops, which to my mind now hold a special place in many children's hearts. Wafers and rolls (chocolate and strawberry) and its variants were as good for eating as they were for role-playing. Sandwiched cookies relished with their halves divided and filling licked off prior to the biscuit being eaten. Semi-circular egg cookies and butter sticks with a shading of pale yellow that hit the right spots.

Figure 3: A display of biscuits in golden tins in an older style biscuit shop.

Source:
www.marilynyeephotography.com. With permission granted by Marilyn Yee.

Miniaturised margarine and sugar toasts, a "biscuit" mimicking a breakfast staple. Cream crackers, especially for older folk, that made for an elegant sufficiency. And perhaps a couple that grew to be among my favourite, the inexplicably shaped savoury biscuits that reminded one of a cross between a mushroom and a spaceship, and a twirl patterned solid biscuit which, with its five-spice powder hints, was sweet and savoury all at once.

My more recent memory took place some thirty years later, in 2013. A friend excitedly brought me to a biscuit shop on Casuarina Road, which she acclaimed to be just like the ones we had encountered as children. Indeed, the biscuits were placed in the very containers I immediately recognised, bar one factor: the biscuits had already been packed and vacuum-sealed into calibrated weights and pack sizes. Ah, very clever and practical, I thought to myself. This was to tarry any effect of *lau hung* (leaking air) that the humidity in Singapore brings, so often resulting in biscuits losing their crunch and going soft. This shop was not set in the "heartlands" or where one expected there to be heavy foot traffic. It could be safely assumed that the biscuits would be bought in larger quantities and expected to keep for longer. However, it also seemed to speak to other (somewhat related) factors. A normalised hygiene concern in which the biscuits' pre-packaging meant that biscuits were not picked up with what was often a tired-looking plastic bag that had been used and reused over an extended period of time. The packaging itself, furthermore, signalled a step up in tidiness and professionalism, displaying a more modern take to a setup that otherwise was invoking of nostalgia.

The simple technology of the vacuum sealer (and perhaps the plastic packaging) provide a way of transitioning the biscuits from past to present. It allows us to partake in the biscuits that we remember, in a form we recognise, albeit with a small modification which suits practical aspects, ranging from the "freshness" of the biscuit to good business sense. These two memories — while seemingly banal — also framed for me a (creative) tension that lies at the heart of the relationship between snacks, more broadly, and the Singapore snackscape. On one side lies *taste* in the sense of it being palatable, tasty, delicious, and desirable. Whether one is hankering for the old or the novel, the taste test is a likely indication of the snack's staying power. On the other side lies *technology* in the sense of the mechanisms that allow a snack to be amenable to the modern denizen. This technology resides in things such as material (plastic containers, adhesive tapes) and machines (sealers, food mixers), all the way to the processes that facilitate their being consumed. One may include as a process, for instance, the making of standardised *ondeh ondeh* (pandan flavoured glutinous rice balls) or chicken chop pieces for cooking time precision, all the way to the modes of operation in snack franchises. Somewhere along this spectrum are the negotiations for each snack type and each snacking demographic.

Biscuits in Singapore have arguably performed this balancing act for a long time, often in the shadows of other more salubrious snacks. From the golden tins to the imperialistic Jacob's biscuits to the local brands such as Khong Guan, they have also occupied the spaces of snacks and snacking in persistent but somewhat marginalised ways. Their role should be given prominence, for not only are they good analogies as an aggregate of the snack category, they are entities worthy of discussion in and of themselves. Biscuits are, in fact, very Singaporean. They beat closely to the heart of the nation, being accommodated and accommodating extremely well to its rhythmic nuances and activities.

Thus far, I have alluded to the importance of time (and timing) in discussions regarding snacks (and snacking). I have also mentioned how biscuits are a particularly Singaporean snack. I will now extend this assertion to consider how the way one goes about daily life in Singapore, the way one understands time, is inextricably linked to practices of snacking, and how biscuits are extremely good examples to think with.

One way of going about this is to think about how there is a co-existence of multiple periodicities (Shrove *et al.* 2009) within a circumscribed period of time (for instance, a day) as within a particular space (for instance, a shopping centre). However, that is not to say that all periods or times are equal. Work times, for example, may be more dominant. The movement of morning traffic works in synchrony with a number of things: ERP charges, bus lane restrictions, school bus timetables, dropping off schedules, holiday routines. School-going children and teenagers may follow a similar routine: schools begin at particular times, and when they end, other timings and schedules such as extra-curricular activities, tuition, and homework take over. Dominant time is overlapping, accumulative, structured, practised, and more often than not, efficient time. This is time that is lived day to day as it is time that follows an order (most commonly, clock time). It is what Lefebvre (2013 (1992)) refers to as lived time intersecting with mechanistic time. Bodies that participate in dominant time cleave to rhythmic routines and training — what he calls "dressage" — that are wholly or partially defined by mechanistic time.

Unless time for snacking has been factored into dominant time, it remains on the periphery, waiting to be called on, slipped in between schedules, or "stacked" with other activities should the need arise. Biscuits, in their compactness and portability, are an easy snack that may be carried along and/or purchased in a range of accessible places. Indeed, the travails of a pack of biscuits may be long, for such are the working hours in Singapore that more often than not, the workday — dominant time — is stretched. Biscuits here play the role of tiding one over as work is tidied and finished up for the day. Biscuits mould to the performance of work. In fact, one would be hard pressed to find an office worker who has not compartmentalised off a portion of her/his drawer for snacks, and specifically biscuits. While the contents of these drawers may be an interesting sociological study in and of themselves, biscuits are a prominent staple that is most likely featured here. This contingency planning echoes the forward thinking (and experience) of a worker as it demonstrates the prioritisation and importance of work in the rhythm of daily living.

There are also those who may not be considered to follow dominant time, but whose time is nonetheless structured and determined by it and its demands. Here I refer to those who wait or wait on their employers or family members to return from work or school: carers, domestic helpers, and grandparents, for instance. Should they be delayed in returning home for a meal, biscuits are a tried and true means of staving off (hunger) time. Similarly, there are those for whom work only begins outside society's dominant time. Cleaners, sweepers, and others in the service industry often work unsociable hours where food is not as easily purchased on the job, such as in the wee hours of the morning. For these groups, biscuits may transform from snack status to take on the importance of meals. Also, as nightlife economies become more rampant in a twenty-four hour city-state like Singapore, both the formal and informal night economies come to life (Yeo *et al.* 2012), opening up not just touristic and entertainment venues but also minimart pop ups from which one can procure snacks, including biscuits.

Biscuits are a currency. They buy time, but they also allow for future time to be stored in them. As Singapore grows and progresses, the Gini coefficient — a measure of wealth inequality — of income is growing too (Chan 2014). Often, when charities and other volunteer groups carry out visits to the elderly and the financially disadvantaged, care packages as a show of generosity are given out to these households. In them, one may find oil, rice, canned food, and amongst these staples, biscuits as snacks that lend themselves to storage.

Biscuits here hold acts of kindness, and they hold time. Once consumed, however, they are gone until further replenished. Biscuit time is transient.

CONCLUSION

Our snacking landscape — snackscape — is a collective of coherent and incoherent moments. It both reflects and creates proper, dominant time, and informal and in-between time. Snacks such as biscuits survive, evolve and thrive (not all at once, not all the same time) because of the conditions within which they are performed, made delectable and practical.

The story of snacks in Singapore is a story of time. The tapestry of Singapore's snacks is a tale of the city. Eating conforms to the rhythms of a city. The rhythms of the city call upon snacking to sustain it, just as snacks allow for these rhythms to continue. In Singapore, the highly circumscribed rhythms of work, school and leisure give rise to practices of eating that contour to these rhythms. The ingenuity of the snacks that we now consume, this heady mixture of taste, innovation, and labour — and in a country that no longer has any meaningful means of growing food — has meant that the snack form mirrors, and is constituted by the daily living habits, working demands, and general pulse of the nation. It may be fair to say that we are, as a nation, as reconstituted, complex, put together and processed as our choice of food snacks.

REFERENCES

Ariès P (1962) *Centuries of Childhood*. New York: Vintage Books.
Bergson H (1988 (1896)) *Matter and Memory*, WS Palmer and NN Paul (trans.) New York: Zone Books.
Chan R (2014) Income + wealth inequality = More trouble for society. *The Straits Times*, 11 February.
Chua BH and Rajah A (2001) Hybridity, ethnicity and food in Singapore. In: DYH Wu and BB Tan (eds.) *Changing Chinese Foodways in Asia*. Hong Kong: Chinese University Press, pp. 161–200.
Delind L (2006) Of bodies, place and culture: re-situating local food. *Journal of Agricultural and Environmental Ethics* 19(2): 121–146.
Duruz J (2011) Tastes of hybrid belonging: Following the laksa trail in Katong, Singapore. *Continuum: Journal of Media and Cultural Studies* 25(5): 605–618.
Halbwachs M (1992) *On Collective Memory*, LA Coser (trans. and ed.) Chicago: University of Chicago Press.

Kopytoff I (1986) The cultural biography of things: commoditization as process. In: A Appadurai (ed.) *The Social Life of Things: Commodities in Cultural Perspective*. Cambridge: Cambridge University Press, pp. 64–91.

Lai AE (2010) The kopitiam in Singapore: an evolving story about migration and cultural diversity. *Asia Research Institute Working Paper Series No. 132*. National University of Singapore, Singapore.

Lefebvre H (2013 (1992)) *Rhythmanalysis: Space, Time and Everyday Life*, S Elden and G Moore (trans.) London: Bloomsbury.

Rajaram K (2014) Business endeavours in savoury snack industry: Old Chang Kee. *International Journal of Business and Social Sciences* 5(6): 171–188.

Ravenscroft N, Chua S and Keng LNW (2001) Going to the movies: cinema development in Singapore. *Leisure Studies* 20(3): 215–232.

Shove E (2009) Everyday practice and the production and consumption of time. In: E Shove, F Trentmann and R Wilk (eds.) *Time, Consumption and Everyday Life: Practice, Materiality and Culture*. Oxford: Berg, pp. 17–34.

Shrove E, Trentmann F and Wilk R (2009) Introduction. In: E Shove, F Trentmann and R Wilk (eds.) *Time, Consumption and Everyday Life: Practice, Materiality and Culture*. Oxford: Berg, pp. 1–16.

Singstat (2012) *Service Survey Series 2012: Food and Beverages Services*, Singapore: Department of Statistics. http://www.singstat.gov.sg/publications/publications_and_papers/services/sssfnb2012.pdf, accessed 10 December 2014.

Virilio P (1991) *Aesthetics of Disappearance*, P Beitchman (trans.) New York: Semiotext(e).

Yeo SJ, Hee L and Heng CK (2012) Urban informality and everyday (night)life: a field study in Singapore. *International Development Planning Review* 34(4): 369–390.

Chapter 3

Tasting Memories, Cooking Heritage: A Sensuous Invitation to Remember

Kelvin E. Y. Low

Ah Mm's little flat was perpetually filled with this distinctive amalgamation of smells of fried lard, peeled onions, garlic, fried chilli paste and other food she was in the process of preparing. I will never forget that huge wok of lard frying on the stove, so fragrant yet a bit cloying at the same time... Ah Mm also learned to cook curry chicken (page 52)... Hers was delicious in its simplicity — an unforgettable taste of my childhood... As I think about my childhood, especially the year I lived with my grandparents and ate so many meals cooked by Ah Mm, I am filled with warm memories of the simple, yet delicious food we enjoyed as a family (Seow 2009: 44–45).

INTRODUCTION

Identities of self, families, and social groups are contingent on and expressed through memories and embodied recollections of the past. Remembering the past through food experiences imply that food serves as an intermediary that reproduces the social ties which anchor individual and collective membership. Seow's (2009) vivid recollection of her childhood days — mediated by a plethora of sensory qualities of Ah Mm's food preparation and cooking processes — evince the significance of taste and other sensory responses toward triggering one's recollection of childhood days in relation to familial and neighbourly ties. The act of "tasting memories" therefore establishes cultural connections between the then and now. How is the past remembered through food as a vehicle? How is such remembering reflective of memories and heritage that are embodied by and mediated through sensory experiences? What do these sensorial aspects of gastronomic nostalgia mean for social actors?

In the domain of food studies, Sutton (2010) traces the inauguration of food and the senses to anthropologists Levi-Strauss and Douglas. Both discuss the senses and foodways based on structuralist approaches. Where Levi-Strauss (1969) refers to the senses as "operators" in connection with such structural binaries as "silence and noise" and "life and death", Douglas notes how contrasting sensations of sweet and savoury link up with the structural ordering of a meal and its courses (see Douglas and Gross 1981). These structural dimensions were later followed by others who delved deeper into the social salience of the senses, seen for instance in Stoller's (1989: 8) work on the Songhay in Niger where his senses of taste, hearing and sight were essential in his ethnographic research and writing in order to both transcend the "Eurocentric mistake" of emphasising sight as the privileged sense and to offer "[v]ivid descriptions of the sensoria of ethnographic situations". Such situations include the important relationship between taste, sauces and social proximity among the Songhay. Seremetakis's (1994) account of her childhood and eating peaches is another case in point. Recalling with vivid fondness the aroma and taste of the peach, she argues for how the senses are "entangled with history, memory, forgetfulness, narrative and silence" (1994: 2). By examining sensory aspects of history, she has worked toward building an anthropology of the senses. Such a field, when interpellated with investigations on culinary cultures, makes available richer ethnographic elaboration in comprehending lives and everyday experiences (Stoller 1989; Sutton 2010). Furthermore, the senses reflect upon social order and are an important means of cultural representation, thereby leading to a broader frame of how social life is organised and sustained.

The earliest cookbooks in Singapore may be traced to its colonial context (1826–1942) where they prescribed not only recipes but instructions on how to manage servants, maintain the cleanliness of kitchens, and various other guides on domesticity and commensality. In sum, these texts carried with them the values and representations of empire (Leong-Salobir 2011). The recent proliferation of cookbooks in the contemporary context shifts the focus toward the ideological work of cooking authentic Singaporean food that at the same time also disseminates traditional values, thereby reflecting upon Singapore society in terms of its struggles as a new nation, and its identity formation in the context of multiracialism (Tarulevicz 2013). By analysing texts that include cookbooks and other forms of culinary writing comprising food memoirs and biographies, I demonstrate not only the importance of how food and the senses connect to family and collective history, but also how such links are further contextualised within the trajectory of Singapore as a food nation (Tarulevicz 2013). As a form of heritage, culinary practices are reflective of national identities. Such identities are also contested, negotiated, and reconfigured within particular social and cultural milieu. What is it about foodways that make them memorable accounts of past and present family life, as well as ethnic and national heritage? If food and foodways express ethnic identification and belonging, what varying narratives do social actors as well as the state harness in their various culinary modes? Addressing these queries would mean undertaking a careful engagement with how different clusters of memories are both similar and divergent, depending on the context of recollection as well as the motivations for memory- and heritage-making (cf. Duruz 1999).

Beyond its immediate purpose as culinary instruction manuals, cookbooks are regarded as an important trove of memory- and heritage-making "texts". In this essay, I employ them for socio-cultural investigations into the dynamics and processes of memory- and heritage-making in Singapore. As sources of invitation to remember (Duruz 1999), they are therefore examined not merely as culinary texts but as cultural artifacts (Appadurai 1988; Tobias 1998), providing "socio-historic markers" (Parys 2013) with regard to culture, history and society. As an object of scholarly inquiry, the socio-cultural pertinence of these materials is reflected in how these as heritage texts illustrate community building, political and economic life (Garth 2014; Pilcher 1998), nutritional history (Mitchell 2008), and women's lives (Higashiyotsuyanagi 2010; Supski 2013; Theophano 2002), among other "cultural tales" (Appadurai 1988).

Where foodways refer to how culture and food intersect (Camp 1989), cookbooks and other culinary writings accordingly bear witness to how people lived their lives in specific socio-political milieu. They also indicate the importance of familial relationships and the making of a nation's heritage. They serve as indexes of life in pre- and post-war periods, reflecting upon how foodways may have changed, disrupted, or been continued by different persons in the family and across different familial units. Even if such culinary texts may not be readily perceived as historical documents since they were not designed to serve as a repository of historical "facts" (Mitchell 2001), they nonetheless pertinently show how individual and family lives and their foodways ought to be contextualised within such broader milieu of socio-political episodes as wartime (Wong 2009) or in the prosaic activities found in day-to-day routines. As Chen (2014) also reminds us, cookbook writers often register their opinions and sentiments of individual experiences, as well as various social and political events and contexts. In the case of Singapore, these include, among others, the Japanese Occupation of 1942–1945 (Wong 2009) and the Hock Lee bus strike of 1955 (Seow 2009). Paying attention to these varying contexts will further add to a more nuanced comprehension of what foodways and familial ties represent in different environments.

How does gastronomic nostalgia work? Three strands of making sense of food heritage form my central preoccupation in conceptualising the visceral and socio-cultural connections between food, identity and nostalgia. The first locates sensory nostalgia as a way to comprehend how food, the senses, and memory recall work in intersectional ways to shed light on both familial and ethnic identity. The second has to do with what I term sensory discomfort, where social actors' recollections of the past are not uniformly couched in positive, nostalgic terms. Instead, sensory disarray and discomfort also constitute a part of the larger scheme of food heritage production. The final deals with the notion of sensory imagination. This is where the past — be it actually experienced by writers of culinary texts, or imagined on behalf of the readers — is analysed vis-à-vis Appadurai's (1996) idea of "armchair nostalgia". In explicating these conceptual trajectories, I examine nostalgia in its plural and complex forms (Sutton 2001: 155), as opposed to nostalgia as a singular notion. Analysing nostalgia as polyvalent draws attention to how social actors engage with the past in differentiated ways. As a corollary, different facets of culinary nostalgia, as the three strands will elucidate, shed light on varying domains of social life; for instance, food and migratory contexts, food and the experience of place, food and commensal practices in the family, and food and the transmission of sensory-cultural know-hows. In turn, these domains suggest a wider shared sense of commensality and belonging that are inscribed within particular socio-cultural practices, where shared tastes contribute to a shared identity (Walker 2012).

COOKING AND SENSING HERITAGE

As a complex field of inquiry, the politics of heritage is embroiled with the construction of social identities (Bessière 2013) to be deployed as a resource. Heritage is a discourse drawn from history, encompassing a set of values and socio-cultural practices, material and immaterial components, that together possess crucial socio-political functions (Graham 2002; Smith 2006). Such practices can include foodways, which as iterated above, are modes and experiences intimately tied to collective memory and heritage. Theorisations of collective memory suggest that remembering is not merely the act of an individual, but what and how we remember transpire in relation to our membership within particular mnemonic communities, including families, organisations and nations (Lupton 1994; Zerubavel 1996). In this respect, comprehending the process of remembering as being socially enmeshed (Prager 1998) means that claims to a "common heritage presuppose a shared memory" (Chronis 2006: 268). As a resource for the present, heritage forms the bridge between the past and the present, where a sense of continuity is projected. What then is food heritage? Why is food heritage important? What does it do for social actors and nations? I first suggest the following components that form different aspects of food heritage in Singapore: foodways that comprise a range of dietary habits, food preparation processes, cooking techniques, cooking spaces, eating places, social groups and their varied episodes of commensality, institutional structures of food consumption, regulatory agencies and food industries, among many others. In short, food heritage stands for all that traverses domestic and public realms of gustatory experience. While actors can all relate to food in emotionally connected ways in these realms, they do so in manifold ways that are germane to their own subjectivities.

Foodways passed down as "heirlooms" through the generations imply continuity and familiarity and reinforce the role of food in the family. The perceived loss of culinary tradition as a heritage project for people appears to be a perennial concern, thereby constantly emphasising the importance of handing down cooking techniques and recipes for posterity. Seow (2009: 10) explains this in her recollection of home-cooked dishes that have been "consigned to history"; since these dishes would never be found in public eating venues but have been confined to her family for generations, she takes it upon herself as a custodian to bridge "the generation of [her] children" with the generations before them. A further step, Seow (2009: 10) notes, is to carry out the following:

> I decided that I had to do more than just pass on our family recipes. I had to write of the times my grandparents and their children lived in, and when I was a little girl. So, I have written about food that evokes such powerful memories of the past, of intriguing sights, smells and tastes that can, in an instant, transport me to another time, to another place.

Such continuity that is historically contextualised is deemed crucial and valuable not only because foodways are symbolic references to group identity and generational ties, but because there is a perceived anxiety or lament about a vanishing past — or what Holtzman (2006: 367) terms "a lay notion of sentimentality for a lost past" — that needs to be properly recorded for future generations, including the frittering away of culinary skills as an urgently perceived problem to be rectified. These relate to how Bessière (1998: 28) conceptualises heritage as a bulwark to "protect our past... [and] to perpetuate disappearing threatened knowledge and techniques". To take another example, ubiquitous hawker fare that has been a longstanding staple of Singapore's gastronomic landscape has undergone many changes over the past few decades. From street hawkers to the proliferation of hawker centres, followed by food courts (Kong 2007; Tully and Tan 2010), there has been a constant reminder that "the retirement of long-serving hawkers has left voids", "new hawkers have introduced changes to the traditional tastes of dishes", and that "the younger generations are eschewing hawker food for fare that is considered more cosmopolitan or more healthy" (Tully and Tan 2010: 16). Given these various developments, it is thus made exigent that hawker food as an icon of Singapore's national identity be accordingly preserved and protected. As overtly pronounced by Member of Parliament, Baey Yam Keng in the foreword to *Not for Sale: Singapore's Remaining Heritage Street Food Vendors* (Teo *et al.* 2013: 10), hawkers and their stalls need to be accorded recognition:

> We must be proactive in preserving, protecting and promoting our local food culture. This book seeks to record and celebrate hawkers and stalls with the longest history and heritage, and accord them with recognition and the status of national heritage food.

Baey's importunity is about the continuity of hawker apprenticeship, skills transfer, and the handing down of recipes accompanied by traditional cooking ways that therefore encompass "heritage value". All of these are recognised as paramount given that he perceives hawking not only as a form of livelihood but "a piece of art" emanating from "artisan hawkers". Furthermore, hawker centres in Singapore are regarded as "an important common space" since affordable hawker food is enjoyed by people from all walks of life where the "vibrant atmosphere adds to the senses and flavours of the eating experience" (*Ibid.*). Evidently, these aspects of consuming and preserving hawker food exemplify the gastro-politics of collective identity, place and sensory elements in commensal practices.

Apart from such commemorative books or culinary memoirs (see also, Seow 2009; Tan 2012), programmes targeted at continuing the hawker trade and skills transfer are also in place, such as the Hawker Master Trainer Pilot Program jointly launched by the Singapore Workforce Development Agency (WDA) and the National Environment Agency in 2013 (Xue 2013). These different forms of food heritage reflect Bessière's (2013: 277) contention regarding the mechanisms and instrumentality of heritage, where heritage and tradition operate together in providing "constant order amidst continual change". Food heritage is therefore pertinent, not only in providing a foundation from which identities are formed and sustained through the lens of food reminiscences, but it offers a cloak of stability in the face of social change in Singapore. As a resource, food heritage thus serves both as a social bond for actors, as well as a political-ideological tool for the state in instilling a sense of collective identity as a part of nation-building processes.

The sustenance of food heritage, according to state directives, begins with the family unit, for "[j]ust like charity, food heritage begins at home" (Tully and Tan 2010: 18). Such heritage that may be found in the home comprises the various processes of helping out during the day-to-day or special occasion meal preparation, where "one would have had the chance to learn the art of choosing and handling ingredients, [as well as] how to manipulate textures and flavours" (*Ibid.*). The authors then go on to offer a list of 21 suggestions as to how food heritage at home and family traditions, "which is also the country's heritage", may be procedurally honoured. Some of them include both learning how to make and appreciate "heirloom recipes" from senior family members, imparting such culinary knowledge to one's children including the "stories behind the food", continuing food practices by inventing new family food traditions but without losing sight of traditional cooking techniques, "bless[ing] your favourite hawkers with verbal and monetary encouragement", supporting local food businesses as well as efforts to save food heritage, and finally, "guard[ing] your own wellsprings of culinary meaning" by writing your own book (Tully and Tan 2010: 18–19). What this list reflects are complexes of generational ties, culinary skills transfer, community efforts, and the institutionalisation of food heritage. Moreover, given the Singaporean state's approach to national history which has to do with "intertwining the personal with the nation" (Tarulevicz 2013: 114), this thereby illustrates how heritage should be performed through the aforementioned list of suggestions. In order to flesh out these elements that together illustrate what food heritage entails as a system of relationships (Tschofen 2008) and what it does at the symbolic level, the senses are potent arbiters in processes of remembering the past and cooking in the present, including how ethnicity is reproduced in state projects of cooking identities through ethnic food/actor categorisation. The discussion should be comprehended in interrelated ways in terms of the use of history and narration for contextualisation, and the focus on posterity and identity-formation at different levels.

The notion of sensory heritage has largely been debated in tourism studies and how cultures and the past are imbibed through one's sensory experiences, or through embodied encounters of history with sensory re-enactments at tourist sites or museum exhibits. Extant scholarship on the senses in connection with heritage has touched upon the areas of materiality and tangible objects (Chronis 2006), senses and the experiencing of places, cities and modernity (Howes 2011; Kong 2013), and the emotional character of heritage and homelands drawn upon vis-à-vis sensory encounters with objects and places (Kearney 2009). I develop further the notion of sensory heritage to locate foodways as a medium that similarly articulates poignant moments of the past that are meaningful for social actors. Extending from my earlier work on senses, heritage and military history and on identity work (Low 2010; 2013), the senses enable social actors to connect more intimately to the past, for the past is rendered more meaningfully contextualised when mediated by and recalled through sensory moments shared in familial, culinary settings. In this manner, our links to the past are embodied where not only the mind comes into contact with history, but that such links are crucially attached to the physical world and therefore should not be regarded as separated from the body (Merleau-Ponty 1968). Multi-sensory markers found in culinary texts enrich and actualise a "tasting" of the past that create embodied and emotive bonds across past and present times.

DELICIOUS MEMORIES? REMEMBERING THROUGH THE SENSES

While the processes of cooking and eating are highly sensory and embodied activities (Lupton 1996), I move beyond the biological sense — consumption of foods — to locate the socio-cultural meanings that are associated with these evocative processes. They convey familiarity, intimacy, and nostalgic memories which together form the basis for familial if not national recollection and identity formation, because the sensuousness of food serves as a pivotal vehicle of memory (Holtzman 2006). By embarking on an embodied and sensory reading of the different sets of materials considered herein, I demonstrate the importance of the senses in crafting selves and others, serving as memory stimuli that add to the sensations of heritage. Following Korsmeyer and Sutton (2011), such analytical attention devoted to sensory memories broadens the ambit of interrogating identity and selfhood, collective memory and group identity.

If memory is regarded as a social act, then this means that it takes place in a specific milieu in which social actors re-experience food and commensality through the senses. Instead of interpreting sensory memory recollection and emotions as mere accident, one ought to critically examine these as "connectors between actors and social structures" (Tschofen 2008: 48). Abdullah (2010: 172) articulates this point:

> [S]ensory experiences of food contain within them both personal and collective memories, emotions, histories, spaces and moments in time, providing referential points between then and now, and here and there.

Emotional recollections of the past — specifically about family relationships — is both mediated and enriched by the senses in interrelated ways. There is thus an emotional, sensorial and familial connection that is made and experienced through foodways, documented and enlivened through sensory associations in culinary texts. Poly-sensorial moments which are emotionally intense and poignant — not unlike the Proustian moment of a tea-soaked madeleine — are thus idiomatic of how one accesses and engages with the past with the senses as mnemonic agents. These moments, comprising at first physiological experiences of smelling and tasting, translate into how commensality and convivium come with "communicative-socialising functions" (Tschofen 2008) pertaining to foodways. In Sanmugam's (2011: 9–10) depiction of her Amma's (mother) cooking skills, which were learnt from Aatha (her grandmother), her account explicates the significance of commensality, gender roles and the family, as well as communal food sharing as a typical way of life:

> Having learned to cook from Aatha, Amma was almost obsessed with it and she took great joy in serving her food to family members. The aromas of her cooking would fill the air and our neighbours could hardly wait

to be offered some of her food. Those smells permeated our entire home and lingered within the fabric of the cotton *saris* that Amma wore. As a child, I used to wrap myself around her legs and breathe in those delicious perfumes.

Sanmugam's childhood memories of food thus provide glimpses into how cooking responsibilities fell upon women and how the pleasant smells of her mother's cooking provided a safe blanket of comfort. These represent emotional themes of duty, security and happiness (cf. Lupton 1994). Furthermore, such remembrances demonstrate a strong link to familial ties, where culinary skills are inherited across the generations.

Having written her book as a tribute to the "special people" in her life, Seow (2009: 10) recalls with fondness, cooking memories of her grandmother and father:

[M]y grandmother, my Hua Mama, was there right beside me, grinding glutinous rice into a smooth paste, or my father standing by the sink, fastidiously shaking off any excess water from the *chye sim* he had just washed. I have invoked for you my past that is part of my sons' inheritance.

The author's memory-choreography that is textured with familial ties and sensory elements of hand movements and accompanying sounds, is interestingly not just meant for her sons. By invoking the past for "you" (us), the reader, Seow's work exemplifies what Appadurai (1996) notes as a type of "armchair nostalgia" or nostalgia *sans* lived experience; the case here is not so much about re-experiencing a past culinary moment, but an invitation to experience vicariously, someone else's past as an outlet of a sense of shared food heritage. This relates to Duruz's (1999: 236–237) take on how cookbooks may provide "invitation[s] to remember" so that a "comforting narrative of the past" can be invoked through recourse to a fictive, ersatz past. While there is no actual loss, such gustatory nostalgia serves as a window for a fictional and imagined recollection for the unrelated reader, a theme that is also explored by Lupton (1994; 1996) on imagined nostalgic remembering. In other words, there is still a sense of shared food heritage despite the absence of any first-hand experience, where the underlying sentiment of a shared sensory affinity (drawing from Anderson's (1983) mental affinity of imagined communities) is key towards rendering such heritage accessible and resonant.

Apart from culinary memories that intersect with family life, another aspect of such sensory nostalgia also touches upon ethnic heritage of food practices. In this instance, the different dialect groups that together make up the Chinese segment of Singapore's population are first traced to the country's migrant past:

> Singapore is a country built by migrants. After the Malays — who were the original inhabitants of this sleepy little island — some of Singapore's earliest arrivals were the Chinese, who came by the hundreds from Malacca… Others from China followed, arriving by junk along the shores of Telok Ayer, landing among its many sheltered bays (Tan 2012: 6).

Tan (2012: 7) goes on to describe the various occupations that these different migrant groups took up and thereafter proceeded to outline how Chinese migrants connected to their hometowns through food:

> It was the simple tastes of home that nourished the bodies and fed the souls of Singapore's early Chinese diaspora. For the Cantonese, it was comforting double-boiled soups and roasted meats; for the Teochews, watery porridge with large, fluffy grains of rice eaten with condiments like preserved vegetables and salted eggs. The Hokkiens craved braised pork — robust, flavoursome and a reminder of home; and the Hakkas favoured stuffed bean curd and dishes spiked with homemade rice wine.

Ostensibly, the varied "tastes of home" Tan alludes to represent the ways through which food serves as a medium that delineates different identity-relevances; these are based on the contrasting culinary cultures of the aforementioned dialect groups. Dishes and how they are eaten — watery, fluffy, robust and flavoursome — all conjure taste sensations that supposedly signify each dialect group's distinct gastronomic way of life. Correspondingly, Walker (2012) proposes that the associations between food, identity and memory more often than not focus on specific forms of cooked food, as well as the ways of eating them. Additionally, the links between food, place and ethnic significance are also depicted in Tan's book. She notes that while the Chinatown of today has changed dramatically from its yesteryears, there still exists a "common thread that continues to bind the history of Chinatown to its people today", which are "hard work and good food" (Tan 2012: 8). Similar to my earlier discussion on the lamentations of an impending lost, good past, Tan points out that "many of Chinatown's eateries today teeter on the brink of extinction", since the next generation prefer their pay cheques" that come with "less gruelling work". Dividing her book into three categories, Tan speaks of Chinatown in its changing historical contexts ("The Place"), people who have lived their lives and established their businesses ("The Memories"), and a collation of recipes contributed by some of the author's interviewees that "literally offer a taste of Singapore's Chinatown in the comfort of our own homes" ("The Food"; Tan 2012: 9).

One could argue that both social actors and the state employ food as a way to maintain ethnic identities that are historically validated (Holtzman 2006), thereby accounting for the use of historical narratives of ethnic groups in culinary texts. The contradictions of bounded and multi-ethnic culinary heritage is also observed in how culinary writers both operate within ethnic categories in their gustatory narratives and yet simultaneously acknowledge the cross-ethnic influences that have come to bear in the different foodways which they describe. In their work on *Indian Heritage Cooking*, which comes under a series on "Singapore Heritage Cookbooks" supported by the National Heritage Board, authors Sanmugam and Kasinathan (2011: 14) point out distinctions between North and South Indian cuisine, where they also indicate multi-ethnic influences in the cooking of Indian cuisine:

> The early Indian immigrants in Singapore incorporated local ingredients and cooking styles into their traditional cuisines or spiced up Malay and Chinese dishes with an Indian touch, creating dishes unique to Singapore.

Serving up "Indian versions of Malay and Chinese dishes" (*ibid.*), multi-ethnic cooking and eating are perceived through such dishes as the Indian *rojak* (*rojak* is a Malay word that means "mixture"; the authors note that it could be a variation of a Chinese fruit and vegetable salad), *mee goreng* (which the authors suppose may have been adapted from *char kway teow*, a Chinese fried rice noodle dish), and *sop kambing* (where its recipe provided later in the book points toward some Chinese culinary links — "The soup is also served with a sprinkling of fried shallots and chopped spring onions, clearly a Chinese influence" [Sanmugam and Kasinathan 2011: 28]), among others.

As another example, Hyman (1993: 121) waxes lyrical over how there exists an intermingling of the "ethnic foods of the three races". In the process however, she ends up reinforcing if not reifying ethnic culinary proclivities, despite the hybridisation (see Tarulevicz 2013) of such food habits: "The ethnic food of the three races have also intermingled to produce a cuisine incredibly rich in variety and innovation. Singaporean Malays eat noodles doused with curry sauce, Indians perfume their curries with star anise and lemongrass, and the Chinese happily consume quantities of Malay *satays*." (*ibid.*). A similar contention is submitted by Chua and Rajah (2001) who talk about how social actors are the ones who essentialise ethnic identities vis-à-vis foodways and consumption styles, resonating "typifications of food-and-ethnicity" (2001: 190). If so, then multi-ethnic families are equally conscious about how their multiple backgrounds present a mixture of different heritage, as the next passage from *Singapore Family Favourites* (2010: 2) suggests:

> Hervé's French background and my Chinese heritage make for some wonderful fusion recipes. We want our children to better understand and experience both of our cultures and traditions, not only through sight but also through taste as well…We like to infuse new textures and tastes [in]to our cooking while still maintaining a balanced diet for our growing boys.

Another multi-ethnic family featured in the book similarly demonstrates a concurrent awareness of ethnic differences and ethnic overlaps (2010: 16):

> Our team is thus named because we are a multi-racial family, with a Chinese mother, Indian-Chinese daughter, Indian cousin and Malay son-in-law. We are a true representation of Singaporean society… As you can imagine, our multicultural background is strongly represented in our cooking, and we draw from all these influences to create recipes that are often quirky, always original, and never boring!

The above passages indicate that culinary boundaries are more porous than ethnic boundaries (Tarulevicz 2013), where individuals think of identity in ethnically bounded terms and simultaneously cook in hybridised ways. Overall, sensory nostalgia as an aspect of food heritage conjoins social relations, group membership, as well as experiences of place that together illuminate how foodways connect us to the past. Culinary stereotypes are manufactured through state orchestration of the different categories of ethnic cuisines that seem to sideline the reality of more fluid boundaries of ethnic food practices; these may and have arisen in the context of inter-ethnic unions among other factors that alter the family unit from singular to multiple ethnic composites.

In this instance, then, gustemology and the issue of ethnic culinary heritage should not be perceived as contained or bounded in totality. At best, state heritage-making relies on simplistic ethnic categories whereas foodways as lived experiences importantly reflect otherwise (see for example, Chua and Rajah 2001). There are, obviously though, instances where culinary authors also mirror the state's CMIO (Chinese, Malay, Indian, Others) quadratomy in registering memories of ethnic cooking habits. One could argue alongside Appadurai (1988) and Tarulevicz (2013) that boundary making through culinary practices are rendered meaningful both by individuals and the state in concerted efforts to maintain ethnic identity. This chapter can only remain somewhat cursory in its insights on how social relationships are mediated through food practices, and how the dimension of ethnic food heritage reveals the various contradictions of "doing" or "eating" ethnicity; these fields indubitably warrant further deliberation.

As an alternate motif, memories of food can also not be as "delicious" in the nostalgic sense. In the context of Singapore's experience of World War Two between 1942 and 1950, Wong (2009) documents the scarcity of food in times of hardship, where these years saw largely unchanged diets comprising starchy foods such as sweet potato and tapioca. Drawing upon archival research on oral histories, including other memoirs and autobiographies, she also details everyday food and eating habits and survival strategies, as well as a cluster of "wartime recipes" which for her "function perhaps as the most representative relics and memories of everyday life in wartime Singapore" (2009: 14). Notably, the bleak, sensuous clues of economic and political hardships and wartime food can be gleaned from the following passage that depicted the different types of rice and their grades that were available:

> Eating plain white rice was sheer luxury during the Japanese Occupation. Because of the shortage, rice was rationed and graded. There was rice mashed with gravel, tiny sand grains, rice husks, broken rice grains, half-polished rice and decayed grain, the lowest-grade grain smothered with a coat of wriggling maggots. Many British prisoners-of-war (POWs) recalled being given rice preserved in slaked lime. Sergeant Hursley recalled the unmistakable yellow and rotted egg-like odour of the limed rice... Wu Sijing recalled a greyish "cement rice" which no matter how many times one rinsed and washed it, remained the colour of ashes... "Tartar rice" was also a particularly unpleasant memory. Its rotting smell and yellow grains reminded one of rotting teeth and was nauseatingly unpalatable. (Wong 2009: 58–59)

Beyond the context of wartimes, the lack of proper hygiene in eating places also point to the idea of sensory transgression and disgust. Tan's (2012: 96) write-up on Maxwell Road Food Centre in Chinatown clearly demonstrates how sugar cane as a common beverage in Singapore is portrayed in unappealing ways of hygienic-sensory violations. At the same time, different groups of people hold divergent memories of the food centre; where hawkers recalled having enjoyed congregating with fellow stallholders at the common washing area and communicating by "shouting across the stalls", diners "remember it differently". The unsanitary context brings forth an unsavoury recollection:

> Set smack along the main thoroughfare where people ate, the common washing area collected stacks and stacks of dirty dishes that piled up high during peak hours — not a particularly appetising sight. When the crowds ebbed, the hawkers would perch themselves on tiny stools and do their washing up. The oily dishwater ran into clogged drains, which in turn spilled over onto the floors. Poles of sugar cane sat nearby, their porous flesh soaking up the polluted water before heading for the crusher to yield sweet (though terrifyingly unhygienic) sugar cane juice.

Unappealing and distasteful in all of their senses, the textures, tastes, and smells of varying rice grain types depict a negative discourse of disgust and repulsion, denoting hardships in the form of sensory transgressions in otherwise "normal" circumstances. Such sensory discomfort is also evident in the case of sugar cane juice mentioned above. Sensory nostalgia has in this case, translated into sensory discomfort as an alternate theme, revealing how the senses operate both in establishing social order as well as embodied disarray through sensory displacement. Attention paid to sensory discomfort and disgust in food memories acts as a response to Holtzman's (2006) call for moving beyond "pleasant smells and tastes of good food" that remain consonant with Western epicurean views, extending the diverse significance of sensory modalities.

Sensuous ways of recollecting the past through culinary episodes are ineluctably not only about nostalgic, delicious memories. Indeed, a whole platter of pleasant and unsettling remembrances of these episodes are evident, and both types of food heritage structure how we revive if not connect to the past, and how these links are made relevant as important aspects of changing culinary landscapes across the different decades of Singapore in wartime and post-war situations. These various gastro-sensory moments are also to be read within the broader structural milieus that contextualise how they are recalled and registered (cf. Farquhar 2002) — for instance, how wartime food habits were greatly constrained if not altered by such practices of food rationing, the scarcity of food and food services, and how food cultivation was promoted to bring about self-sufficiency, resulting in a farming culture where farming practices took priority over work schedules and were also inserted into the school curriculum (Wong 2009: 21). Similarly, learning about food heritage in the context of Chinatown also comes along with a cursory look into Singapore's migrant past and dialect proclivities, signalling the relationship between foodways and group identity. Culinary texts therefore contextually provide nuggets of socio-historical information that carry tales of how people lived in times past and how these have bearings on comprehending the contemporary context.

Briefly, a final point I raise here has to do with embodying cooking skills and techniques. Bodily memories not only remember how foods tasted, smelled and looked like, but such embodied remembrances are also crucial in the preparation of food. Sensory know-hows are therefore important skills in food practices that are stressed upon. In the commemorative publication on *Not for Sale* (Teo *et al.* 2013), respective references are made by two hawkers pertaining to the senses in terms of the preparatory process for chicken curry noodle and *youtiao* (fried doughsticks):

> Hawkers don't work from recipes, even if I tell you everything, you may not be able to get the same taste. You must experience cooking hands-on, use your eyes to see, your sense of smell and ears to listen in order to master our skills (Teo *et al.* 2013: 65).

> My hands are how I measure the weight, texture and doneness of my dough (Teo *et al.* 2013: 263).

Culinary skills need to be actualised through the conscious use of one's different senses as a skillset (Abdullah 2010). In learning how to cook *bergedil* (potato croquettes), Ali (2013: 75) narrates her job of "mixing and kneading the potatoes thoroughly", where her mother also demonstrated "how to shape the potato croquettes into a perfect, desirable size" by placing the potato mixture onto her palm and forming it into a round ball, only to lightly flatten it thereafter. Ali conclusively declares: "The only way to learn how to cook is from experience, to be completely involved in the cooking process, especially the preparation" (*Ibid.*), this included putting up with earfuls of scolding and going through many rounds of practice and correction. On a separate occasion,

Ali (2013: 78) offers a sensorial recollection of cooking Malay desserts such as *kueh kacau*, a sweet potato base accompanied by coconut milk, eggs and *gula melaka*:

> One day before Hari Raya, my aunt was stirring the batter of *kueh kacau* and asked me to take over the wooden paddle. I was in short sleeves and unprepared for the splattering batter. I got scalded with batter that flew onto my face. From then I realised I had to wear long sleeves and on top of that cover both my hands with cloth to avoid being hurt by hot batter. I also had to shield myself with the lid of the aluminium pot... To stir the batter, a long wooden paddle was used in consistent strokes, allowing the batter to thicken slowly. Once thickened, the *kueh kacau* became a beautiful golden dark yellowish brown, and spread its sweet, beautiful aroma all over the badminton court area.

Clearly, this *kueh kacau* episode brings forth embodied recollections of both sensory dangers (being scalded with the hot batter) and sensory pleasures (remembering the texture of the thickened batter, the enticing hue of yellowish brown, and the wonderful and permeating smell).

Embodied skills and sensory expertise also relate to ethnic identity. As Hyman (1993: 120–121) notes: "Nonya cooks are very proud of their skill when it comes to pounding spices. It is said that an experienced cook can tell from listening to the rhythm of the pounding, whether the person is a good cook or not, and from the sound made by the pestle which spice is [being] pulverised." Together, these examples of embodied cooking throw light upon Sutton's (2001: 135) notion of "embodied apprenticeship", where one remembers not only a set of cooking techniques, but other avenues of "images, taste, smells and experiences" that likewise mediate culinary enskilment and intimate gastronomic memories.

CONCLUSION — THE POLITICS OF EDIBLE HERITAGE

Given the social and emotive characteristics of foodways, cookbooks and other culinary texts form anchoring points that convey and sustain the connections between food practices, propinquity, group identity and heritage. Memorable both as sensory and social experiences, the acts of cooking and of commensality are intimately tied to nostalgic remembering and heritage formation. The appetite for memories and heritage is found in social actors who wish to remember different facets of their lives and family members, as well as states that drive heritage-making projects for ideological purposes. In combination, both forms of remembering add to the construction and maintenance of identity in familial, generational and ethnic manners although the ways of doing so may converge or differ in their content and process. Together, foodways as instruction and as experience "bind individuals together, define the limits of the group's identity, serve as a medium of communication, celebrate cultural cohesion, and provide a context for ritual performance" (Nussel 2006: 958). Food heritage as culinary patrimony is about time past, present relevance, and imaginings of the future, where it connects inextricably to both group membership and kinship (cf. Lupton 1994).

This chapter has considered how culinary texts serve as apropos sources through which the heritage and memories of a nation are captured and storied concurrently as collective identities and individual biographies. Cookbooks and other materials form culinary repertoires of family life, historical events and heritage. In order to make heritage digestible and delicious, families have thus been asked to story their own gastronomic nostalgia by penning culinary writings. In other words, they bring to the plate, their own appetites and remembrances that are relevant and significant for themselves. These writings therefore serve as a locus from which an interplay of family life, the senses and heritage-making within the broader social and cultural contexts of Singapore in different time periods has been identified and analysed. In sum, culinary texts merge or reflect upon both private familial memories and collective narratives that in conjunction shed light on identity politics.

Sensory and ethnic embodiment of heritage lends further credence to consider how these different forms of engagement with the past are important in various dimensions of social life. Through these forms, foodways, as captured in the texts that I have examined, wield significant cultural heritage import. Culinary narratives found in these texts, informed by sensory attention and by ethnic dimensions, connect people to their familial ties and to their ethnic identity. This chapter thus shores up interesting questions pertaining to whether and how analyses of foodways may intersect with heritage and sensory studies towards realising the importance of different social ties and how the past is made relevant in embodied and sensorial gustatory ways.

REFERENCES

Abdullah N (2010) Comfort food, memory, and "home": senses in transnational contexts. In: D Kalekin-Fishman and KEY Low (eds.) *Everyday Life in Asia: Social Perspectives on the Senses.* Surrey: Ashgate, pp. 157–176.

Ali A (2013) *Sambal Days, Kampong Cuisine.* Singapore: Ate Ideas Pte Ltd.

Anderson B (1983) *Imagined Communities: Reflections on the Origin and Spread of Nationalism.* London: Verso.

Appadurai A (1996) *Modernity at Large: Cultural Dimensions of Globalisation.* Minneapolis: University of Minnesota Press.

Appadurai A (1988) How to make a national cuisine: cookbooks in contemporary India. *Comparative Studies in Society and History* **30**(1): 3–24.

Bessière J (2013) "Heritagisation", a challenge for tourism promotion and regional development: an example of food heritage. *Journal of Heritage Tourism* **8**(4): 275–291.

Bessière J (1998) Local development and heritage: traditional food and cuisine as tourist attractions in rural areas. *Sociologia Ruralis* **38**(1): 21–34.

Camp C (1989) *American Foodways: What, When, Why and How We Eat In America.* Little Rock: August House.

Chen Y (2014) Recreating the Chinese American home through cookbook writing. *Social Research: An International Quarterly* **81**(2): 489–500.

Chronis A (2006) Heritage of the senses: collective remembering as an embodied praxis. *Tourist Studies* **6**(3): 267–296.

Chua BH and Rajah A (2001) Hybridity, ethnicity and food in Singapore. In: DYH Wu and CB Tan (eds.) *Changing Chinese Foodways in Asia.* Hong Kong: The Chinese University Press, pp. 161–200.

Douglas M and Gross J (1981) Food and culture: measuring the intricacy of rule systems. *Social Science Information* **20**(1): 1–35.

Duruz J (1999) Food as nostalgia: eating the fifties and sixties. *Australian Historical Studies* **113**: 231–250.

Farquhar J (2002) *Appetites: Food and Sex in Post-Socialist China.* Durham, NC: Duke University Press.

Garth H (2014) "They started to make variants": the impact of Nitza Villapol's cookbooks and television shows on contemporary Cuban cooking. *Food, Culture and Society* **17**(3): 359–376.

Graham B (2002) Heritage as Knowledge: Capital or Culture? *Urban Studies* **39**: 1003–1017.

Higashiyotsuyanagi S (2010) The history of domestic cookbooks in modern Japan. In: EC Rath and S Assmann (eds.) *Japanese Foodways, Past and Present.* Chicago: University of Illinois Press, pp. 129–144.

Holtzman JD (2006) Food and Memory. *Annual Review of Anthropology* **35**: 361–378.

Howes D (2011) Vienna: sensory capital. In: M Diaconu, E Heuberger, R Mateus-Berr and LM Vocisky (eds.) *Senses and the City: An Interdisciplinary Approach to Urban Sensescapes.* Vienna and Berlin: Lit Verlag, pp. 63–76.

Hyman GL (1993) *Cuisines of Southeast Asia: A Culinary Journey through Thailand, Myanmar, Laos, Vietnam, Malaysia, Singapore, Indonesia, and the Philippines.* New York: John Wiley and Sons.

Kearney A (2009) Homeland emotion: an emotional geography of heritage and homeland. *International Journal of Heritage Studies* **15**(2/3): 209–222.

Kong L (2013) Creating urban spaces for culture, heritage, and the arts in Singapore: balancing policy-led development and organic growth. In: C Grodach and D Silver (eds.) *The Politics of Urban Cultural Policy: Global Perspectives.* London: Routledge, pp. 154–164.

Kong L (2007) *Singapore Hawker Centres: People, Places, Food.* Singapore: National Environment Agency.

Korsmeyer C and Sutton D (2011) The sensory experience of food. *Food, Culture and Society* **14**(4): 461–475.

Leong-Salobir C (2011) *Food Culture in Colonial Asia: A Taste of Empire.* London and New York: Routledge.

Levi-Strauss C (1969) *The Raw and the Cooked.* Translated from the French by John and Doreen Weightman. New York: Harper and Row.

Low KEY (2013) Olfactive frames of remembering: theorising self, senses and society. *The Sociological Review* **61**(4): 688–708.

Low KEY (2010) Summoning the senses in memory and heritage making. In: D Kalekin-Fishman and KEY Low (eds.) *Everyday Life in Asia: Social Perspectives on the Senses.* Surrey: Ashgate, pp. 87–113.

Lupton D (1996) *Food, the Body and the Self.* New York: Sage.

Lupton D (1994) Food, memory, and meaning: the symbolic and social nature of food. *The Sociological Review* **42**(4): 664–687.

Merleau-Ponty M (1968) *The Visible and the Invisible.* Evanston, IL: Northwestern University Press.

Mitchell J (2008) New Zealand cookbooks as a reflection of nutritional knowledge, 1940–1696. *Nutrition and Dietetics* **65**(2): 134–138.

Mitchell J (2001) Cookbooks as a social and historical document. A Scottish case study. *Food Service Technology* **1**: 13–23.

Nussel J (2006) Heating up the sources: using community cookbooks in historical inquiry. *History Compass* **4/5**: 956–961.

Parys N (2013) Cooking up a culinary identity for Belgium: gastrolinguistics in two Belgian cookbooks (19th century). *Appetite* **71**: 218–231.

Pilcher J (1998) *Que vivan los tamales!: Food and the Making of Mexican Identity.* Albuquerque: University of New Mexico Press.

Prager J (1998) *Presenting the Past: Psychoanalysis and the Sociology of Mis-Remembering.* Cambridge, MA: Harvard University Press.

Sanmugam D (2011) *Tricks and Treats and other Childhood Tales.* Singapore: Ate Ideas Pte Ltd.

Sanmugam D and Kasinathan S (2011) *Indian Heritage Cooking.* Singapore: Marshall Cavendish.

Seow JM (2009) *Soya and Spice: Food and Memories of a Straits Teochew Family.* Singapore: Landmark Books.

Seremetakis CN (ed.) (1994) *The Senses Still: Perception and Memory as Material Culture in Modernity.* Boulder, CO: Westview.

Singapore Family Favourites: Recipes from the Fairprice Family Cook Off (2010) Newport, NSW: Big Sky Publishing.

Smith L (2006) *Uses of Heritage.* London: Routledge.

Stoller P (1989) *The Taste of Ethnographic Things: The Senses in Anthropology.* Philadelphia: University of Pennsylvania Press.

Supski S (2013) Aunty Sylvie's sponge: foodmaking, cookbooks, and nostalgia. *Cultural Studies Review* **19**(1): 28–49.

Sutton DE (2010) Food and the senses. *Annual Review of Anthropology* **39**: 209–223.

Sutton DE (2001) *Remembrance of Repasts: An Anthropology of Food and Memory.* Oxford and New York: Berg.

Tan A (2012) *Savour Chinatown: Stories, Memories and Recipes.* Singapore: Ate Ideas Pte Ltd.

Tarulevicz N (2013) *Eating Her Curries and Kway: A Cultural History of Food in Singapore.* Chicago, Illinois: University of Illinois Press.

Teo A, Guan B and Dashow S (2013) *Not for Sale: Singapore's Remaining Heritage Street Food Vendors.* Singapore: Good Food Syndicate.

Theophano J (2002) *Eat My Words: Reading Women's Lives through the Cookbooks They Wrote.* New York: Palgrave.

Tobias SM (1998) Early American cookbooks as cultural artifacts. *Papers on Language and Literature* **34**(1): 3–18.

Tschofen B (2008) Of the taste of regions: culinary practice, European policy and spatial culture — a research outline. *Anthropological Journal of European Cultures* **17**: 24–53.

Tully J and Tan C (2010) *Heritage Feasts: A Collection of Singapore Family Recipes.* Singapore: Miele Pte Ltd.

Walker I (2012) Ntsambu, the foul smell of home: food, commensality and identity in the comoros and in the diaspora. *Food and Foodways* **20**(3/4): 187–210.

Wong HS (2009) *Wartime Kitchen: Food and Eating in Singapore 1942–1950.* Singapore: Editions Didier Millet and National Museum of Singapore.

Xue J (2013) Preserving Singapore's hawker heritage with apprenticeships. *The Straits Times*, 21 October.

Zerubavel E (1996) Social memories: steps to a sociology of the past. *Qualitative Sociology* **19**(3): 283–299.

Chapter 4

Placing Pig Farming in Post-Independence Singapore: Community, Development and Landscapes of Rurality

Harvey Neo

INTRODUCTION

The pace and depth of restructuring in an array of agro-food industries have been remarkable in the past decades. The drivers behind such transformation, which are fundamentally aimed at increasing profit, are nonetheless fuelled by the interplay of changing economies/technologies and shifting consumer demands. The latter is especially underpinned by changing social norms and expectations. Regulatory institutions also play important roles in managing and guiding the direction of these complex changes. The interplay of economy, regulation and culture must thus be recognised in understanding the geographies of food production and consumption.

In this chapter, the role of regulation in shaping and mediating the economies and cultures of food production in the first three decades of Singapore's independence is examined. The focus is on the pig farming industry, which was completely eradicated in Singapore by the late 1980s. Drawing largely from archival materials, I trace the tumultuous years from the mid-1970s to the late 1980s where policies pertaining to the development and future of the pig farming sector in Singapore proved to be unstable and prone to unexpected changes. At a more general level, not unlike many other countries grappling with the basic security issue of food provision, post-independence Singapore struggled to determine the future of agriculture. Should policies stimulate the productivity of agriculture? Or should domestic food production be de-emphasised in favour of an import strategy? Today, Singapore is not self-sufficient in any of the major foods that the country consumes. However, "local production [remains] an important secondary strategy in ensuring food supply resilience for Singapore" and the country continues to produce a modest amount of fish, eggs and vegetables as this provides "a buffer against supply disruptions" (AVA 2013). As an illustration, in 2013, 5.6% of the country's demand for fish was met by local production while the corresponding figures for eggs and vegetable were 35% and 4.2% respectively (AVA Food Imports 2013 and AVA Local Production 2013).

That agricultural production persists even at a level which is arguably symbolic and can hardly act as a buffer suggests that one must probe deeper for the reasons behind the eradication of pig farming in post-independence Singapore. In other words, why could Singapore not have a limited pig industry that supplies about 5% of local demand? Are the reasons related to environmental well-being? Did pig farming obstruct development in ways which are hard to mitigate? More importantly, what impacts did such eradication have on former pig farmers, their life worlds and their sense of community and purpose? What does the eradication of pig farming portend for the future of agriculture in Singapore? This chapter attempts to address these questions, and in so doing, illuminate the interconnections between food consumption, culture and community in the changing landscapes of post-independence Singapore.

The empirical data used in this chapter draw from English- and Chinese-language newspaper reports (especially those published in the 1970s and the early 1980s). In addition, I accessed three recordings of oral history of pig farmers and regulators which are stored in the National Archives of Singapore. To supplement these secondary and archival resources, I also managed to speak to two former pig farmers (who are in their 70s) and draw on their memories of their days as pig farmers. Both are my distant relatives who used to rear pigs in the 1970s and 1980s in Seletar and Punggol.

Following this introduction, I will elaborate on the key concepts that will ground my discussion of the ebb and flow of pig farming in Singapore. Next, I will detail the history of pig farming in Singapore, focusing on the 1970s and 1980s — the two decades that saw the most dramatic changes in the fortunes of pig farmers. I will attempt to explain the underlying drivers for these changes and their impacts on people, places and sense of community. I will conclude this chapter with the hindsight gained in the 30 years since pig farming was eradicated in Singapore, to evaluate its rightful place in the Singapore nation-building narrative.

PURITY, REGULATION AND COMMUNITY

The idea of purity is pertinent in food studies and especially for this research. Purity, in the anthropological, metaphorical sense used and made famous by Mary Douglas' seminal work *Purity and Danger* in 1966, is the "enemy of change, of ambiguity and compromise" (2002: 200). However, conventional understanding of purity, when applied to the agricultural and food industry, can simply mean a desire for more "wholesome" foods, in rejection of modern destructive means of food production. Yet others have taken both meanings of purity to analyse the complex changes in food production and consumption. In tracing the early efforts of Heinz to sell its canned products around the world, Domosh (2002: 10) argues that advertisements in which white women are feminised as icons of purity conflated and colluded with the message of Heinz products as "pure in the strictest sense of the word".

Moreover, invocations of purity are often attempts to create and sustain a boundary between us and the "other", most often seen in discourses of racial purity (Horwitz 2001). Taken to the extreme, such "othering" and boundary drawing become a discursive legitimisation for genocide — perhaps the most infamous example of which was Nazi Germany (Scales-Trent 2001). More apropos to this chapter, social scientists, including geographers, have long maintained an interest in the nexus of space, ethics and human beings' instrumental use of animals (for food and other purposes). *Animal Geographies* (Wolch and Emel 1998) and *Animal Spaces, Beastly Places* (Philo and Wilbert 2000) represent the two definitive books on human-animal relations. Nonetheless, the majority of the chapters in these edited collections deal with "wild" animals even as humans beings' relationship with animals are more commonly defined in terms of consumer and the consumed. In 2011, nearly 60 billion chickens, 13 billion pigs and 3 billion cows were slaughtered for human consumption (Foodtank 2014: 2). Livestock production is thus in part a relation between animals and humans (for example, farmers, consumers, regulators).

The issue of food taboo, which springs from human beings' particular attitudes towards certain animals, is similarly predicated upon the idea of purity and boundaries between human and (non-human) animals, amongst other things. As Rouse and Hoskins (2004: 236–237) sum up succinctly:

> Food taboos exist simultaneously as a method for blending the physical and the moral; as a form of social control or a way of delineating order; as a way of reducing ambiguities; as a way of embodying resistance to disintegration (personal and social), and as a method for ascribing sacredness.

In an early review essay on the geography of food consumption, Grigg (1995) chose to look at spatial variations in food consumption habits around the world. He attempted to explain these variations through broad structural reasons like the developmental state of individual countries/regions and cultural preferences for food. Simoons (1994), a social anthropologist, has more specifically focused on the spatial distribution of food taboos. The most systematic and codified of all food taboos are the Muslim halal and the Jewish kosher dietary laws. Given that Singapore has a sizeable minority of Muslims, it is surprising that (as will be discussed later) religious sensitivity was not a key reason for the eradication of pig farming. This is in contrast to the Malaysian pig industry where cultural politics was a key complicating factor in the development and restructuring of the industry (see Neo 2009; Neo 2012). This is not to say that other lines of division which are centred on notions of purity and cleanliness have not been evoked in the development and subsequent demise of the pig farming sector in Singapore. For example, as will be discussed, pig farming has often been viewed as a particularly polluting activity.

Besides this motif of purity (and cleanliness), this chapter highlights the role of regulation (or the lack thereof) in the development of the pig industry in Singapore. In the political-economic tradition of food studies, a popular focus is to look at the impacts that changing regulatory regimes at various spatial scales have on the production and consumption of food. In the United Kingdom context, Harrison et al. (1997) have analysed the tensions in implementing national food policies and regulation at the local level. However, by far, the most popular studies have been those which look at how changing regulations have caused agro-food firms to seek opportunities elsewhere or restructure their operations to achieve greater profits (see Wolf and Bonanno 2014; Cheshire and Woods 2013).

More relevant for this chapter are works that attribute changing regulatory regimes as partly the result of social-political imperatives. Neo (2009) details how the institutions governing the Malaysian pig industry are often reactionary to broader social politics in the country; hence, decisions made with respect to the industry might at times seem inconsistent. Guthman (1998) has shown how cultural constructions of food and nature are integral to the formulation of the regulatory regime of organic farming in California. Mansfield (2003) in her comparative study of the American and Vietnamese catfish industries similarly emphasises the importance of cultural constructions and political rhetoric in the formal and informal regulation of the American catfish industry. In other words, the catfish is imbued with contested meanings that are place rooted; insofar as they are similar — biologically and taste-wise — catfish from Vietnam are constructed as being less desirable than those from the United States. As food is an intimate component of culture, it is not surprising that the regulation of food production and consumption is imbued with cultural meaning, as these various examples indicate. In terms of specific regulation over pollution control, Ramsey *et al.* (2013) in their comparative study of Spain and Canada have highlighted how environmental regulation of the pig industry is intimately tied to the broader political economy. These studies all point to the fact that regulation of the agricultural sector is not an objective, value-free, economistic endeavour (Selfa *et al.* 2010).

Last but not least, community is a key idea that recurs in this chapter. In recent years, there have been concerted attempts to draw closer research programmes in rural studies and agriculture/food studies. The rationale is empirically self-evident. Changes in the modes of production in much of the agro-food sector have clear ramifications on the livelihoods and spaces of rurality. The latter in turn is intimately tied to the construction of community. Numerous studies have attempted to draw the links between a sense of (farming) community and the material aspects of rural change. These studies focus empirically on fishing community (Macken-Walsh 2012), family farmers (Mincyte 2011), elderly livestock farmers (Riley 2011) and first generation farmers (Ngo and Brklacich 2014), amongst others.

More apropos to this chapter, for example, is the continuing demise of the small farms. Globally, 67% of poultry production and 42% of pork production now come from industrial factory farms (Foodtank 2014: 2). In the United States alone, the number of pig farms has decreased drastically from 2 million in 1950 to 73,600 in 2005 (Nierenberg 2005: 15) while the number of pigs produced in the same period rose from 80 million to 100 million. Ikerd (2003: 34–38) argues that such intensification processes involves the "economic colonisation of the rural areas", a colonisation, he avers, that should be resisted by rural people so as to "preserve their priceless rural culture ... and to pursue a different strategy of 'sustainable' rural development" (see also Kietavainen 2014). Anthropologist Walter Goldschmidt concurs. Reflecting on the industrialisation of the rural pig industry in Iowa which has pushed out numerous family owned farms, he notes that the "sense of community, the ideals of mutuality and the social value of civility" are eroded by the changing systems of production (Goldschmidt 1998: 185). Notwithstanding the remnant romanticism in such writings, they at least prove that economic imperatives, politics, regulation and culture are very much inter-related in the transformation or demise of livestock industries in rural spaces.

When framed within the body of work pertaining to the agrarian transition (Harrison 2001; Buttel 2002), these studies are united in their aim to explain the complex reasons behind the refashioning of the rural landscape and to detail its subsequent impacts. In such ways, early concerns about food production have grown to include broader inquiries into the ethical relationship between agro-food and the changing faces/spaces of culture, rurality and altered livelihoods (Welsh *et al.* 2003; Buttel 2002). Hence, the livestock sector, such as the pig farming sector that was present in Singapore cannot be fully understood solely from an economic-developmental perspective. The ramifications on lives, community and, indeed, a broad sense of place concerning rurality must be addressed concomitantly.

Conceptually, the study of the pig industry in Singapore is grounded in an understanding of historical contingencies, the cultural politics of food production/consumption as well as the local regulatory regime and issues of governance. It will become apparent that the history of the pig industry is a synecdoche of the Singapore developmental narrative. Relating the fate of the pig farming sector in Singapore with the economic trajectory of Singapore reveals to us the remaking and unmaking of the community and national psyche, underpinned by the ideology of modernity and the soft authoritarianism of an exemplary developmental state. The next section will briefly outline the development and demise of the pig industry in Singapore post-independence. I then examine this chequered history by focusing on the regulation of the industry and its impact on community, before concluding.

PIG FARMING IN POST-INDEPENDENCE SINGAPORE

The predecessor of the Agri-Food & Veterinary Authority of Singapore (AVA), the Primary Production Department (PPD), was the government agency that oversaw all agricultural matters. In the early years of independence, agriculture was a significant sector by various measures. In 1967, just two years after Singapore's independence, it provided for the livelihoods of more than 20,000 families; it took up nearly 20% of all land use in Singapore; contributed to 4% of its GDP and the country was even self-sufficient in pork and poultry (Department of Statistics 1967: 19). Ten years later, in 1977, farms in Singapore produced 1.25 million pigs valued at $197.5 million (*The Straits Times*, 3 Oct 1977: 6). This figure ensured Singapore's continued self-sufficiency in pork. The change in the fortunes of the agricultural sector as a whole was dramatic, given that it was only another decade or so later that the entire pig farming sector in Singapore was all but decimated. What happened in the years between 1977 and 1989?

The Growth of the Pig Farming Sector: From Colonial to 1970s Singapore

In 1932, a *Straits Times* reader lamented the lack of a modern pig farming sector in Singapore. Amongst other things, he noted that farmers in Singapore did not get much help from the (colonial) government:

> I wish that individual farmers on [sic] here would get as much assistance from the authorities as is the case in the Philippines and Dutch East Indies. There the government not only maintains a highly trained staff of veterinary assistants who are placed at the disposal of the farmers whenever necessary, but whenever epidemics are threatened also supplies the necessary serums and vaccines either free or at a most moderate cost ... What has been done on [sic] that place could be done in Singapore and I am sure that there are still immense possibilities for a large pig farm on the island, run on up-to-date scientific methods (*The Straits Times*, 6 Aug 1932: 5).

The call by this letter writer was not followed up on expeditiously and it was only in the twilight years of the colonial administration, in 1959, that the Primary Production Department was set up to coordinate and promote agricultural development in Singapore. Moreover, it would be years after the

PPD's establishment that his suggestion of scientific modernisation of pig farming materialised. In any case, by the time Singapore gained independence (after leaving the Malaysian Federation) in 1965, almost all pig farms in Singapore were family-owned small holdings, rearing less than 100 pigs each (De Koninck 1975). These farms were spatially dispersed and could be found in many parts of Singapore, including Lim Chu Kang in the west, Yio Chu Kang in the north and Changi and Tampines in the east. Most of these family farms practised mixed agriculture and did not exclusively rear pigs. One of my interviewees, describes her farm (which closed in the mid-1980s) as follows:

> We did everything. We had pigs but not many — maybe about hundred plus? It was considered small. But we had a lot more layers [hens reared for their eggs] and also ducks. We even had a pond of fresh water fish, but that's more for personal consumption, and we grew water hyacinth in the pond too. That can be used to feed the pigs. We reared organic pigs [laughs] only because I did not want to spend too much money on commercial feed for the pigs. Also, our main business was selling eggs.

To be sure, the regulation of and policy governing pig farming in Singapore mirrored the experience of elsewhere in the world. For example, the twin concerns of improving productivity and managing environmental impacts are never far from the minds of the regulators and planners. In their influential study of the Oklahoma pig industry, Lyford and Hicks (2001) stressed the need for more certainty and less fluidity in the legislative environment so that all concerned parties can benefit. Legislation is thus seen as a major driving force behind the expansion (or contraction) of the pig industry (see also Savard and Bohman 2003). This was true for the Singaporean pig farmers too.

In a triumphant 1977 article, the PPD reflected on its role in modernising the pig industry as "a remarkable achievement, considering the limitations of land area which over the past decade had been further whittled down as a result of massive industrial and housing development" (*The Straits Times*, 3 Oct 1977: 6). Citing the Punggol Pig Farming Estate as its most ambitious and successful project, the PPD noted that it "ha[d] been in the forefront in revolutionising animal husbandry in Singapore" and even planned for an eventual number of up to 1,000 pig farms in Punggol by 1982, up from the less than 200 in 1977 (*Ibid*). There were also plans to allocate 235 hectares of land in nearby Jalan Kayu for more pig farms.

In retrospect, 1977 marked the peak of a geopolitical cum developmental ideology of self-sufficiency. It was an ideology that took root in 1965 when a country with no natural resources and a small population was forced to survive. This critical juncture formed the roots of Singapore's developmental strategy. With the loss of the hinterland in Peninsular Malaysia, the three key inter-related "survivalist" motifs of "small size", "vulnerability" and "planning" emerged. Perry *et al.* (1997) have noted that "one of the hallmarks of modern Singapore lies in its intensively planned environment". Others have similarly observed that "the bottom line is that given Singapore's environmental limitation, the country has very little margin for error" (Savage 1991: 197). The immediate survivalist need to feed a growing nation meant that the government in the 1960s was obligated to promote food self-sufficiency. Besides such pragmatic concerns, Puah (2013) has argued that in the early years of post-independence Singapore, the People's Action Party struggled to consolidate power against the breakaway faction of Barisan Sosialis who counted the rural areas as their strongholds. Lee Kuan Yew was reported to frequently "visit farms in PPD land-rovers ... to show that the government cared for the farmers" (Puah 2013: 19). This is not to say that the twin goals of achieving food self-sufficiency and establishing political legitimacy are not mutually exclusive (for the former is arguably a component of the latter). However, it does suggest that once political legitimacy is concretised, fundamental policies towards agriculture can be changed without fear of losing the support of the electorate, as was the case at the start of the 1980s.

The Demise of the Pig Farming Sector: 1970s–1980s

By the mid-1970s, the freewheeling growth of the pig farming sector was coming to an end. Concerns about the environmental impacts of pig farms which were lightly regulated led to plans to relocate farms into a central pig farming area and the consequent push for greater intensification. The chief source of environmental pollution came from excretion. Nitrates and phosphates from the manure and urine of pigs that were improperly disposed of were the main pollutants. It did not help that fresh water was (and still is) a core survivalist need for Singapore. In its annual report in 1974, for example, the PPD noted the indiscriminate disposal of pig waste into water bodies around the farms.

In other places, manure of pigs in small mixed use farms are used to fertilise the soil for crops to supplement or even supplant inorganic fertilisers (OECD 2003). However, given that the implicit policy in Singapore was for greater consolidation and intensification, which would result in mega-farms, such an environmental friendly way of disposing manure became untenable because "large operations are more likely than smaller operations to have an insufficient land base for utilising manure nutrients" (Thu and Durrenberger 1998: 17). Manure then became a form of waste rather than a potential resource.

Faced with the twin concerns of fresh water provision and food self-sufficiency, it became quickly apparent which was deemed more critical, as when E.W. Barker, then National Development Minister remarked in Parliament: "water first, before pigs" (Rahim 2009, cited in Puah 2013: 25). With this, all pig farms began a process of resettlement, away from catchment areas and mostly into the centralised pig farming area in Punggol. This major initiative did not suggest that the state meant for the eventual demise of the pig sector — not yet, anyway. If anything, the few years following 1974 saw a host of regulations and celebratory rhetoric about the pig farms which often seemed contradictory. The reality also did not bear out the rhetoric.

First, while the concern for environmental pollution (particularly the pollution of water bodies) was the key rationale for the resettlement of pig farms into centralised areas like Punggol and despite the congratulatory tone of the drive towards intensification, many family farms that resettled continued with both the scale of the farms (i.e. small) and production practices (i.e. lackadaisical attitude towards environmental protection with minimal technological innovation) (*The Straits Times*, 31 Mar 1978: 8). Second, contrary to the image of a well-planned state, newspaper reports between 1977 and 1985 show that when it came to pig farming policies, the government was unable to formulate a consistent and long-term developmental plan for the pig farming sector. Indeed, it would appear that even a short- to medium-term plan was not apparent.

For example, in October 1977, a newspaper article lauded the achievement of self-sufficiency for pork in Singapore, especially highlighting how the PPD's ambitious project in the Punggol Pig Farming area would make it the most technologically advanced farming area in Singapore (*The Straits Times*, 3 Oct 1977). Yet, barely two years after this celebratory news, it was announced that a new pig farming area would be built in Lim Chu Kang and all pig farms in Punggol would be shut down by 1989 (*The Straits Times*, 24 Sep 1979). In the three years after this announcement, it appeared that the decision to relocate the Punggol pig farms was again stayed or reversed, with newspaper reports once more highlighting the virtues of the Punggol pig farming area. For example, in 15 February 1981, an article headlined, "Punggol pig farms: a model of efficiency", highlighted the high regulation standards of the pig farms in Punggol (*The Straits Times*, 15 Feb 1981). More news of a similar nature was to come in the next two years when the inaugural graduates of the nine-month pig farm manager course taught by the new PPD-established Punggol Pig Centre was publicised (*The Straits Times*, 15 Jun 1982). The Director of PPD was quoted as saying that he hoped the graduates would be able to "meet the challenging demands in the next two years when large industrial pig farms will be fully set up in Punggol." By early 1984, even before large industrial farms had materialised, the survival of pig farming was in serious jeopardy.

A possible reason for the shifting policy towards pig farming could be that the government then had fierce internal disagreements with regards to the future of pig farming. This is most evident in the fact that the policy towards pig farming made a complete turnaround almost as soon as Dr Goh Keng Swee took the helm at the PPD. As late as December 1983, the government was still encouraging farmers to apply for the capital grant to build waste treatment plants (*The Straits Times*, 23 Dec 1983). However, less than three months later in March 1984, the complete phasing out of pig farming was mooted in parliament (*The Straits Times*, 13 Mar 1984). To quote at length Dr Ngiam Tong Tau, who took over the Directorship of PPD after Dr Goh Keng Swee took charge of it:

> So I think we roughly gave them $20 per pig for infrastructure cost to build pig waste treatment plants... Some of them were already building the plants and the government suddenly declared they were going to phase out pig farming. *Came out of the blue. It was kept very hush hush... up in high levels of government. On the ground we didn't know anything. Then one fine day, we were told that, "Oh now the policy is to phase out pig farming immediately." I said, "What? You are giving farmers so much hope and money to build treatment plants and they've already built all the modern farms"... and the government declared, "phase out"...* And at that time, Dr Goh Keng Swee came into the picture because he was instrumental in coming with this law to phase out pig farming. The policy to phase out pig farming in Cabinet, so they were really tough. They removed the then Director, Dr Siew, from office. They more or less told Dr Siew to retire. So Dr Siew resigned and went to work for the private sector (Ngiam, A003117/08 Reel 01, Oral History Centre, National Archives of Singapore, emphasis added).

The extended quote shows that the decision to phase out pig farming was a surprise to even people who were working to modernise the pig farming sector. It is clear that regulatory policies towards pig farming in Singapore had undergone dramatic change in the fateful months between mid-1983 and early 1984. It is beyond the scope of this chapter to attempt to probe the real reasons behind the reversal of policy except to note that notwithstanding the potential of building a high-tech pig sector that can fit into a modernist discourse, it was eventually decided swiftly and resolutely that the sector has no place in the continuing developmental plans for Singapore. The olfactory nuisance of pig farming and the lingering doubts about a truly clean pig industry, coupled with the perennial fear of spatial constraints eventually sounded the death knell for the pig farming sector. It was moreover an unexpected end to a sector that at various points in its chequered history looked set to stay. Beyond these regulatory and policy shifts and turns, what has been relatively muted in this history are the voices of the pig farmers, and how the changing fortunes of pig farming (which were exacerbated by inconsistent policies) have impacted their sense of identity and community. I turn to this in the next section.

PIG FARMERS AS COMMUNITY AND FAMILIES

The Singapore Livestock Farmers' Association was formed in 1964 by a group of Chinese poultry farmers but expanded quickly to include all kinds of livestock farmers, including pig farmers. Mr Lim Chor Hau, a founding member of the association, recalls that the impetus for the creation of the association was to provide a community of learning and self-help amongst livestock farmers:

> About 1963, I pioneered some new techniques in my poultry farm and many farmers heard about it and came to look at my farm. Some of these farmers became my friends and we started to keep in contact with one another. Then a few of them told me: "Us farmers, we are so dispersed and disorganised, most of us do not know anyone and those who do, have very few friends. *Why don't we set up an organisation, to build friendships, to share farming knowledge, and we can interact with the government as a unified group too?* (Lim, A001164/11 Reel 09, Oral History Centre, National Archives of Singapore, emphasis added and translated from Chinese by author).

Such ground-up initiative from farmers which promote solidarity is not uncommon. In Malaysia, for example, the Federation of Livestock Farmers' Associations of Malaysia, is a key lobby group that has taken the lead to address grievances and chart growth in often very hostile operation climates in Malaysia (Neo 2012; Neo 2009). This is mirrored in Singapore. Despite a far more restrictive political climate in the early 1980s, the Singapore Livestock Farmers' Association attempted to resist the government's bombshell announcement of the phasing out of pig farming. In solidarity, and likely also in fear of a similar fate befalling them, poultry farmers stood firm with their pig farming counterparts.

Mr Toh Joo Ee, a vice-chairman of the Association, told the media then that "the plans drawn up by the PPD to restructure pig farming had all along been correct" (*The Straits Times*, 22 Mar 1984: 10). Amongst other things, he questioned if Dr Goh Keng Swee's strategy of importing pigs from other places like Malaysia and Indonesia was prudent, arguing that there can be "no assurance that [Singapore] will get overseas supplies" (*Ibid.*). The subtext of this is that trade relations are subject to broader geopolitical ties and Singapore might be risking too much if we were to totally rely on food imports. Ironically, Mr Toh's suggestion of maintaining a limited local supply of food against unexpected disruptions in food imports aligns with the present food policy of AVA, described in the introduction.

In the months that followed, pig farmers continued to make various arguments against the complete phasing out of pig farming. A pig farmer appealed to the government to allow small farms which would supplement meat imports, at least until the current generation of farmers passed on. Drawing on the sense of identity and community as farmers, 55 year old Poh Ah Leck who had been resettled twice, lamented that "I have been farming since I was 18. What other work can I do? This is my life and I have raised eight children" (*The Straits Times*, 21 Apr 1985: 10). In other words, there was a palpable sense of "losing oneself" with the phasing out of pig farming where farmers spoke not solely about the pragmatism of *livelihoods* but the very core of *living*.

The spokesperson of one of the biggest family-run pig farms, felt a deep sense of loss even as the family was already diversifying into other businesses like food processing, food and beverages and the operation of supermarkets (they remain the owners of the present-day Prime Supermarkets). Speaking not so much about the economic loss, Mr Tan Hong Chiew wondered how the 59-member family could stay together and noted, "it will be a very, very painful experience when the family breaks up" (*Ibid.*).

A sense of identity thus resided in both a functional entity such as the Singapore Livestock Farmers' Association as well as at the more intimate scale of the family — which encompasses both functional and intrinsic values. Other farmers drew even more broadly on their sense of loss in the inevitable transformation of their ways of life. A letter writer to the now defunct Chinese daily, *Nanyang Siang Pau*, reminisces about his days as a former farmer:

> Every day after school, I had to give up all after-school activities and quickly return home. That time, our farm had a few 70 kg or so pigs. Every afternoon, I had to shower and wash the pigs. We could not afford mechanised sprinklers so I had to draw pails of water from the well to deposit into the tank beside the pig sty. That tank could hold 65 gallons of water. Using little buckets I then splashed water on the pigs to prevent them from over-heating ... Whenever we managed to sell some pigs, the whole family would be so happy, because we had earned our keep ... Although rearing pigs and vegetables were really tough, we managed to survive pretty well [despite my father's early passing]. This was really a miracle led by my mother and my siblings, my family. Writing about this, I am once again intoxicated by the memories of my simple, halcyon days in the village (Piao 1973: 13, translated from Chinese by author).

In less lyrical terms, one of my interviewees when asked about how she and her family felt about giving up farming and moving into a Housing Development Board flat, answered:

> We were in Jalan Kayu, we had to give up pig farming first but we knew it would be a matter of time before we ha[d] to stop everything completely. No more chickens, no more ducks too. My two elder daughters and my only son [third child], they always help[ed] in the farm. After school definitely, and often even before they [went] to school in the morning — there [was] just so many things to do. When we had to move eventually (in the late 1980s), I c[ould] tell they d[id] not know what to do with their free time [laughs]. Also, in the kampong, our house might be messy but it was a big house, and so much space. Of course this is an executive flat — the biggest HDB flat, but it still feels so small. I never worked again after giving up farming. My husband and I, we get by with our savings and playing the stocks. But my children, the three eldest ones, I think for them, adjusting was also not easy. *It is just such a different world, different life.*

Such evocations of community, family and "the simple life" encapsulated within the "small farm" present a more favourable image of farming (albeit arguably romanticised) against the view that farming is backward and has no place in modern Singapore. Indeed, as Singapore develops further, such discursive constructions of family, community and roots are increasingly used to challenge the presumptive economic-developmentalist path that Singapore takes. This can also be seen in the call for the conservation of nature, where environmentalists frame nature as heritage that will enrich the community at large (Neo 2007).

While these family-run farms found no place in the modernist, developmentalist state, the irony remains that the development of big modernised farms did not fit perfectly either. The attempts to latch onto the broader developmental and modernising ideology and discourse of Singapore by investing heavily was an attempt to show that the existence of pig farms did not contradict the broader developmental project of the Singapore state. Indeed, for most of its existence, the PPD adopted this view as well. As evinced in the discussion earlier, such a narrative failed to save the pig farms. How then can one think of agriculture in Singapore now? In the next concluding section, I suggest how rural landscapes in general and pig farming specifically can be located in the broader questions of community and development in post-independence Singapore.

CONCLUSION

For years since the eradication of pig farming and the spatial consolidation of other forms of agriculture, Lim Chu Kang in the western part of Singapore has remained one of the last bastions of rural landscape and agriculture. This is set to change with the recent announcement by the government that the area will be cleared to build the Tengah New Town (*The Straits Times*, 1 Nov 2014). All 62 farms in Lim Chu Kang are set to be relocated by 2021 to places yet to be determined but with reduced leases and smaller plot sizes. Some of these farms have invested heavily in high-tech farming (e.g. a vertical vegetable farm). This seems to be treading on all-too-familiar ground — and a replay of the fate of the pig farming sector two decades ago.

Writing at the cusp of Singapore's 50th year of independence, we are in a better position to reassess the events spanning the decade from the mid-1970s to the mid-1980s which led to the shutting down of the pig industry and valorise other voices which have not been heard as clearly. As alluded to earlier, pig farmers were not a homogenous group. Smallholders which formed the majority were unable to modernise and upscale their operations. The main reasons for this inability were their limited capital and lack of desire to produce more pigs. Related to this was the fact that most family farms practised mixed farming and readily considered giving up pig farming rather than investing more into this economic activity, particularly when the future of the sector became more ambiguous from the late 1970s onwards. On the other hand, bigger farms enthusiastically adopted the language of modernisation and had hoped (to no avail) that with better intensified production technologies and the ability to manage the environmental impacts of pig farming, there might be a future for them.

Yet, as can be seen from the recent resettlement notice for the far less pollutive farms in Lim Chu Kang, the question of environmental protection is but one of the several considerations when assessing the future of agriculture in Singapore. The multiple demands for space is arguably the key factor at work. Presently, in a far more interconnected world, where flows of goods/foods has become easier and cheaper, the almost complete reliance of food import might not be such a risky policy idea. Not least, it is virtually impossible for Singapore to even strive for food self-sufficiency anyway, given its expanded population.

Future land-based farms in Singapore will face heightened regulation over their production methods and output, with at least 90% of their land mandated to be directly involved in production (*The Straits Times*, 26 Aug 2014). This resolutely productivist and developmentalist drive towards agriculture might seem commonsensical at first glance. However, when set against the fact that Singapore is likely to depend on food imports, regardless how productive and intensified local farms can be made to be, it compels us to think about what other roles agriculture can play — beyond the functional and pragmatic.

Echoing the pig farmers' lament about losing their lives (beyond mere economic livelihoods), a soon-to-be-resettled Lim Chu Kang farmer was quoted as saying: "This is a growing community of farmers and people interested in farming ... The *kampung* spirit is very much alive here. We have a WhatsApp group that we update each other on and will turn up at anyone's farm if they need help." Another remarked in resignation: "I have seen farms move before but this particular one feels like a revolution. Many farmers I know who watched me grow up are ending their businesses. It's a sad thing to know they are going into history" (*The Straits Times*, 21 Nov 2014).

With the impending demise of the farms in Lim Chu Kang, there remain five other pockets of farming areas in Singapore, the most famous of which is the Kranji Countryside. Therein lies a likely albeit modest future space for farming in Singapore. It is a future that aims to expand the productivist language of agriculture to include the notions of eco-tourism, education, recreation and heritage conservation — what Wilson and Rigg (2003) termed "pluriactivity" of farms. As stated in the Kranji Countryside Association website:

> Every child should be brought up to appreciate and cherish our natural environment, to understand where food comes from, and to live a life of health and sustainability. We hope to impart a green consciousness to one and all, and to encourage Singaporeans and visitors alike to return to nature and its treasures. We also believe that the countryside should be a place with a soul, and that challenged Singaporeans should be able to find employment and empowerment on the farms. Join us in our vision to keep this part of Singapore wild, beautiful and caring.

It is telling that in their mission statement, the Kranji Countryside Association makes no mention of food security, knowing full well that in reality local agricultural production has been consigned to a light supplementary (almost symbolic) role within Singapore's main strategy of diversified food imports. Given this, their vision is actually realistic and commendable because it speaks of a place (both physically and metaphorically) which ties food, nature and community. The nurtured and continual existence of such a place can only enrich Singapore in the years to come.

REFERENCES

AVA (2013) Promoting Local Produce. http://www.ava.gov.sg/Promoting+Local+Produce.htm, accessed 10 November 2014.

AVA Food Imports (2013) Food Imports. http://www.ava.gov.sg/docs/default-source/tools-and-resources/yearly-statistics/food-imports, accessed 15 March 2015.

AVA Local Production (2013) Local Production. http://www.ava.gov.sg/docs/default-source/tools-and-resources/yearly-statistics/local-production, accessed 15 March 2015.

Buttel FH (2002) Some reflections on late twentieth century agrarian political economy. *Sociologia Ruralis* **41**: 165–181.

Cheshire L and Woods M (2013) Globally engaged farmers as transnational actors: navigating the landscape of agri-food globalisation. *Geoforum* **44**: 232–242.

De Koninck R (1975) *Farmers of a Small City State: The Chinese Smallholders of Singapore*. Montreal: Canadian Sociology and Anthropology Association.

Department of Statistics (1967) *Year Book of Statistics*. Singapore: Government Printing Office.

Domosh M (2002) Pickles and purity: discourses of food, empire and work in turn of century USA. *Social and Cultural Geography* **4**: 7–26.

Douglas M (2002 (1966)) *Purity and Danger*. USA: Routledge.

Foodtank (2014) *Rethinking Industrial Animal Production*. https://www.scribd.com/doc/247019882/Rethinking-Industrial-Animal-Production, accessed 15 November 2014.

Goldschmidt W (1998) The urbanisation of rural America. In: KM Thu and EP Durrenberger (eds.) *Pigs, Profits and Rural Communities*. USA: State University of New York Press, pp. 183–198.

Grigg D (1995) A geography of food consumption: a review. *Progress in Human Geography* **19**: 338–354.

Guthman J (1998) Regulating meaning, appropriating nature: the codification of California organic agriculture. *Antipode* **30**: 135–154.

Harrison CM, Flynn A and Marsden T (1997) Contested regulatory practice and the implementation of food policy: exploring the local and national interface. *Transactions of the Institute of British Geographers* **22**: 473–487.

Harrison G (2001) Peasants, the agrarian question and lenses of development. *Progress in Development Studies* **1**: 187–203.

Horwitz H (2001) Uses of racialism: hybrids, race and cultural legibility. *Western Humanities Review* **55**: 43–64.

Ikerd J (2003) Corporate livestock production: implications for rural North America. In: AM Ervin *et al.* (eds.) *Beyond Factory Farming*. Canada: Canadian Centre for Policy Alternatives, pp. 29–38.

Kietavainen PG (2014) Narrated agency and identity of settlement farmers in the changing circumstances of modern society. *Sociologia Ruralis* **54**: 57–70.

Lim CH A001164/11 Reel 09, Oral History Centre, National Archives of Singapore.

Lyford C and Hicks T (2001) The environment and pork production: the Oklahoma industry at a crossroads. *Review of Agricultural Economics* **23**: 265–274.

Macken-Walsh A (2012) Operationalising contemporary rural development: socio-cultural determinants from a strong local fishing culture. *Human Ecology* **40**: 199–211.

Mansfield B (2003) From catfish to organic fish: making distinctions about nature as cultural economic practice. *Geoforum* **34**: 329–342.

Mincyte D (2011) Subsistence and sustainability in post-industrial Europe: the politics of small-scale farming in Europeanising Lithuania. *Sociologia Ruralis* **51**: 101–118.

Neo H (2012) 'They hate pigs, Chinese farmers … everything!': beastly racialisation in multiethnic Malaysia. *Antipode* **44**: 950–970.

Neo H (2009) Institutions, cultural politics and the destabilising Malaysian pig industry. *Geoforum* **40**: 260–268.

Neo H (2007) Challenging the developmental state: nature conservation in Singapore. *Asia Pacific Viewpoint* **48**: 186–199.

Ngiam TT A003117/08 Reel 01, Oral History Centre, National Archives of Singapore.

Ngo M and Brklacich M (2014) New farmers' efforts to create a sense of place in rural communities: insights from southern Ontario, Canada. *Agriculture and Human Values* **31**: 53–67.

Nierenberg D (2005) *Happier Meals: Rethinking the Global Meat Industry*, Worldwatch Paper 171, Worldwatch Institute.

OECD (2003) *Agriculture, Trade and the Environment: The Pig Sector*. Organisation for Economic Co-operation and Development.

Perry M, Kong L and Yeoh BSA (1997) *Singapore: A Developmental City State*. New York: Wiley.

Philo C and Wilbert C (2000) (eds.) *Animal Spaces, Beastly Places*. London: Routledge.

Piao Y (1973) 那段养猪种菜的日子 (Those days of rearing pigs and growing vegetables). 南洋商报 (Nanyang Siang Pau), 20 November 1973, p. 13.

Puah YK (2013) *Pig Farming and the State: Re-thinking rural development in post-independence Singapore*, Unpublished Honours Thesis, Department of History, National University of Singapore.

Ramsey D, Soldevila-Lafon V and Viladomiu L (2013) Environmental regulations in the hog farming sector: a comparison of Catalonia, Spain and Manitoba, Canada. *Landuse Policy* **32**: 239–249.

Riley M (2011) 'Letting the go' — agricultural retirement and human-livestock relations. *Geoforum* **42**: 16–27.

Rouse C and Hoskins J (2004) Purity, soul food and Sunni Islam: explorations at the intersection of consumption and resistance. *Cultural Anthropology* **19**: 226–249.

Savage VR (1991) Singapore's garden city: reality, symbol and ideal. *Solidarity* **131/132**: 67–75.

Savard M and Bohman M (2003) Impacts of trade, environmental and agricultural policies in the North American hog/pork industry on water quality. *Journal of Policy Modelling* **25**: 77–84.

Scales-Trent J (2001) Racial purity laws in the United States and Nazi Germany: the targeting process. *Humans Rights Quarterly* **23**: 259–307.

Selfa T, Fish R and Winter M (2010) Farming livelihoods and landscapes: tensions in rural development and environmental regulation. *Landscape Research* **35**: 595–612.

Simoons FJ (1994) *Eat not this flesh: food avoidance from prehistory to the present.* Madison, Wisconsin: University of Wisconsin Press.

The Straits Times (2014) Kampung spirit alive in Lim Chu Kang: farmers there a close-knit group but must start vacating area in three years, 21 November.

The Straits Times (2014) Lim Chu Kang farmers in limbo as land leases run out, 1 November.

The Straits Times (2014) $63 million fund, new criteria for farming, 26 August.

The Straits Times (1985) Picking up the pieces after Dr Goh's bombshell, 21 April, p. 10.

The Straits Times (1984) 'Keep the better livestock farms, no assurance that we'll get overseas supplies': Farmers, 22 March, p. 10.

The Straits Times (1984) Days of the pig farm numbered, 13 March, p. 1.

The Straits Times (1983) Waste plants for 21 more pig farms, 23 December, p. 11.

The Straits Times (1982) You're the pioneer farmers, 20 told, 15 June, p. 10.

The Straits Times (1981) Punggol pig farms a model of efficiency, 15 February, p. 7.

The Straits Times (1979) Lim Chu Kang earmarked for pig farming, 24 September, p. 11.

The Straits Times (1978) Respite for the Punggol pig farmers, 31 March, p. 8.

The Straits Times (1977) Intensive farming: Singapore is now self-sufficient in pigs and poultry, 3 October, p. 6.

The Straits Times (1932) Pig farming, 6 August, p. 5.

Thu KM and Durrenberger EP (1998) (eds.) *Pigs, Profits and Rural Communities.* USA: State University of New York Press.

Welsh R, Hubbell B and Carpentier CL (2003) Agro-food system restructuring and the geographic concentration of US swine production. *Environment and Planning A* **35**: 215–229.

Wilson G and Rigg J (2003) Post-productivism agricultural regimes and the South: discordant concepts? *Progress in Human Geography* **27**: 681–707.

Wolch J and Emel J (1998) (eds.) *Animal Geographies.* USA: Verso.

Wolf SA and Bonanno A (2014) (eds.) *The Neoliberal Regime in the Agri-Food Sector: Crisis, Resilience and Restructuring.* USA: Routledge.

Chapter 5

The Kopitiam in Singapore:
An Evolving Story about Cultural
Diversity and Cultural Politics

Lai Ah Eng

(with Contributions by Lee Shuyun Michelle and Lim Jialiang)[1]

INTRODUCTION

Hundreds of *kopitiam*s (coffee shop in local Chinese dialects) are found throughout Singapore. While both old and new ones are found in the city areas, the majority are located in the town and neighbourhood centres of all HDB (Housing and Development Board) public housing estates in which 83% of Singapore's population live. A quintessential feature of Singapore public culture and everyday life, the *kopitiam* is an institution and space within which are embedded dynamic aspects and processes of economics, social-cultural diversity and cultural politics, set within the larger contexts of change, localisation and globalisation throughout Singapore's recent history. In origin a small-scale village, street or neighbourhood setup serving cheap foods during the colonial period of mass migrations, the *kopitiam* has since evolved and

---

[1] Some sections of this chapter appear in an earlier work: Lai AE (2013). For this chapter, the author wishes to acknowledge Lee Shuyun Michelle's contributions in the sections on Hainanese *kopitiam*s and *kopitiam*s' historicisation and commoditisation, as well as Lim Jialiang's contributions on the appeal to authenticity and nostalgia in *kopitiam* heritage and on some market trends.

experienced much change over several distinct broad periods: pre-World War Two until the early 1970s, massive resettlement of communities into HDB public housing estates in the 1970s and 1980s, and rapid urbanisation and globalisation since the early 1990s.

This chapter is divided into four sections. The first examines the *kopitiam*'s evolution of its social-cultural distinctiveness and diversity through the foods and peoples involved. It explicates the historical, social and cultural evolution of the *kopitiam* as a site of Singaporean ethnicities and multiculturalism derived from the continuous inputs and interactions of generations of (im)migrants, entrepreneurs and customers over time.[2] The second section documents some features of the HDB "heartland" *kopitiam* today, focusing on foods and community. The third section examines several forces and trends since the early 1990s — market trends and official policy, *kopitiam* heritage commoditisation and reinvention, and consumer tastes and preferences — that have dramatically affected *kopitiam* economics and cultures. The last section concludes with a discussion of future possibilities in the *kopitiam* story.

Background

This chapter is mainly empirical in substance,[3] with several broad theoretical parameters framing its discussion: a socio-historical perspective and its significance to the life of a locale or local community; the economic, social and cultural dimensions of local life constructed through migration, settlement, adaptation and reinvention; and the local-global nexus.

Two periods of mass migration, the first throughout the late 18th, 19th and early 20th centuries and the second since the 1980s, set the contexts for the *kopitiam*'s development through diverse populations and their cultural

---

[2] I move between *kopitiam*s in general and those in public housing estates.

[3] Research employed historical, sociological and anthropological approaches. Secondary data is drawn from books, journals, archives, reports and media documents (newspaper reports, and "amateur" history and heritage-related blogs). Primary fieldwork (July–Nov 2008, Nov 2014) was based on conversational interviews and observations at *kopitiam*s in several public housing estates: Marine Parade and Bedok — these are all "first generation" housing estates built under the government's resettlement scheme of the early 1970s. Their populations are socially mixed and multi-ethnic, comprising Chinese (majority in every case), Chinese Peranakan, Malays, Indians, Eurasians and various other backgrounds, many of whom were first resettled from surrounding villages, squatter areas and rental quarters. I did not encounter any major problems with observations, mainly because of the openness of *kopitiam*s and local familiarity as resident, familiar customer, and interested documenter of food cultures.

inputs and interactions. In the first period mainly under British colonialism, diverse peoples, chiefly from China, India and the Malay Archipelago, came to Singapore and Malaya in massive waves to work and live in the ports, mines, plantations and emergent villages and towns, with migration flows stopping only just before World War Two. Singapore grew rapidly from entrepot port to town with rich hinterlands in Malaya and Southeast Asia. In the second period, migration to Singapore since the mid-1980s took place in a new era of post-colonial economic globalisation. Coming with varied levels of skills for various occupations, immigrant settlers and transient migrant workers now originated from more varied Asian and worldwide sources.

The *kopitiam*'s story also illustrates the local-global nexus which characterises various spaces, places and communities of a city or nation-state drawn into globalisation processes. In Singapore, the *kopitiam* stands out as a unique institution with its particular local-global nexus of economic, social and cultural inputs, ingredients and infusions, through the generations of diverse people who inhabit it and through the foods and activities that they bring and partake of. Its neighbourhood location — spontaneous, open and public — provides multifaceted insights into the local: everyday life as habitable reality (de Certeau 1984) and reality par excellence (Berger and Luckmann 1966); meanings and experiences of culture and community (Geertz 1975; Cohen 1982); modes of interaction, negotiations of similarities and differences (Cohen 1982; Heller 1984); and civil and moral order (Suttles 1968; Whyte 1993; Lai 1995). Simultaneously, its location makes it a well-placed institution to provide glimpses into local-global connections and into the social life, landscape and heritage of the open and globalising city that Singapore is.

THE *KOPITIAM* IN HISTORY

In Early Settlements During the Colonial Period

The *kopitiams* had humble origins as small-scale economic enterprises. Found in early settlements of workplace, village, street or neighbourhood in 19th and early 20th century colonial Singapore,[4] they sold cheap drinks and meals to poor migrant workers, and they were run by individuals or small teams of men and,

---

[4] Here, I omit earlier forms of public eateries that must have existed to serve the maritime trading communities in Singapore in pre-colonial times.

later, families. Known as *han*, *tong* and *tan* in Chinese dialects and *gerai* and *sarabat* in Malay, most were no more than carts or makeshift structures, often with itinerant hawkers operating alongside. In the pepper and gambier *kangkar* (plantation) Chinese settlements, the forerunner of the *kopitiam* was probably set up alongside the liquor, provision and pawn shops run by the *kongsi* (the work association usually run along clan lines). As populations and demands grew, some expanded into modest-size "eating houses", with proprietors selling both drinks and food or only drinks and teaming up with/renting out stall space to food operators.

Early *kopitiam*s and food stalls assumed a strong ethnic dimension in their spatial distribution and cuisine as they "followed" migrant workers and met their desires for culturally familiar foods. By 1900, the Chinese had become the majority population, and Chinese "eating" houses/stalls became numerous. They typically sold a range of noodles and fresh pre-cooked "economy rice" — affordable combinations of rice with dishes such as salted eggs, fish and vegetables — such foods cooked in their distinct versions by place origin. When meats became affordable, place origin versions followed suit, such as Cantonese roast meats and Teochew duck. Some *kopitiam*s and stalls offered *tze char* (literally "cook-fry") cook-to-order dishes which approximated home cooked meals. In the enclaves settled by Indians and Indian-Muslims, similar eateries referred to as *kedai makan Mamak* (Indian/Indian-Muslim food shop) sold breads (*prata*, *thosai*) and meals of rice combined with various curries, while *sarabat* stalls sold coffee, teas and snacks. Similarly, *kedai-* (shop) and *gerai-* (stall) *makan* (eat) in areas settled by Javanese, Sumatrans, Boyanese, Bugis and Madurese sold various *nasi* (rice) dishes such as *padang*, *rawan*, *jenganan*, *lemak* and *sambal*, spicy meats and vegetables, and various cakes and cuisines from their homelands. Such ethnic food stalls found in the pluralistic areas and edges of town, such as the old Esplanade and Selegie-Rochor-Serangoon vicinities, also catered to the increasing diverse tastebuds.

With the sale of food and drink, the *kopitiam* gradually became a social centre for the largely male immigrants. Among the Chinese, its early forms were probably their only alternative gathering place to brothels and alcohol, opium or gambling dens. When public gambling farms under British licences were outlawed in 1829 by the colonial government on grounds of immorality, some *kopitiam*s served as fronts for betting and gambling dens. Some also served as meeting places for secret society members. In the main, most *kopitiam*s were simple eateries where, besides food, customers sought rest, company and recreation. It was also a place for men, as women immigrants were relatively few and were expected to remain at home or in women's quarters. Among women, usually only hawkers, workers and servants were found in workplaces and markets, while only prostitutes, dancers, escort girls and mistresses were seen in recreation places frequented by men; women did not sit around in *kopitiams* to chat and idle.

As social centre, the *kopitiam* was the place to meet and gather for news, chats, stories and a games of chess or cards, its strategic location simultaneously providing a view of people and the world passing by.[5] News of the outside world — on immigrants' homelands, Singapore and Malaya, and elsewhere — came via vernacular newspapers subscribed to by the *kopitiam* owners and from which reports were read, alone or aloud to others many of whom were illiterate. When *Rediffusion* (the first commercial and cable-transmitted radio station in Singapore) started broadcasting services in various Chinese dialects and Malay and Tamil languages in 1949, many *kopitiams* subscribed to it to attract customers. *Rediffusion* not only offered news but also stories, songs and music of various linguistic and cultural traditions, from the classical to contemporary pop, and it provided many hours of free and favourite entertainment to customers. As many households could not afford the installation and subscription charges, the *kopitiam* became the location where they could enjoy the new radio station.

Hainanese *Kopitiams*

The early history of *kopitiams* is incomplete without understanding the significant part played by the Hainanese *kopitiam*.[6] The dominance of the Hainanese in the Chinese *kopitiam* business is an interesting tale of the latecomer and minority immigrant group whose survival skills later gave them an unexpected edge. Arriving later than the other dialect groups that had already occupied various occupational niches backed by exclusivist clan associations, the numerically smaller and marginalised Hainanese found employment in despised or difficult work as farmers, rubber tappers, seamen, cooks, waiters and servants. Throughout the 19th and early 20th centuries, those who worked as cooks and domestics in European/Peranakan households built up a reputation

---

[5] Chua (1995) elaborates on the *kampung* (village) *kopitiam* as the location par excellence for collective idling by males.
[6] Some details in the discussion on Hainanese *kopitiam* in this section are drawn from the work of Lee Shuyun Michelle (2009), Hainanese Gobidiams in the 1930s–1950s: Food Heritage in Singapore.

as loyal and reliable Hylam/Hainan "houseboys" and "cookboys", and they came to be in great demand for their ability to help support colonial and rich lifestyles.

Changing economic and political conditions during the turbulent pre- and post-war periods saw the gradual demise of the Hainanese domestic workers. Their growing demands for better work conditions and competition from well-organised Cantonese single women immigrants (the *ma-tsae*) from the 1920s onwards greatly reduced their appeal, their decline in this sector culminating during the exodus of the British in the immediate pre-war, post-war and pre-independence periods (Lee 2009: 13). Many were forced to enter new occupations, and they turned to what they knew best — foods, beverages and services. Striking out on their own individually or in small teams of relatives or friends, Hainanese men tapped on their culinary, housekeeping and personal service skills cultivated from domestic work to set up *kopitiam*s, bakeries, eateries, canteens and related food and beverage businesses such as coffee processing and food catering, under new conditions of self-employment. Others found waged employment as cooks and waiters in Western-style hotels, clubs, restaurants and cafes, while yet others started their own small hotels. Other Hainanese immigrants entered the *kopitiam* trade directly, picking up skills along the way. Their economic niche-building was further strengthened by the common ideal among Chinese immigrants to exit arduous waged labour into *ka-ki-kang* (self-employment) and, even better, to be a successful entrepreneur through hard work.

The 1920s–1950s thus became a period of growth during which the Hainanese carved out and consolidated their distinct *kopitiam* business niche (Lee 2009:14–15). The now famous Killiney Kopitiam chain (Killiney Kopitiam 2007), for example, was opened as a humble shop in Killiney Road in 1919 by a Hainanese immigrant. Similarly, the now famous Ya Kun Toast (Ya Kun 2014) began with 15-year old Hainanese immigrant Loi Ah Koon who arrived in Singapore in 1926 and first worked as an assistant in a Hainanese coffeestall before setting up his own. Yet Con, Chin Chin and Swee Kee, all renowned for chicken rice and other Hainanese dishes, started operating in 1931, 1935 and 1949 respectively. The famous Chin Mee Chin Confectionery in Katong was opened in 1925 by a Hainanese, Mr Tang, while the Red House Bakery and Confectionery nearby, first started by Jewish Jim Baker in 1925, was taken over in 1931 by a Hainanese seaman Tan Siang Fuan (see Chapter 6 of this volume). Hainanese *kopitiam*s numbered between 20–30 along the main streets of the Hainan town enclave and "Coffee King" Lee Chang Er owned seven *kopitiams* (Lee 2009: 18). Hainanese *kopitiams* also sprang up in other locations such as Telok Ayer, Siglap, Chai Chee, Thomson and Nee Soon, while Hainanese cafes served mainly British and Commonwealth troops and their families in the Seletar, Sembawang and Portsdown military bases.[7] The firm establishment by Hainanese in the food and beverages industry by the early 1930s led to the formation of the Kheng Keow Coffeeshop and Eating House Owners Association in 1934, later renamed the Kheng Keow Coffee Merchants Restaurants and Bar-Owners Association (新加坡琼侨咖啡酒餐商公会) in 1952 to reflect the expansion of the business and related trades during the 1950s which was considered the peak of the Hainanese *kopitiam* business.[8]

The core attraction of Hainanese *kopitiams* and eateries was their foods. Drawn from their culinary backgrounds working in European households, some distinct dishes were hybridised creations with Hainanese-Western roots, such as breakfast comprising coffee,[9] *kaya*-butter toast and half-boiled eggs, pork chops and assorted confectionery (developed from the original British breakfast, Western pork chops and Western confectionery respectively). Other dishes were chicken rice, curried chicken and beef noodles. The early Hainanese *kopitiams* and eateries may thus be credited with introducing to the public Hainanese, Western and hybridised Hainanese-Western foods, many of which have now become iconic or favourite Singapore foods. They may also be credited for being foundational in developing the *kopitiam* into a public institution and the strong public culture of eating and drinking by the 1950s, during which the *kopitiam* landscape was made up of hundreds of operators. But where the Hainanese *kopitiam* business became a successful niche, so did it attract other newcomers and competitors such as from the Foochows.[10]

Indian and Malay Eateries

Paralleling the Chinese *kopitiams* and eateries were *kedai kopi* and *sarabat* stalls set up by Indians, Indian-Muslims and Malays which catered to demand for

---

[7] For two other outstanding examples — Jack's Place and Han's — see www.jacksplace.com.sg and www.hans.com.sg.

[8] Membership rose from 61 at its inception to 221 in 1940 and 505 in 1950 (Lee 2009: 16–17).

[9] Hainanese coffee merchants and *kopitiam* operators also developed their special recipes and distinctive forms of roasting coffee beans and brewing coffee.

[10] Among the Chinese *kopitiam* operators the numerically larger group of Foochows expanded so rapidly that they set up the Singapore Foochow Coffee Restaurant and Bar Merchants Association (新加坡福州咖啡酒餐商公会) which had about 600 registered members by the 1950s (Lee 2009: 18).

ethnic foods by the expanding Indian and Malay populations. For example, Zam Zam, which opened in Jalan Sultan as early as 1908, sold Indian-Muslim foods such as *briyani*, *murtabak* and *prata* (with different curries and meats) and drinks such as coffee and teas such as *teh alia* (ginger tea) and *teh tarik* ("pulled" tea). The first Indian vegetarian eatery Ananda Bhavan (now a chain of four across "Little India") was founded in 1924 by Indian immigrant Bhavan within the Indian enclave of Selegie (Ananda Bhavan 2013), while vegetarian restaurant Komala's was opened in 1947 by Murugiah Rajoo and brothers, immigrants from Tamil Nadu, South India, after Rajoo had first worked as a waiter for ten years at Komala Vilas vegetarian restaurant in the Indian enclave in Serangoon (Komala Vilas nd). Such eateries sold Indian vegetarian foods such as *prata*, *thosai*, *vadai*, pancakes, as well as sweets in their diverse varieties. Sabar Menanti restaurant in the historically ethnic Kampung Glam and Kampung Jawa districts, famed for *nasi padang* and other Minangkabau dishes, was first set up around 1958 as a food stall by an immigrant from Sumatra (Omar 2006). Indeed, Indian-Muslim and Malay stalls and eateries, although smaller in numbers, have equally contributed to the making of the Singapore *kopitiam* as a public institution and to the public culture of eating and drinking.[11]

Resettlement into the HDB Estates and the Rise of the Multicultural HDB *Kopitiam*

The *kopitiam* underwent much change in the immediate years of nation building, from the mid-1960s until the mid-1980s. This was a period of massive and hurried urban renewal and rural resettlement, under which the HDB was tasked with meeting Singapore's housing redevelopment needs and with resettling populations from sometimes overcrowded and dilapidated urban areas, slums and squatter settlements, as well as rural villages into high-rise blocks of flats in HDB housing estates and new towns. Large plots of land with numerous settlements and farms were targeted for clearance for public housing and schemes such as industrial estates, and their entire populations

---

[11] The historical evolution and individual stories of Indian, Indian-Muslim, Malay and other eateries within the contexts of the social history of Singapore and their respective communities need to be researched and told alongside the Chinese ones, for a more complete and inclusive story of *kopitiam*s and food heritages in Singapore's multiculturalism.

were moved out into new instant and highly planned neighbourhoods.[12] Along with these new public housing estates was born a new type of *kopitiam*.

Designed as part of basic facilities in the HDB estate's town and neighbourhood centres, this new *kopitiam* was typically located at each end of a shophouse row and close to hawker centre and market facilities, serving drinks and cooked food as before. Most of the first operators of the new *kopitiam*s were likely *kopitiam* operators and others displaced by resettlement and offered priority HDB accommodation and the option of relocation into or priority allocation of HDB business premises at concessionary resettlement rental rates (Lim and Lim 1985: 311–316, 326–328). Others were individuals seeking new business opportunities. Similarly, the many itinerant hawkers and makeshift stallholders who found themselves compulsorily licensed and resettled as part of the government's town cleansing, public health, urban renewal and resettlement programmes, also took up new stalls in the new *kopitiam*s, hawker centres and markets in the new estates.

The *kopitiam* in the new public housing estate was also new in another sense — through its multicultural makeup. Where previously, the *kopitiam* was largely ethnic-based in location, cuisine and clientele, this new *kopitiam* was clearly multi-ethnic, mirroring the new multi-ethnic composition of the new estate whose populations were resettled from previously mainly ethnic-based areas. This feature became an instant reality as the *kopitiam* naturally became one of the first public gathering sites for those disoriented by resettlement and for reorienting them. Through it, co-residents and neighbours from former communities were reunited with one another, strangers became recognisable as familiar faces, and yet others befriended as members of a new social network and co-residents of the new community. The *kopitiam* operator now had to provide food and drink for an enlarged and ethnically mixed clientele even as the majority in every housing estate was Chinese, and he quickly adapted the old formula in which he sold drinks and rented out stalls selling a variety of ethnic foods. Residents themselves also began to develop a multi-ethnic and cross-cultural taste for foods due to regular exposure in the *kopitiam*. "Multicultural" thus became the unwritten formula for the *kopitiam*'s survival, growth and success in the new multi-ethnic neighbourhood, and in doing so

---

[12] See Lim and Lim (1985) for details of resettlement policy, process and pact and Chua *et al.* (1985) for a detailed longitudinal case study of resettling a village. Unfortunately, the latter study did not track the resettlement consequences for the village's one and only coffee shop. See also Neo, Chapter 4 of this volume, on the resettlement of pig farmers.

it reinvented itself as a public place for the cultural confluence of cuisine, clientele and community in local everyday life that persists to this day.

THE HDB *KOPITIAM* TODAY

There are an estimated 1,963 food courts, coffee shops, eating houses, cafes, coffee houses and snack bars and 322 coffee shops in Singapore today, among which hundreds of *kopitiam*s are found in the HDB estates.[13] Their manifestation as a public site of multiculturalism is best understood by way of the kinds and flows of foods, people and activities found in them.

Foods, Foods and More Foods

The common comment "what to eat today?" attests to the variety of foods sold in the HDB *kopitiam*. Culturally, they range from Chinese to Malay, Indian/Indian-Muslim, "Western" and international, derived from migration flows of people and their foods. Individual items such as chicken rice, noodles, *prata* and *nasi padang*, once identified as ethnic and introduced by/for immigrants, are now iconic Singapore foods readily available in most *kopitiam*s as basic and popular items. The Hainanese-Western breakfast set is now standard fare. The "economy rice" stall that originally offered a cheap combination of rice and dishes to immigrants retains its status as the *kopitiam*'s "anchor" stall while the *tze char* stall is now effectively a small restaurant serving a wide range of dishes. The Indian/Indian-Muslim food stall selling *prata*, *chapati* and meat dishes, the Malay stall selling *mee rebus, nasi lemak* and meat dishes, the "Western" stall offering local versions of Western foods (chops, steaks, grills, fries) are at least three other "must-haves" for a *kopitiam* to be "complete" or at least "decent". Traditional ethnic foods abound and so do hybridised and cross-cultural versions of individual items, such as noodles (Chinese, Indian and Malay in dry, fried or soup versions and by Chinese dialect group); rice (Chinese, Malay and Indian, each with a range of meats and vegetables); curries (Chinese,

---

[13] http://www.business.gov.sg, http://www.thegreenbook.com, both accessed 3 July 2009. Total membership of outlets registered with the Keong Keow and Foo Chow associations vary between 700 and 1,100, while there are 800 HDB coffee-shops and 550 pre-war coffee-shop houses (National Environment Council 2004).

Hainanese, Malay, Indian); breads (Chinese, Malay, Indian and Western); and *rojak* (Chinese, Malay, Indian). A diversity of drinks match this food "fair" and are often ordered in their hybridised Singlish names. Most customers have developed at least a mildly multicultural taste, and it is common practice for individuals to rotate different ethnic dishes among their meals and for a family to be eating different dishes together.

A *kopitiam's* range of ethnic foods also varies by ownership, location and customer base. For example, stalls in Chinese-owned 128 Kopitiam, Bedok, besides offering common dishes such as roast meats and noodles, also serve distinctly traditional Chinese dishes such as Teochew porridge, Szechuan duck, black chicken, pig's innards and trotters, and frog legs and turtle soups. The stalls in nearby Mukmin Restaurant serve a range of Malay and Indian-Muslim foods and desserts, the classics being various kinds of rice with spicy meats and vegetables, breads and cakes as well as Malay and Indian hybridised versions of Western foods such as burgers.

Some HDB *kopitiam*s and stalls have also attained fame for their foods within the estate or beyond, "appearing" on food and heritage trails by word of mouth and through the internet[14] (see Tan, Chapter 8 of this volume, for a discussion of food blogs) and are sites sought out by eager "foodies". Mukmin Restaurant, for example, was and still is well known for its range of Malay *kuih-muih* (cakes and desserts) and, according to one stallholder, "people from all over Singapore, from as far as Woodlands, will come here to eat and buy our food". Similarly, the *tze char* stall formerly in MP59 Kopitiam in Marine Terrace (and now relocated to Bedok) attracts crowds from beyond the estate. Their claims to fame and sometimes ownership of a particular dish are based on "first" setup, originality, authenticity, heritage and tradition, special skills, styles and ingredients, and sometimes simply being the offspring of an original stall, or due to an award received or positive media coverage by food tasting experts, while patronage or visits by celebrities or politicians are given prominent publicity through pictures and pinups.

Since the 1990s, the range of foods that have shaped and substantiated Singapore's diverse culinary landscape (Chua and Raja 1997: 1) have been further infused with new ingredients and inputs by locals and new immigrants. In the Marine Parade and Bedok *kopitiam*s surveyed, the traditional "Western"

---

[14] See for example, www.foodlane.sg, www.makansutra.com, www.hungrygowhere.com, www.makantime. com, soshiok.com, www.goodfood.sg, www.yebber.com, www.ieatishootipost.blogspot.com and www. eateatenate.blogspot.com.

food stall now additionally serves burgers, pizzas and spaghetti, besides chops and steaks; Indonesian *ayam penyet* and Thai *tom yam* are popular in Malay cuisine; the Korean and Chinese noodles stall in MP59 Kopitiam is well patronised; while Japanese and fusion foods (e.g., XO brand fried rice) was offered by fusion food Asia.Com stall in VStar. A Botak Jones outlet serving American foods set up shop in a Marine Parade *kopitiam* in July 2009 and was doing brisk business initially. Its parent company, set up by an immigrant American and his Singaporean wife, was born out of the observation that there is a "definite lack of availability of good, well-made western food in the industrial and heartland areas".

> Botak Jones is always finding ways to bring the quality of food and service into a more comfortable, everyday setting, which translates into coffee shops and eating houses, where people feel at ease and can dress as they wish and be themselves ... everyone should have the opportunity to taste what the world has to offer no matter where and how they live (Botak Jones nd).

Some dishes and stalls "die" in Singapore's fiercely competitive culinary environment and amidst rapidly spiralling business costs (for example, fusion food Asia.Com stall closed after a year; Botak Jones has reduced its number of outlets; MP59 Kopitiam changed hands in 2013). However, the concept of "multicultural" in the *kopitiam* is firmly established — it has to offer a wide range of ethnic, hybridised and even "national" foods that meet the ethnic, multicultural and international palates of customers and at affordable prices. In turn, it is the strong public culture of eating, first initiated through meeting immigrant needs and developed to now include "foodies" and food heritage trails, which sustains the multicultural *kopitiam*'s survival and success.

People of the *Kopitiam*

Customers and community[15]

In contrast to an earlier time when the *kopitiam* was a male domain, the *kopitiam*'s customers today are families, schoolchildren, groups and individuals

---

[15] For a fuller discussion on various aspects of a local HDB community, see Lai AE (2012) A neighbourhood in Singapore: ordinary people's lives 'downstairs'.

(all of whom are mainly local residents) frequenting it according to their everyday life schedules and needs. Now a taken-for-granted scene, women, including Muslim women, eat and drink in the *kopitiam* in same-sex or mixed groups or alone. "Latchkey" schoolchildren whose parents are out working can safely eat there. The down-and-out, the storyteller and the joker too can find their own spaces in the *kopitiam*. This is the public home ground of the *Ah Laus*, *Pakciks* and *Makciks* (the elderly in local Chinese and Malay referencing) and *Ah Bengs*, *Ah Lians*, *Mats* and *Minahs* (the Chinese and Malay youngsters in local referencing). The *kopitiam* that is opened every day from early morning till late at night is at once a place of intense colours, sounds and activities. Customers queuing for food, stallholders shouting orders, cooks preparing foods, cleaners clearing tables, people eating and chatting, the television screening programmes — these are the everyday scenes of the multicultural public site that the *kopitiam* has evolved into within the local community. As if in a play about everyday life, they all make their appearances at different times to perform on the stage that the *kopitiam* is. It is a site where HDB "heartlanders" of various age, ethnic, income and work backgrounds frequent to eat, drink, socialise, idle or simply to feel the presence of others. A shared space, it offers a sense of being open and equal to all (Chan 2003: 132, 135), with social boundaries temporarily removed or well negotiated within an order of civility honed over time. The professionally dressed worker and the pyjama-clad *auntie* (elderly lady), the retired *pakcik* and the young student — all may enter and share space in the *kopitiam*. It is normal to ask "can I sit here?" and unthinkable to reply "no, you cannot".

As a social centre, the *kopitiam* remains, as in the past, a window to the world through media access. There is always something to watch on cable television (which replaced *Rediffusion since the 1980s*), from international news to cartoons, soap operas, documentaries, sitcoms and reality shows. Highlights are "live" sports events such as local and international soccer league games, when men in particular, fathers and sons, foreign workers and beer drinking groups, turn up to watch, and from which new Singlish terms are spawned, such as Pang-Pow (cannon-firing in Hokkien) for Arsenal and Tok-Tok-Ham for Tottenham Hotspurs soccer teams. Indeed, the *kopitiam* is one of the few public places where local languages may still be heard and the multicultural Singlish language further developed, such as "palata" (prata), "who man say?" (who said so?) and "you sit I bring" (please sit, I will bring your order). Here too, chats and discussions about world and local events, jokes, stories, personal histories and various matters significant or otherwise continue to take place in the true tradition of coffee shop talk. The heartland HDB *kopitiam* is a place that provides a sense of social intimacy and community.

The practices of religious diversity and negotiations of religious boundaries in the *kopitiam* attest to the strength of equality, tolerance, respect and developed codes of civility within its multiculturalism and sense of community. Visually and symbolically, these are manifested by the peaceful coexistence of Muslim-run stalls' signboards, which typically display icons of mosques, moon and star and Arabic inscriptions about Allah, and Chinese *kopitiams'* altars for the deities deemed important for peace and prosperity. Religious boundaries around food are maintained along halal/non-halal lines for Muslim and others foods. Stalls observe these boundaries in food preparation and service, such as with colour coded crockery, while customers demarcate eating spaces within an unspoken but well understood code when eating halal/non-halal dishes at a shared table. Some events further highlight religious diversity and its negotiation. During Ramadan, Mukmin Restaurant opens close to breaking fast time when there is a frenzied sale of foods by the stalls and the owner offers free food to the needy as a gesture of almsgiving. It is also a time for non-Muslim customers to savour the special foods of the season. For Chinese *kopitiam*s and stalls, offerings are made daily and on auspicious occasions such as the Seventh Month Festival, while the *tze char* stall offers special dishes such as *lou hei* (a salad toss for blessings) and visiting lion dance troupes perform for prosperity during the Lunar New Year. In general, the code of civility for respecting and accommodating cultural and religious needs, practices and taboos in the *kopitiam* are well understood and developed by stallholders and customers alike, honed through everyday practice over time.

Kopitiam owners and stallholders

The white singlet and striped pyjama pants-clad *kopitiam* proprietor making coffee was a common sight until the 1980s. Today's *kopitiam* owner is likely an absentee landlord who owns several *kopitiams* in various parts of Singapore and even abroad — a consequence of intense competition and capital movements in which older founding proprietors unable to keep up with competition or wishing to retire have sold their shops to new and aggressive investors in what has become a highly lucrative business (elaborated in the third section). Similarly, *kopitiam* stallholders tell a complex story of small family business formations and adjustments to economic pressures since the 1990s.

Kopitiam stalls have historically been run by a sole proprietor or as a small family or team enterprise. Father-son, husband-wife, siblings and friends teams were common. But stallholders' upwardly mobile children, like those of *kopitiam* owners, are reluctant to take over their parents' trades with the long hours, hard work and low status. As a result, there has been some loss of culinary skills and secrets and some stalls have closed when their operators retired (Huang 2008, Yen 2008). More seriously, since the late 1990s, rising costs have led many stalls to close or relocate, some several times, to areas with lower rents. The 30-year old Malay food stall in one Marine Terrace *kopitiam* closed when it changed ownership and rents were raised twice. Father-sons team of a popular chicken rice stall moved out of Marine Parade to Katong and then Bedok because of rising rents; another Hainanese chicken rice stall in Bedok, in the same business for 30 years, has moved several times within Bedok to neighbourhoods with cheaper rents. Lao Feng Turtle Soup's stallholder in Block 128 Coffee Shop Bedok intends to retire after several decades in the business as rents and costs of ingredients have spiralled, and also because his "highly educated" son never had any interest in the business. Younger generation members of family-run stalls in Mukmin Restaurant hold full-time jobs and only assist after work or during the Ramadan peak hours. Marine Parade Laksa run by a husband-wife team in Block 128 Coffee Shop Bedok is a classic stall story. Starting as itinerant hawkers carrying their food ware on shoulder poles in Joo Chiat/Katong in the 1950s, they relocated from their Katong shop where they had been for decades to Marine Parade when rent controls were lifted, and then to Bedok following rental rises. Now in their early 80s, their last move from a S$3,000 per month rented stall in Marine Parade to their current S$1,500 one in Bedok might well be the last, although their grandchild is running a similar stall in Katong where "*laksa* wars" among competing stalls have occasionally erupted.

Hard work, long hours and low wages in the *kopitiam* and food stall trades — a constant feature since their early days — has meant a shortage of local workers, particularly throughout the last decade. The solution has been the hiring of cheap foreign workers, sometimes illegally and which has been fraught with problems of exploitative work conditions.[16] However, this too has run into problems due to official policy changes since 2013 to reduce overall

---

[16] For a discussion on the hiring of cheap foreign workers and their cultural implications, see Lai (2013: 220). Under existing law, the services sector must employ a minimum nine Singaporeans or permanent residents before they can hire foreign workers, while only Singaporeans and permanent residents are allowed to work in food stalls, including *tze char* stalls. See also *The Straits Times* (12 Dec 2007a) (12 Dec 2007b) (5 Jul 2009a) (5 Jul 2009b) (16 Oct 2009).

dependence on cheap foreign labour. The labour shortage continues and the hiring of cheap local elderly labour by *kopitiam*s appears to be another short-term solution.

A NEW CHAPTER IN THE *KOPITIAM* STORY: THE 1990s AND BEYOND

*Kopitiam*s have entered a new era in their evolution since the early 1990s. There are unprecedented changes and tremendous competitive pressures, with frequent changes of *kopitiam* ownership and food stall tenancy amidst a general trend of spiralling costs and prices. The demise of many old *kopitiam*s and stalls will probably go unremembered. What dominates the scene are the success stories of early immigrants' *kopitiam*s and eateries which had a headstart and are now run by subsequent generations of family, through inheritance and intergenerational skills transfers but changed by rebranding, modernised management systems, new ideas of public eating culture, and reinvented and hybridised dishes — such as Jack's Place, Hans, Killiney and Ya Kun (all Hainanese), Bhavan and Komalas (South Indian) and Sabar Menanti (Indonesian/Malay). There are also new "rags-to-riches" success stories, such as that of Pang Lim, the 13-year-old kitchen-helper who became Koufu food court's chain boss[17] and Lim Bee Huat, the once nine-year-old *kopi kia* (coffee boy) who became *kopi king* of the Kopitiam chain[18] and who dreams of "a *kopitiam* on every street" and hopes to "fill the street corners with coffee, *kaya* toast and eggs". These enterprises have expanded locally through the establishment of outlets all over Singapore, as well as regionally and internationally, such as in the case of Komalas, Kopitiam, Hans and Ya Kun whose staff are effectively a class of international "circulating migrant" entrepreneurs. There are also numerous food courts in shopping malls, "new generation" *kopitiam*s and "hipster" cafes mushrooming in gentrified town areas and older HDB estates that have undergone physical upgrading programmes. Underlying this changing *kopitiam* landscape are several forces

---

[17] Pang worked variously as kitchen helper, street hawker, fruit seller and coffee shop stallholder before opening his first coffee shop in 1990 with his younger brother and uncle. Pang's Koufu chain operates about 30 food courts, five coffee shops and five cafes, mainly in HDB estates. See Tan (2007) and Koufu (nd).

[18] Lim Bee Huat started as a coffee stall assistant who harboured entrepreneurial ambitions and made acute observations about the trade along the way (http://www.kopitiam.biz/our-success-story/).

which have significantly affected the *kopitiam* as a complex economic and cultural site: market behaviour and official policy changes, coffee shop heritage commoditisation, as well as consumer tastes and preferences.

Market Behaviour and Policy Changes

Since the late 1980s, structural economic changes, together with state deregulatory measures followed closely by private capital mobilisation in the property markets, have affected old *kopitiam*s. In particular, the removal of the Control of Rent (Abolition) Act in 2001[19] displaced or spelt the death of many small businesses that were unsustainable without low rents, resulting in their shuttering or relocation. An influx of capital quickly entered the *kopitiam* sector and intensified, with *kopitiam* chains such as Kopitiam, Koufu and S11 purchasing *kopitiam*s around Singapore. In HDB estates, the consolidation of major *kopitiam* operators was made possible by another policy change at about the same time: the privatisation of ownership of HDB *kopitiam*s, where they were previously only rented out under HDB's management since resettlement days. This trend was started by the founder of the Kopitiam chain when he bought his first HDB *kopitiam* in Bishan with a "jaw-dropping" bid of S$2.01 million in 1988, a sum that buckled industry expectations then. The shop's value later rose to S$6 million while the chain quickly expanded to about 70 outlets by 2009.[20]

The rapid and widespread extent of buying *kopitiam*s had the overall economic effect of soaring prices of *kopitiam* properties for sale or resale. It was a period of consolidation for the major *kopitiam* operators, in which the *kopitiam* became as much a property investment or speculation as a business (Han 2013). The bullish market has also created the urge for investors to see *kopitiam*s as targets for "flipping". This process begins with the sale of a newly purchased *kopitiam* to another owner, who then takes the opportunity to renovate the space (even if it was renovated fairly recently by the previous owner) so as to justify increased rents onto the tenants. Rather than work for

---

[19] The Rent Control Act was passed in 1947 to prevent profiteering by landlords due to the housing shortage then. However, it has been phased out gradually, firstly through the Controlled Premises (Special Provisions) Act, in 1970, and then in 1989. This allowed owners to recover possession of their properties if they have development plans approved by the Urban Redevelopment Authority, and owners and tenants will have to negotiate to reach a settlement.

[20] The Kopi Tiam King www.kopitiam.biz/our-success-story, accessed 1 July 2015.

a return, the new owner may simply hold the *kopitiam* for a few years (or in some extreme cases, months) and sell it to make a quick buck, and the process continues. This is seen in the increasing regularity of *kopitiams* being bought and sold for millions, such as the case in which six *kopitiams* in Hougang were sold during 2011 for a combined value of SGD$60 million, while another, Coffee Express 2000, sold for a record SGD$23.8 million in 2013 (Huang and Cheong 2011; Wee and Lim 2013; Chan and Kua 2007). In June 2016, Yong Xing Coffee shop in Bukit Batok was sold for a record of S$31 million (almost 10 times the original price of $3.38 million 20 years ago) to a brother of the founder of coffee shop operator Chang Cheng Group which owns the Chang Cheng Mee Wah chain of coffee shops (Lin 2015). Several *kopitiams* observed in Marine Parade and Bedok (W326 Coffee Shop, 123 Coffee Corner, MP59) changed hands at least thrice since the late 1990s. MP59 Coffeehouse and VStar Coffeehouse in Marine Terrace changed ownership around 2004 and 2006 respectively, and each again changed ownership twice around 2010 and 2012. Another example is the *kopitiam* at Block 18 Bedok South Road, which has changed owners three times from 2010–2014.

The overall economic effect of this trend on stallholders and customers has been the rapid rise in rentals and food prices. The sale of a *kopitiam* at Jurong East in 2007 at SGD$12 million to Koufu netted an increase in rents of SGD$1,000 for the economy rice stall (Chan and Kua 2007). The sales of *kopitiams* in Marine Parade over an estimated ten-year period from 2004 to 2012 led to several rises in rental and food costs. Rental for one *kopitiam*'s *roti prata* stall rose by about $1,000 per month (about 30%) and the price of *roti prata* rose ten cents (about 20%) with each change of ownership, while prices of other stalls' dishes have risen variously by about 30%–70% and the price of a cup of coffee rose by nearly 100% from fifty cents to one dollar. The steep rise in rents has also meant a movement of stalls to places with cheaper rents and a hollowing-out of some *kopitiams*. Rather than full occupancy, some *kopitiam* operators have failed to attract stall tenants as rents have become too unsustainable. This appears particularly true for stallholders whose clientele bases are more limited. It is now common to hear that Malay foods are harder to find as some Malay food stallholders find rents too high and move elsewhere. Two long-time Malay stalls in the Marine Terrace *kopitiam* moved out when it was bought over by a new owner in 2012. The original tenants of Bedok Block 18's *kopitiam* simply moved out as rents were raised with each change in ownership. Under the current fourth owner, none of the original tenants, except for the *tze char* stall, are still at the *kopitiam*. Food prices also average around S$3.50–$4.00 per plate in this *kopitiam*, which is markedly higher than those at around S$2.50–$3.00 at the hawker centre nearby.

Simultaneous cutbacks in the building of HDB *kopitiams* (and also traditionally adjacent facilities such as hawker centres and wet markets) in new housing estates such as Ponggol and Sengkang further favoured shopping mall food courts funded by big capital. Thus, while prices of sale/resale *kopitiam* properties, stall rentals and food prices soared, some newer HDB estates additionally faced a dire lack of *kopitiams* (also hawker centres) selling foods at lower prices. One 2013 report noted that in Sengkang, the majority of stalls in Kopitiam Square, Singapore's first privately built and owned food centre and wet market under the Kopitiam chain, were unoccupied (about 40 out of 60) due to high rents and lack of customers. Renaissance Properties, a subsidiary of Kopitiam, had earlier in 2009 won the tender to run the centre at $500,100 a month — more than double the next highest bidder's offer. Even at that time, Sengkang residents had expressed concern that the high tender bid would result in higher rent and food prices, and indeed customers complained of high prices (and poor food quality), and 15 food stalls and three wet market stalls left within a year (Ee 2013).

By 2012, high prices and costs of living, including of food, had become a serious social and political issue. Although the Ministry of National Development said there was no evidence of speculation in the market for HDB shops,[21] there was indirect acknowledgement of the problem through policy changes. HDB, probably in response to the property investments/speculation in *kopitiams* after its policy change to private ownership and to the complaints of the lack of *kopitiams* (and hawker centres), quietly returned to its old policy of only renting out newly built *kopitiams*. It was also announced that new towns Sengkang, Hougang and Sembawang will have a new hawker centre in each of their neighbourhoods by 2017.[22]

---

[21] The Ministry of National Development (MND) revealed, in a written parliamentary reply, that, of the 216 HDB shops sold in 2012, only 14 — or 6% — were resold within one year of purchase. "This does not suggest a speculative element in HDB shops", see *The Straits Times,* 16 Oct 2012).

[22] This was announced by the Ministry of Environment and Water Resources (*The Straits Times,* 21 Oct 2012).

Shophouse kopitiams: redevelopment and gentrification

The effects of market and policy changes on shophouse *kopitiams* elsewhere in old city areas such as Tanjong Pagar, Chinatown and Joo Chiat deserve a brief note here. The removal of rent control in these areas and a simultaneous policy change in land use that "established zoning which favoured commercial and other non-residential uses" (Ho and Hutton 2012: 235) led to big capital moving in to purchase old shophouses for conversion into offices, hotels and cafes. Such redevelopments first took place in phases in the financial district and surrounding areas in the 1970s and 1980s. The passing of the Control of Rent (Abolition) Act in 2001 sounded the death knell for the remaining rent-controlled premises out of which 68% operated low-value commercial businesses such as coffee shops and eating places.[23] The overall result has been the gentrification of commercial properties. The pressures of gentrification have in turn forced rentals up, especially in areas like Keong Saik Street and Tiong Bahru and those near the Central Business District. *Kopitiams* in these areas face high rents as well as possible buyouts for other more high-value uses. Tong Ah Eating House in Keong Saik Street was bought over by a hotelier for SGD$8 million after operating at its premises for 75 years (Lee 2013). Similar trends have forced several *kopitiams* in Tiong Bahru to close or change their business operations. These *kopitiams* now include restaurants so as to continue running their businesses. Hua Bee, which sells fishball noodles, now houses the upscale Japanese *yakitori* restaurant Bincho. Similarly, 01–46 now opens in the evening as a pizzeria named Two Face (Tan 2012). A strategically located old *kopitiam* in new heritage site Joo Chiat has been bought over, redeveloped and renamed Alibaba R based on a "hawker bar" concept but several of its former tenants have moved elsewhere due to high rents (see Duruz, Chapter 6 of this volume, for a fuller discussion of AlibabaR). Similarly, the stallholders in another *kopitiam* nearby moved out when it was acquired and turned into German-themed beer-bar-restaurant Brotzeit.

Kopitiam Heritage: Historicisation, Commoditisation and the Appeal to Authenticity and Nostalgia

In today's relentless *kopitiam* competition, elements of *kopitiam* culture and heritage are being invoked to maximise business claims and opportunities by

---

[23] Bill, *Control of Rent (Abolition)*, 2nd Session, 9th Parliament, Singapore 2001.

kopitiam operators who consciously appeal to specific elements of tradition, culture and heritage which play on memory, nostalgia and even pride. *Kopitiams* have also been swept along with and contributed to the wave of nostalgia sweeping Singapore amidst its rapid economic, social and cultural changes.[24] Indeed, the "local *kopitiam*" as an institution is now cast as part of tradition, culture and heritage. It has undergone sufficiently long evolution to have built up history and tradition and there is now sufficient space for recreating the past, historicising it and invoking memory and nostalgia, while the appeal to social ties and locale intimacy through its social role and location further lend a sense of historical and contemporary meanings. Thus for example, the Koufu chain claims to

> reinvent the coffee shop traditions with a fusion of eastern and western techniques so that the company can evolve through modern management concepts and yet stay true to good old coffee shop traditions,

and "to preserve the uniqueness of authentic Singapore hawker cuisines". It also claims to be able to personalise service with "friendliness and intimacy" because its shops are located in housing estates (Koufu nd). Killiney chain *kopitiams* recreate the atmosphere of the old coffee shop with period furnishings, décor and historical memorabilia. Its mission statement is "to keep the '*Kopitiam*' tradition going for this generation and for the many generations to come", while its tagline is "Welcome to the good old days". Ya Kun's branding lies in its belief that "a good toast binds kinship, friendship and partnership" and its mission includes "to preserve its unique and rich heritage". Both Killiney Kopitiam and Ya Kun have received "heritage" as well "spirit of enterprise" awards in recent years. It is of little surprise that a legal case involving the use of the name "Kopitiam" by two such operators took place in 1988 when the competition first began.[25]

In the claims of tradition, culture and heritage, the "ethnic" and multicultural elements in each *kopitiam*'s history and foods sold are capitalised

---

[24] Blogs and Facebook sites such as yesterday.sg, iremember.sg, Remember Singapore, Nostalgic Singapore, On a Little Street in Singapore, and Singapura Stories all attempt to document some memories, sights and sounds of the past. A sense of urgency pervades cultural preservation and heritage work.

[25] The legal tussle between Kopitiam Singapore Restaurant and the company Kopitiam Pte Ltd over the exclusive use of the name "Kopitiam" resulted in the latter's favour as it was ruled that the term "*kopitiam*" was generic and could be used by anyone.

on, and originality, authenticity and diversity are emphasised. In this, the Hainanese operators' claim to both *kopitiam* and culinary heritage is an outstanding example by virtue of having been among the first to start and to contribute through their unique fusion foods. Indeed, the "Hainanese *kopitiam*", considered foundational in "tradition" and "heritage" have become legendary within the now developed larger *kopitiam* culture.[26]

At the same time, operators are aware that *kopitiams* (also food courts) must remain diverse/multicultural in their foods and their appeal to customers. Thus, Kopitiam set up the Banquet halal food court chain (which, however, closed in 2013) and Hans runs several halal Hanis Café and Bakery outlets. For Koufu, it

> ... want[s] to nurture the inherent joy of sharing a meal or drink with family and friends, by providing friendliness and a spark of inspiration in the everyday life of people of all ages, social classes and ethnic backgrounds,

while Komala's restaurant claims that

> it is the commitment to such values [quality, value-for-money authentic Indian food, commitment to cleanliness and hygiene] that earned Komala's popularity with the Indians, Malays, Chinese and tourists throughout its 50-year history in Singapore.

Needless to say, foods and food cultures themselves have become part of heritage. Clearly traceable to migration origins and histories, food specialisation and hybridisation continue to be a dynamic part of this living heritage, sustained by and in turn sustaining, exciting and enriching the strong public eating culture. Some new, reinvented, hybrids and further hybrids of food dishes have even triggered food crazes and the occasional culinary war between, such as over *kaya* toast, *laksa*, chicken rice, bean curd, *nasi padang* and chilli crab.[27]

---

[26] One recent television sitcom revolved around the *kopitiam* and was titled "Hainan Kopi Tales".

[27] Yakun makes and sells its own brand of Hainanese *kaya* (*The Straits Times*, 9 Mar 2009), while Hans continues the Hainanese tradition of hybridising dishes and confectionery. For examples of the *kaya* craze, *kaya* toast wars and food feuds, see *The Straits Times* (5 Dec 1999), *The Straits Times* (22 May 2005) and *The Sunday Times* (11 Jan 2009). Competing food heritage claims in the competitive local and tourism sectors have recently also threatened to take a regional dimension between countries in Southeast Asia such as Malaysia, Singapore and Indonesia where foods have followed migration and developed into local versions, igniting even nationalist sentiments in what may be alternatively seen as shared heritages.

Finally, occupational pride and prestige have contributed to the push for recognition of the *kopitiam* as tradition and heritage. The low status of the *kopitiam* is fast changing, the success stories of Koufu, Ya Kun, Hans, Kopitiam, Bhavan, Komalas, Zam Zam and Sabar Menanti have undoubtedly contributed to this change. Lim Bee Huat, the "kopi king", still has a mission to accomplish:

> to make the coffee shop or hawker business respectable in the eyes of the people ... to change the image of the coffee shop as a 'low grade' business ... because the children of the '*kopitiam*' men are afraid people will look down on them (Kopitiam nd).

The issue of *kopitiam* authenticity is especially relevant in a time of nostalgia and search for identity.[28] While both HDB and brand name *kopitiams* are sites of cultural production, HDB *kopitiams* are "endowed" with working class origins and characteristics and do not need to appeal to nostalgia or manufacture authenticity.[29] The HDB *kopitiam*'s historical origins and everyday life provision of cheap foods for the working class and "common folk" in a "common" space is firmly established, its "heartland" location and social role further enabling its authenticity and "timelessness" to endure. On the other hand, "nostalgia" *kopitiams* such as Ya Kun, Killiney and Toast Box which have been gentrified through décor, utensils, pricing and clientele have to endeavour to tap on nostalgia and to offer elements of an authentic past. Thus, Toast Box

> ... is a reflection of the coffee shops from the 60s and 70s ... This warm, nostalgic concept was reinvented to bring back fond memories for those who missed the good old times, and for the younger ones to experience the feel and flavours of a bygone era (Toast Box 2014).

Toast Box, a subsidiary of a local bread company BreadTalk, is an interesting case as it does not have a history like Ya Kun's or Killiney's. How it positions itself is therefore through its fidelity towards the past — its décor includes wooden stools, heritage items and a "butter mountain" (a huge conical shaped

---

[28] The discussion in this section on nostalgia and authenticity is drawn mostly from Lim Jia Liang (2014).
[29] The media further reifies this working class nature of the HDB *kopitiam*. The "state of the *kopitiam*" is essential, in which the prices of coffee are heavily scrutinised. Thus, the price rise of a *kopi-o* from 60 cents to 70 cents in 2006 was met with two articles, the second explaining that *kopitiam* associations did not collude to raise prices together. See Lim D (2006) and Lim WC (2006).

block of butter), and it also conducts Nanyang coffee appreciation workshops (Gurkhason 2013).

Pastiche appears to dominate nostalgia *kopitiams* despite their adherence to the "good old days". Toast Box employees wear uniformed frocks, working amidst sacks of coffee strewn around. Jameson defines pastiche as borrowing without intent, where artists (and in this case, interior designers) borrow from the past in a "random cannibalisation of past styles". Ornaments are devoid of use value and serve only as cultural symbols hinting at an idealised past. The recreation of the past through the use of specific material objects and pop culture also circumscribe presentations of the past, leading Jameson (1991: 25) to call these representations "pop history". On the other hand, it can be argued that pastiche as they may be, the local history these *kopitiams* draw from and the nostalgia they create are attempts at placing the local in the global and expressing Singapore's position and identity in a globalised society through food, especially in the face of fierce competition from global branded coffee chains such as Starbucks and Coffee Bean. Indeed, there was a period in the 1990s when it appeared that global brands were replacing local *kopitiams*, especially in city areas and shopping malls. "Food Talk" that speaks of eating locally can be seen as an assertion of (local) agency in a globalised world, and the creation of such deliberately local eateries and cladding them in nostalgia is therefore a reaction and response to globalisation, "a hunt of agency in a moment of change" (Thompson 2012: 58–70).

A note should be made here on food courts in shopping malls, as they have become the new site of fierce competition. The shopping mall food court has been a development in Singapore since the late 1980s. Arguably, the food court is the *kopitiam*'s concept (also the hawker centre's) extended and redeveloped to a new level of public eating culture. Based on the same principle of combining food and drinks under one roof, the food court in a huge space and providing the choice of a wider range of foods in air-conditioned comfort quickly became a successful form and venue by the mid-1990s, particularly when situated in a shopping mall that itself has become a site of consumption culture in Singapore.[30] While there has been a proliferation of shopping malls all over Singapore (Gallezo 2013), their main food court operators are the same dominant players Kopitiam, Koufu and Food Republic which compete through differentiation. Thus for example, Food Republic claims to overturn

---

[30] See Chua (2003). Picnic Food Court was the first food court in Singapore. It opened in 1985 at the now-defunct Scotts Shopping Centre.

"old perceptions of food court dining to fresh outlooks at new heights", and aims to "dish out the best of hawker and restaurant fare under a single platform" (Food Republic 2015). The décor of each of its food courts has a different theme and, more importantly, it has approached famous hawker stores to franchise their products. Boards explain each stall's legacy, and even if it were a generic one without any history behind it, a marketing narrative would be created. These concepts eagerly embrace the cultural capital that is historically provided by *kopitiams*.

Changes in Consumer Behaviour and Preferences

A third trend in the changing landscape are consumers who have become more complex in their preferences and tastes. *Kopitiam* culture is firmly established as part of an everyday lifestyle and habitual affair that cuts across all class and ethnic backgrounds. But unlike the past, there is now a huge variety of *kopitiams* and food outlets competing to keep up with customers' changing tastes, as well as create new expectations of the coffee shop and eating experience. Customers have tremendous choice of *kopitiams* and food outlets and are not limited to neighbourhood ones unless they are locale-bound or cash-strapped. For ordinary HDB residents, the neighbourhood *kopitiams* remain a place of choice in everyday life, with the smaller ones in quieter neighbourhoods still better able to offer a sense of intimacy and community that the larger crowded ones may not. For the more mobile, patronising different types of coffee shops can be a choice of moving between a nostalgic local past and a "hip", globalised, cosmopolitan and gentrified present. Depending on occasion, need and context, these consumers move flexibly between the HDB and gentrified *kopitiams* and between local and international coffee shops, consuming a range of local and international drinks and foods.

Whither the *Kopitiam*?

The story of the *kopitiam* is deeply embedded within a larger historical and social narrative of migration and cultural diversity. Born out of the necessity for food and company among male immigrants of various ethnic backgrounds in colonial Singapore, the *kopitiam* served as a simple eating place and social centre, and it became an economic niche for those with culinary and service skills or who had little choice but to work long hours at low wages in this low status trade. Reflecting ethnic dimensions in terms of spatial locations, foods sold and customer bases, the *kopitiam* also evolved to become the social centre in local communities across the island, serving as the focal point of everyday life and at the same time providing links to the outside world. Through resettlement into public housing estates and over time, the monocultural *kopitiam* reinvented itself into a multicultural institution that is a confluence of cuisine, clientele and community. The multicultural heartland *kopitiam* today remains, together with hawker centres, *the* institution of local community and everyday public life. Open to all, it displays the public culture of eating and talking that is considered by some as the national pastime; and it satisfies the need for replenishment, rest and recreation through culturally familiar foods, friends and fraternities.

The confluence of cuisine, clientele and community in the *kopitiam* makes it a particularly significant site, within the larger politics and dynamics of diversity in Singapore. Cuisine itself is one particularly outstanding dimension of this diversity. Closely associated with *kopitiams* (also hawker centres and restaurants) and constituting heritage with migration roots, Singapore's food diversity has been taken to new levels in recent years and popularised simultaneously as ethnic, national and multicultural. While some dishes may vanish and cooking secrets die out, there are enough intergenerational transfers of cuisine skills, recorded recipes and creative players to ensure continuity. Indeed, the thriving food diversity and hybridisation with its seemingly endless possibilities attests to Singapore's unique multicultural food culture and contribution to the world. The *kopitiam* provides the social and public setting for sustaining this heritage and its further development. *Kopitiam* community similarly displays dimensions and dynamics of the diversity narrative in Singapore, through the meals and meetings the *kopitiam* provides and enables in everyday life.

So how will the story of the *kopitiam* unfold in future? So long as there are cultural flows and interactions, there will be a multicultural *kopitiam* that is the confluence of cuisine, culture and community. And so long as there is a working class, there will be a heartland *kopitiam*. Even as mobile customers and residents now move about for food and company in varied settings, *kopitiam* culture remains a way of everyday life and makes the *kopitiam* a quintessential Singapore experience and a living heritage site. And so long as love of food and public eating cultures remain strong, the multicultural *kopitiam* will continue to thrive and evolve.

The new dimensions of *kopitiam* heritage with its historicisation, commoditisation and the appeal to nostalgia and authenticity speak to larger issues and senses of identity and belonging. Pastiche notwithstanding, *kopitiam* spaces both old and new undoubtedly provide comfort, and the preservation of a part of the old, reinvented as it might be, create opportunities for Singaporeans to reaffirm their identity and belonging in the face of rapid globalisation and change. It appears ironic that many of the *kopitiam* chains are located in shopping malls — a celebration of the old in the space of the new. Yet, this shows the *kopitiam*'s endurance as a site of authenticity and nostalgia as well as dynamism amidst the competition from many new, "hipster" and "new generation" coffee shops and global coffee chains.

Finally, how can the *kopitiam* story be appreciated in context? Like Lao She's famous Chinese "Teahouse",[31] the *kopitiam* is like a miniature society and a metaphor for Singapore, telling a story of its migration and social histories and that of ordinary people and their lives, capturing their struggles for livelihood and the evolution of Singapore's multiculturalism and identity. The story is far from concluded; it continues to unfold with dramatic developments of a local-global nature before our very eyes today.

REFERENCES

Ananda Bhavan (2013) http://www.anandabhavan.com/, accessed 23 May 2015.

Berger PL and Luckmann T (1996) *The social construction of reality: a treatise in the sociology of knowledge*. Harmondsworth: Penguin Books.

Bill, Control of Rent (Abolition), 2nd Session, 9th Parliament, Singapore 2001. http://sprs.parl.gov.sg/search/topic.jsp?currentTopicID=00067956-ZZ&currentPubID=00069884-ZZ&topicKey=00069884-ZZ.00067956-ZZ_1%2Bid014_20010316_S0002_T00031-bill%2B, accessed 20 December 2014.

Botak Jones (nd) http://www.botakjones.com, accessed 23 May 2015.

Chan SC (2003) Consuming food: structuring social life and creating social relationships. In: KB Chan and CK Tong (eds.) *Past Times: A Social History of Singapore*. Singapore: Times Editions, pp. 123–135.

---

[31] For Lao She, "a big teahouse is like a miniature society", and his famous play "Teahouse" can be read as a metaphor for China. It spans 50 years of modern Chinese history, witnessing the disintegration of the Qing Empire and the beginning of the struggle to build a modern nation-state through the portrayal of *xiao renwu* — ordinary characters — from all walks of life who frequented the Chinese teahouse. Singapore playwright Kuo Pao Kun (Kuo 2001) attempted to do the same for Singapore with his play "*Kopitiam*" which was performed in 1996.

Chan F and Kua ZY (2007) Record price for coffee shop means higher rents. *The Straits Times*, 5 December.

Chua BH (2003) The emerging culture of consumption. In: BH Chua (ed.) *Life is Not Complete Without Shopping: Consumption Culture in Singapore*. Singapore: NUS Press, pp. 17–38.

Chua BH (1995) That imagined space: nostalgia for kampungs. In: BSA Yeoh and L Kong (eds.) *Portraits of Places: History, Community and Identity in Singapore*. Singapore: Times Editions, pp. 222–241.

Chua BH and Raja A (1997) Hybridity, Ethnicity and Food in Singapore. Unpublished Academic Work. Singapore: Department of Sociology, National University of Singapore.

Chua BH, Sim J and Low CW (1985) Resettling Soon Hock village: a longitudinal study. In: AK Wong and SHK Yeh (eds.) *Housing a Nation: 25 years of Public Housing in Singapore*. Singapore: Maruzen Asia for Housing and Development Board, pp. 335–374.

Cohen AP (1982) Belonging: the experience of culture. In: AP Cohen (ed.) *Belonging: Identity and social organization in British rural cultures*. Manchester: Manchester University Press, pp. 1–18.

de Certeau M (1984) *The practice of everyday life*, S Rendall (trans.) Berkeley: University of California Press.

Ee D (2013) Business poor at Sengkang food centre. *The Straits Times*, 3 January, p. B1.

Food Republic (2015) About Us. http://foodrepublic.com.sg/about, accessed 12 November 2014.

Gallezo K (2013) 13 major mall projects in the pipeline through 2017. *Singapore Business Review*.

Geertz C (1975) *Local Knowledge*. New York: Basic Books.

Gurkhason (2013) Toast Box Presents Nanyang Coffee Appreciation Workshop @ BreadTalk IHQ (Tai Seng), 1 August 2013. http://www.gurkhason.wordpress.com/2013/08/01/toast-box-presents-nanyang-coffee-appreciation-breadtalk-ihq-tai-seng/, accessed 10 November 2014.

Han FK (2013) HDB coffee shops are not district 10 bungalows. *The Sunday Times*, 14 July, p. 40.

Heller A (1984) *Everyday Life*. London: Routledge and Kegan Paul.

Ho KC and Hutton TA (2012) The cultural economy in the developmental state: a comparison of Chinatown and Little India districts in Singapore. In: PW Daniels, KC Ho and TA Hutton (eds.) *New Economic Spaces in Asian Cities: From Industrial Restructuring to the Cultural Turn*. New York: Routledge, pp. 220–236.

Huang L (2008) Going, going gone? *The Sunday Times*, 3 August, p. 24.

Huang L and Cheong D (2011) Six coffee shops sold for nearly $60m; hefty price tag may be due to stable return on investment: analysts. *The Straits Times*, 2 July.

Jameson F (1991) *Postmodernism, or, The Cultural Logic of Late Capitalism*. London: Verso.

Killiney Kopitiam (2007) http://www.killiney-kopitiam.com, accessed 23 May 2015.

Komala's Restaurant (2015) http://www.komalasweb.com, accessed 23 May 2015.

Komala Vilas (nd) http://web.singnet.com.sg/~komala/, accessed 23 May 2015.

Kopitiam (nd) The Kopi Tiam King. In S-files: Stories behind their success. Singapore: Success Resources Pte Ltd. http://www.*kopitiam*.biz/content/showcontent.asp?section=success, accessed 22 September 2008.

Koufu (nd) Profile History. www.koufu.com.sg/company/koufu-s-journey-mr-pang-lim, accessed 1 July 2015.

Kuo PK (2001) *Kopitiam. In Images at the Margins: A Collection of Kuo Pao Kun's Plays*. Singapore: Times Books International.

Lai AE (2013) The *kopitiam* in Singapore: an evolving story about migration and cultural diversity. In: AE Lai, FL Collins and BSA Yeoh (eds.) *Migration and Diversity in Asian Contexts*. Singapore: Institute of Southeast Asian Studies: pp. 209–232.

Lai AE (2012) A neighbourhood in Singapore: ordinary people's lives 'downstairs'. In: L Hee, B Davisi and E Viray (eds.) *Future Asian Space: Projecting the Urban Space of New Asia*. Singapore: National University of Singapore Press, pp. 115–137.

Lai AE (1995) *Meanings of Multiethnicity: A Case Study of Ethnicity and Ethnic Relations in Singapore*. Kuala Lumpur: Oxford University Press.

Lee D (2013) Pre-war Keong Saik Road coffee shop moving out. *The Straits Times*, 13 July.

Lee SM (2009) Hainanese Gobidiams in the 1930s–1950s: Food Heritage in Singapore. Unpublished Paper submitted for the Independent Study Module. Singapore: Department of History, Faculty of Arts and Social Sciences, National University of Singapore.

Lim D (2006) Kopi-O likely to cost more soon. *The Straits Times*, 25 February.

Lim HY and Lim KH (1985) Resettlement: policy, process and impact. In: AK Wong and SHK Yeh (eds.) *Housing a Nation: 25 Years of Public Housing in Singapore*. Singapore: Maruzen Asia for Housing and Development Board, pp. 305–334.

Lim JL (2014) Kopitiams: A Cultural History. Unpublished Essay for HH3001, Historiography: Theory and Methods, School of Humanities and Social Sciences, Nanyang Technological University.

Lim WC (2006) Coffee price hike not cartel action. *The Straits Times*, 11 March.

Lin M (2015) Bukit Batok coffeeshop 'sold for $31m'. *The Straits Times*, 16 June.

National Environment Council (2004) Clean toilets in our garden city. News Release no. 082/1999, date of issue: 11 August 1999. In: *National Environment Report*, 7 February. http://www.env.gov.sg/info/press/ENV, accessed 1 September 2009.

Omar M (2006) *Sabar Menanti Restaurant*. Singapore: National Library Board.

Othman D (2008) Filipinos are your new servers. *The Straits Times*, 14 July. http://www.straitstimes.com/Free/Story/STIStory_257417.html, accessed 1 September 2009.

Suttles G (1968) *The Social Order of the Slum: Ethnicity and Territory in the Inner City*. London: University of Chicago Press.

Tan HY (2012) Posh nosh — two face. *The Straits Times*, 23 December.

Tan T (2007) From illegal hawker to food chain boss. *The Straits Times*, 14 April. http://wineanddine.asiaone.com/Wine%252CDine%2B%2526%2BUnwind/Features/Topics/Story/A1Story20070622-14990.html, accessed 25 August 2009.

The Straits Times (2012) 3 towns to get new hawker centres by 2017, 21 October.

The Straits Times (2012) No speculation in market for HDB shops: MND, 16 October.

The Straits Times (2009) Your Insights, 16 October, p. A25.

The Straits Times (2009a) Tze char stalls need foreign workers, 5 July.

The Straits Times (2009b) Are locals shunning jobs at tze char stalls? 5 July.

The Straits Times (2009) Toast to sweet success, 9 March.

The Straits Times (2007a) Taking jobs away from locals, 12 December.

The Straits Times (2007b) Language problems in service, 12 December.

The Straits Times (2005) Now who's the toast of the town? 22 May. http://www.smu.edu.sg/news_room/smu_in_the_news/2005/sources/ST_20050522_1.pdf, accessed 25 August 2009.

The Straits Times (1999) Spread some love around, 5 December.

The Sunday Times (2009) Famous food feuds, 11 January.

Thompson JR (2012) Food talk: bridging power in a globalising world. In: JJ Frye and MS Bruner (eds.) *The Rhetoric of Food: Discourse, Materiality, and Power*. New York: Routledge, pp. 58–70.

Toast Box (2014) About. http://www.toastbox.com.sg/about.html, accessed 10 November 2014.

Wee CF and Lim YH (2013) Too much for a coffee shop. *The Straits Times*, 7 July.

Whyte WF (1993) *Street Corner Society: The Social Structure of an Italian Slum (4th ed.)*. Chicago: University of Chicago Press.

Ya Kun (2014) http://www.yakun.com, accessed 23 May 2015.

Yen F (2008) Makan mashup. *The Straits Times* National Day Special, 9 August, p. 17.

Chapter 6

The Taste of Retro:
Nostalgia, Sensory Landscapes
and Cosmopolitanism in Singapore

Jean Duruz

> You can restore vanished buildings with visual records but… [o]nly smell can evoke the atmosphere, the aura of a place and plunge us back in time. A mere whiff can intuit the past with more primal immediacy than the laminated prints of old places sold in antique and curio shops… (Boey 2009: 178–179).

> Even though Le Café's pineapple balls and bean curd tarts have become extremely popular, they still continue to make… retro-licious Butter Cream Cakes… in their kitchen behind because they do not want to lose their traditions to modern-day fads (Ang 2013).

This chapter focuses on relations of time, place and nostalgic returns as means to reflect on Singapore's rapidly changing built environment and culinary cultures. The quotations above, with their resonances of "whiffs" and "retro-licious" tastes, set the scene. The first is from Kim Cheng Boey's *Between Stations*, an elegy to a "lost" Singapore of the late 1960s and 1970s, as well as a lament for a "lost" father, a fleeting figure in a son's memories of ambivalent interactions. The second, a very different form of memory mapping, tells of a blogger's quest to uncover "old-school" cake shops that "had survived the test of time through the 60s". Such a project is shaped as a tribute to cake-making as an emotionally sustaining ritual of childhood and family life. The bitter-sweetness of nostalgia — its regrets, its pleasures — in such remembering is, in many ways, unsurprising (Wilson 1991: 101–102), with food and its sensory moments as anchor points. However, my own interest is in Singapore's more recent "past" and its "present", traced through the material culture of the Katong neighbourhood, and in a different kind of return.

I have been coming to Katong (the name often used to include its neighbouring district, Joo Chiat) on Singapore's east coast regularly for about ten years, with some of these visits extending to several months. During the last year or so, changes to the landscape have struck me more forcefully than usual, even viscerally, with the speed of such changes from one year to the next being almost breath-taking. The long boarded-up Katong Bakery (popularly known as the Red House Bakery) has metamorphosised into expensive apartments; the iconic *laksa* stall on the corner of Ceylon Road no longer exists; many shop fronts of traditional food businesses are now empty, or replaced by upmarket bakeries, chocolate shops, coffee shops and bars. Perhaps Katong, like other "ethnic" neighbourhoods such as Chinatown and the *kampongs* [Malay for villages, neighbourhoods] near the Port, is experiencing the effects of Singapore's *tabula rasa* approach to urban development? Is the east coast yet another example of the mythical "world we have lost" — an example of the imagined "village" of inter-ethnic food exchanges and support, discussed by scholars such as Chua (1995: 238), Kong and Chang (2001: 108), Imram (2007: 14, 17) and Lai (2009) and poignantly drawn from memory by life-history writers such as Josephine Chia (2002: 166–167)? In contrast to the feelings of melancholy engendered by a sense of "lost" spaces, tastes and communities, however, the discourse of city food guides, food blogs, websites and tourism advertising suggests images of plenitude: these forms of promotional culture persist in celebrating the richness and diversity of Singapore's foodscapes, with Katong as its quintessence ("All of Singapore is a food paradise, but the East is her kitchen") (Mok 2007: 71).

For the moment, setting aside the dichotomy of mourning lost worlds on one hand and revelling in a cornucopia of tastes on the other, this chapter looks for other ways to shape theoretical understandings of Singapore's changing food cultures. Many questions haunt me in the process: how are meanings of the "past", and particularly the very recent "past", performed through the food cultures of a supposedly "young" nation-state; how are specific tastes and smells of this "past" memorialised in the landscapes of everyday life; how might analyses of "grounded" and "visceral" cosmopolitanism address the theoretical space between institutional constructions of culinary heritage and people's own engagements with the "past"; how might a returning "outsider" have some claim on the tastes of an "other's" remembered "past"? These questions in total represent a larger project than the space here allows, and in fact, flow through much of my writing on Singapore to date. However, they are also significant in suggesting my drift for this chapter.

Before touring specific sites in search of "whiffs" of history and "retro-licious" tastes of place, we need a sense of what is distinctive about the history of Katong and the east coast to merit the title of "food paradise" and Singapore's "kitchen", and of the changes that some see as cause for palpable concern. Newspaper headlines ranging from "Can Katong's Laid-back Charm be Saved?" (James 2000) to the more recent "Let's Keep Katong's Legacy Alive" (Loh 2013) and "Is Katong Too Cool?" (Quek 2014) suggest more than niggling anxiety about the neighbourhood's re-development and the materiality of its losses. Here some narrative backtracking is necessary.

RETURN TO THE "VILLAGE" OF "MIXED" TASTES

From pre-colonial times onwards, the island to which we now refer as the nation-state of Singapore has been distinguished by its "mixed" racial/ethnic history. Emerging from the fourteenth century trading city of Temasek, "Singapore, even within a colonial context [1819–1959], exalted a sense of cosmopolitanism, richness in cultural diversity and the proliferation of commercial activities" (Velayutham 2007: 21, 23). There is criticism of a national narrative that is, selectively, built on the strengths of culinary colonialism (Tarulevicz 2013: 38). Nevertheless, there is no doubt that, from a *longue durée* viewpoint, the effects of this history on Singapore's food cultures have been profound. Elsewhere I have argued that examples of "confluence" might be traced in intercultural marriage and culinary hybridisation in Singapore, food sharing amongst neighbours in multi-racial neighbourhoods and a collective awareness of the diverse origins of Singapore's food as the nation's cultural capital, as well as of the ethnic and religious constraints that govern its consumption (Duruz and Khoo 2015).

While all of Singapore could be considered remarkable for such "confluences", Katong, nevertheless, is seen to possess this quality in heightened form. Reflecting on this neighbourhood's distinctiveness from culinary perspectives, Phua and Kong comment:

> Katong offers a wide variety of cuisine… Although this is generally available in other parts of Singapore, what makes it unique here is the *concentration of that variety in a geographically small area* along East Coast Road, colloquially referred to as Food Street (Phua and Kong 1995: 123, emphasis added).

Dawn Mok, author of an alternative guide to Singapore, agrees. Referring in lip-smacking prose to the east coast's "potluck of authentic dishes dotingly cooked up by the island's diverse Peranakan, Eurasian, Chinese, Malay and Indian cultures", Mok concludes that in Katong "[t]he traditions and charm of the old kampong days are very much alive here" (Mok 2007: 6, 71). On the other hand, it seems that the "traditions and charm" of Katong/Joo Chiat have also suffered some interruption in the past twenty years. These, according to Kong and Chang, are now being interpreted in "different, more upmarket ways". In addition, "new" cuisines are appearing on the streetscape — Western/Chinois, Italian, Greek, Mexican, Thai and Japanese, for example — signalling Singapore's embrace of "modern" forms of cosmopolitanism, despite its own long history of "mixed" peoples and food cultures (Kong and Chang 2001: 81).

In 2008, walking down Joo Chiat Road and East Coast Road, I was inclined to accept this portrait of the neighbourhood as culinarily distinct, despite incursions from "outside". Following my own *laksa* trail, I had set out to trace the tastes and aromas of this spicy soup (of coconut milk, garlic, chillies, ginger, *laksa* leaf, *belachan*[1]…) (Hutton 1999: 68), as a dish resulting from marriages of Chinese traders to local women chiefly in Malacca prior to the 19th century and brought by descendant generations to Singapore (Duruz and Khoo 2015: 125–127). In addition to the search for *laksa* as symptomatic of the area's "unique mix" of street food, I wanted to map the diversity of dishes associated with Katong's Peranakan heritage. However, walking this version of the *laksa* trail, I unravelled a much more complex story of ownership of this iconic dish, together with its heritage meanings and nostalgic attachments, than I had anticipated. Traditions of working for, or "marrying into", Peranakan families, for example, or rituals of exchange of festive foods and recipes between

---

[1] *Belachan* is a fermented shrimp paste with a pungent odour and piquant flavour and is used in cooking throughout Southeast Asia and Southern China.

neighbours, had all permeated the boundaries of dish ownership. The state too had played its part with the taste of *laksa* firmly embedded in the discourse of tourism associated with Peranakan material culture and, specifically, with Katong itself. At the same time, meanings of "authenticity" were certainly not uncontested, especially when commercial concerns were at stake (Duruz 2011). At the end of my trail, near the site of the infamous 1999 "*laksa* wars" in which competing food stalls laid claim to serve the "original" and "real" Katong *laksa*, I had cause to speculate on the distinctiveness of this dish, the mobility of its meanings and of those of Katong as a "place":

> [P]erhaps a different identity for laksa emerges? … Has laksa escaped from its Nyonya[2] cooks, even in its "ancestral" home in Katong, to assume a new place-bound identity…? Is Katong Laksa, after all, simply a taste of this place — a place of multiple narratives, of eclectic "borrowings" and, perhaps, unlike some of Singapore's other urban villages…, of refusals of touristic attempts at ethnicised homogenisation… (Duruz 2011: 611)?

The extent of such refusals of "ethnicised homogenisation" remains to be seen. Meanwhile, a second culinary tour along East Coast Road brings me to the shop front of Kim Choo Kueh Chang. This is where the foundational narrative of Madam Kim Choo underpins the sale of the business's iconic *nyonya* dumplings, delicately packaged to meet the requirements of culture selling "in different, more upmarket ways". It is here that Raymond Wong, grandson of Madam Choo and a director in this family business mourns the loss of the "*kampong* effect" — the loss of supportive village relationships, the seizure of the "local" landscape through the arrival of different kind of food businesses (that is, businesses without historical links to the area and with different approaches to community relations). In addition, there are other kinds of losses, such as the spectre of Katong as theme-park: the excessive thematisation of the neighbourhood for tourism purposes, as has happened elsewhere, for example, in the rebuilding of Singapore's Chinatown or, in Geylang, the construction of a faux *kampong* — the (now-demolished) Malay Village (Yeoh and Lau 1995; Duruz and Khoo 2015: 138–139).

The architect William Lim, however, is more optimistic about the fate of this neighbourhood. He designates Joo Chiat and nearby Katong and

---

[2] In the Peranakan community, women are referred to as "Nyonyas" and men as "Babas"; in addition, "nyonya" refers to the cuisine resulting from the historical mix of Chinese and "local" ingredients in the Straits Settlements of Malacca, Penang and Singapore.

Geylang as examples of Singapore's "spaces of indeterminacy". These, I suspect, conceptually are not unlike Foucault's imagined heterotopias — "mixed" spaces in which multiple "other" meanings challenge these spaces' dominant and hegemonic ordering (Edensor 1998: 218–219). Responding to the architect Rem Koolhas' criticisms of Singapore's approach to urban policy-making and planning — to the built fabric's continual cycles of demolition and rebuilding — Lim says:

> [T]abula *rasa* in Singapore is not complete. ...In actual fact, Joo Chiat, with its numerous shophouses [shops/workshops with accommodation for workers], some beautifully conserved, others dilapidated, has withstood rapid usage changes, and is characterised by mixed usage and fragmented spatial arrangements. In both Joo Chiat and Geylang, local residents, newly immigrant communities as well as prostitutes and the customers are equally visible on the rugged urbanscape. Spaces of indeterminacy are anchored in the postmodern; pluralistic, fuzzy and complex (2005: 165).

It is now 2014. With intermittent returns to Katong since my various culinary epiphanies, I am eager to discover whether Lim's "mixed usage and fragmented spatial relationships" still characterise this neighbourhood. To what extent do the streetscapes resist over-determination by reductionist culinary and cultural narratives associated with economic development and tourism promotion (narratives such as Katong as, distinctively, the home of Peranakan "style" and heritage, despite the shift of Peranakans to other parts of the island, and other groups' presence in the neighbourhood)? Are these spaces flexible in meaning, allowing the "pluralistic, fuzzy and complex" to reside here still? Is the mix of "local residents, newly immigrant communities as well as prostitutes and the customers [still] ... equally visible", as Lim suggested, a decade ago (2005: 165)? And to return to my reflections at the beginning of the chapter, I want to add: how are meanings of the "past" negotiated through the food in this place of "mixed" histories and sensory geographies — how are specific tastes and smells of this "past" (however "mixed" and "fragmented") memorialised in these landscapes of everyday life?

The moment I arrive for this year's visit to Katong, friends are full of dire warnings: "It's been over-run by expats; it's another Holland Village," I am told on several occasions . This analogy reflects assumptions of expatriate communities' preference for "international" rather than "local" cuisines and for cultures of wine-drinking and other kinds of alcohol consumption. "It's now full of bars with stools too high, while the traditional coffee shops are disappearing" is another comment from a not-so-tall friend, as she negotiates the furniture of the "new" eating places in her neighbourhood. "You won't recognise it," say others, "as many of the businesses you remember have closed down." "No more Yummy Crabs [a favourite haunt]!" ... "The Red House apartments are too expensive"... and so on.

Of course, all neighbourhoods are subject to change over time. Furthermore, nostalgia for "lost" spaces is connected in complex ways with yearning for "lost" times — for the best moments (usually) of youth, no longer recoverable except in memory or "whiffs". The rapidity of the changes, however, is at issue here. Even I, as a casual visitor to this place, feel some sense of ownership and loss when "my" remembered Katong appears to change before my eyes. "Where Did My Katong Go?" asks a blogging mother who grew up here in the care of her grandmother in the 1980s. Eager to retrace the steps of childhood, "Gingerbread Mum" visits the site of her former home, a bakery, a coffee shop, the church and school she attended, and she concludes: "Just a post by a girl who misses the Katong she grew up with" (2012).

Such losses too might be captured, theoretically speaking, in Pierre Nora's discussion of memory and history as separate entities: "We speak so much of memory because there is so little of it left", he says. Nora then distinguishes, critically, between the conscious fabrication of monuments to the "past" [*lieux de mémoire*] to assuage a sense of loss, and "real environments of memory" [*milieux de mémoire*]. In other words, as practices of organic remembering and ritual observance decline, the tangible expression of a "past" to replace these practices becomes imperative (Nora 1989: 7). In Singapore, this construction of a visible, collective past might take the form of museums, galleries, renovated shops and shophouses, themed restaurants, food courts, hotels and neighbourhoods, or even something as simple as Boey's "laminated prints of old places". Meanwhile, and reminiscent of Nora's imagery of fabricated versus "real" memories, Yeoh and Kong make a further, useful distinction regarding the state's approach to memorialising Singapore's history. Commenting on urban planning's tendency to prioritise "meticulous restoration of the physical fabric in historic districts", these authors claim:

> [P]lace is invoked as a concrete showcase of history rather than as an active process. Emphasis is given to the visual qualities, the facades and concrete forms which constitute place rather than the lifeworlds integral to the making of place. Part of the reason for this could be that while lifeworlds are much less susceptible to state control ..., built forms are easily amenable to sprucing up to reflect an idealised picture of the past (1999: 142).

As I set out to explore some of the changes that have taken place in Katong during the last couple of years, I am wondering how arguments like Nora's, and like Yeoh and Kong's as well, might sit in this setting, especially when food is added to the mix. After all, as Wong reminds us, it is food's very corporeality that might be at issue here, and might strike a different chord from mere renovation of buildings: "It is the *sensorial* experience of food that endures in one's memory bank, long after the context in which it is consumed disappears or changes" (Wong 2007: 120, emphasis original). So, while it is possible that themed restaurants and the like might be criticised for presenting a static and homogenised view of history ("a concrete showcase"), in walking Katong again, I am alert to those fragmentary "whiffs" that memory accumulates. These, in fact, might prove indicative of meanings of place and their mobilities, and indicative too of the dynamics of lifeworlds (the "active process[es]") inscribed by these meanings.

SCENTS OF PLACE: THE SWEET, YEASTY SMELL OF BAKING

Visiting Katong in 2013, after moving to a different neighbourhood three years before, Serene Goh, a *Straits Times* journalist, experiences a strong sense of displacement by its current "scene" of "trendy hotels and retailers, fancy pet groomers, yuppies sipping exotic wines". To counter feelings of no longer belonging in the district, Goh seeks out reminders of her childhood and growing up there: "*kopitiam* uncles who remember their regulars, stalwart businesses that have survived soaring rentals, kaya toast from Chin Mee Chin Confectionary". Goh continues:

> That's when it hit me: Katong isn't just a physical place any more, but an emotional yearning. As a monument to collective imagination, it represents a part of Singapore's history when lifestyles were more focused on the beach than bounty, when bibiks rode trishaws and policeman wore shorts (2013).[3]

---

[3] "Uncle" and "auntie" are terms of respect used by young people for older men and women, respectively. A "*kopitiam* uncle" would be the proprietor of the local coffee shop. "Bibik" is generally synonymous with "auntie" but also refers to an older female in a Peranakan household. It often has grandmotherly associations.

While this ode to the "village" and to childhood has a familiar (and poetic) ring, it also suggests more than Goh's mythologising the past in terms of "emotional yearning". Instead, people, practices and places figure in this account in quite active ways (uncles remember regulars, bibiks ride trishaws and so on). At the core of this remembering is Chin Mee Chin Confectionary, where one can literally "taste" the "past" from the comforts of the "present".

Chin Mee Chin is possibly quite unusual along this stretch of East Coast Road as an icon of survival. Mok refers to it as a "charming and time-defiant *kopitiam* [coffee shop]". Furthermore,

> Chin Mee Chin has been in this spot for over 60 years, dishing out simple but soul-satisfying eats accompanied with strong coffee or tea — served in requisite porcelain cups. It's a favourite with locals who love the fact this stretch hasn't been Starbucked, and the shop hasn't given up its ceiling fans and old-world mosaic tiles… (Mok 2007: 78).

Other guides to Katong agree. There is rarely a walking tour that does not mention Chin Mee Chin, especially since the closure in 2003 of its main competitor, the Red House Bakery. This is the case even though the "new" Red House project, together with apartments built on the site, includes plans for a bakery and heritage gallery in its redevelopment.

Back at Chin Mee Chin, bloggers are anxious to attest to its "old school" credentials: "[It's a] tiny 'old times' coffee shop which has been serving the most authentic breakfasts in Singapore for who knows how many years" (Metropolasia nd). "One of the last remaining Hainanese coffee shops of old, Chin Mee Chin…still retains an authentic 1950s ambiance" (Markhsx 2012). "[T]his nostalgia old school confectionary is always packed with breakfast crowd" (a post on Openrice 2014). Quite apart from the actual food, however, Chin Mee Chin provides its own version of ("old school") service rituals. "Regulars" explain for the benefit of the uninitiated:

> The pastries at Chin Mee Chin are displayed at the front of the shop. This is where the chaos start: you … can pile as many as you want on the pretty plate and then just start eating. … You can eat whatever pastries you want, however much, and then declare it later when it's time to foot the bill (Kumory 2014).

Apart from the seeming eccentricity of the service (in fact, forms of self-service), members of staff themselves contribute to this performance of nostalgia: "Chin Mee Chin is a traditional coffee shop where you can find kopi [coffee], pastries and soft-boiled eggs, prepared by (grumpy-looking) aunties with their permed hairdo[s] and uncles in their sheer white tees" (Kumory 2014). This "grumpiness" seems to have acquired the status of legend, although other customers are quick to deny or justify it: "Service was efficient, but hey, we don't expect kopitiam waitresses to flirt as if they were in a diner, do we?"; "The reason the staff are arrogant cos they've been around a long time. But if you ask me it adds to an authentic experience" (a post on Openrice 2014).

It seems that Chin Mee Chin, in its steadfast maintenance of tradition (even in hairstyles of female staff) offers itself as one of Nora's *lieux de mémoire*. As "old school" *kopitiams* disappear from the landscape, Chin Mee Chin itself becomes a singular memorial to "the good old days" — a solitary presence and a poignant reminder of others' absence. However, I am not entirely convinced by this argument, especially after my own nostalgic returns there recently. Even though, as an occasional visitor, my "returns" are limited, they are not without a sense of ritual, sensory content or the layering of "real" remembrance. Walking into Chin Mee Chin, I am almost overwhelmed by the sweet, yeasty smell of baking. This is not surprising as the ovens are at the back of the store and the workers removing trays of buns and pastries from these ovens are in full view. After arriving for breakfast every morning of my recent ten-day visit, there is tacit acknowledgement from the staff and assistance with finding a seat. (The "grumpiness" looks like a taut sense of crowd management to me, and I am touched that once, when I vary my pattern — I opt to "take away" and not "eat in" — there is surprise and recognition that this is less usual. Is this a little like "kopitiam uncles who remember their regulars", perhaps?) And then, of course, there is the food itself — the now-familiar nutty taste of *kaya* [coconut jam], the cold slab of butter melting into a soft, fresh-baked roll, the heart-stopping strength and sweetness of *kopi* [coffee].

In breakfasting at Chin Mee Chin, I am certainly acknowledging its iconic qualities as heritage. At the same time, I am firmly grounded in the textures of my own memories while acutely aware of the sensory landscapes and culinary histories of others. The sensory connection to this memory-layering and nostalgic recall is particularly important, as captured by online comments of customers to Chin Mee Chin: "Every time I go there, I will buy back 2 tubs of the home made kaya. Being a Hainanese, it feels at home to be there" (a post on Foursquare, Chin Mee Chin 2014); "The kaya was smooth and you could taste the richness of the eggs, while the bread was soft, warm and fluffy" (ThreeHungryCats 2013); "I have always loved ... [Chin Mee Chin's] good ole chocolate cupcakes. I have had them for as long as I remember ... . If Katong dwindles away slowly, at least I'll always have cupcakes. I hope?" ("Gingerbread Mum" 2012). These fragments of remembering and imagining suggest to me that this coffee shop is not simply a quaint heritage site that maintains its eccentric rituals for commercial interests but a source of connection in a quite deep, visceral way to "real" "pasts", however varied — and fragile — these connections and their stories might be. Will the taste of chocolate cupcakes be all that remains of Katong at the end of the day?

LAKSA MOURNING: SHOPHOUSE STYLE MEETS PLOUGHMAN'S LUNCH

Walking along "Food Street", I arrive at the corner of Ceylon Rd, a site saturated in food memories and disputes. On this corner and opposite it, famously, the three main contenders in the "*laksa* wars" fought for supremacy, each claiming to be the most authentic and original "Katong Laksa" (Duruz 2011: 609). Now one of the three "warring" food businesses, 49 Katong Laksa, has moved, I believe, to the western side of Singapore and I hardly recognise the building this business has vacated. Instead of a rather cramped, traditional *laksa* stall — tiled floors, hawker-style furniture, walls plastered with photographs and tributes of satisfied customers, and, of course, the air heavy with the dish's aromatic presence — sited in a somewhat crumbling 1920s building, I find that an elegant edifice has emerged from the renovation. Upstairs, there are several boutique "suites" offering upmarket holiday accommodation while downstairs in the space of the former *laksa* stall is a decidedly British gastro-pub/restaurant. Alluding to the "merrie England" of stately homes, gamekeepers and feudal relations, this restaurant is, somewhat quirkily, named Rabbit Carrot Gun.

   Shophouses, of course, have always had their spaces defined by commercial interests, with workers and tradespeople living above, or behind, the shop or workshop. Recently, however, it is the case that the structures themselves — their aesthetics — are receiving recognition. This valuing of the "look" and "captured" history of buildings is evident, for example, in the state's restoration of the corner buildings on Koon Seng Road, with their pediments "richly adorned with plasterwork" or in the rows of shophouses nearby, "representative of the 'Singapore Eclectic Style' — characterised by mixed architectural influences of the Malay, Chinese and European traditions" (Grêlé 2004: 97).

Furthermore, such sites now offer attractive spaces for touristic performances: for settings and activities that are very different from the confined and densely occupied cubicles that comprised these buildings and the multitude of trades originally plied in these. In contrast, in listings on airbnb [a worldwide homestay network for discerning travellers], accommodation suites in the Rabbit Carrot Gun building are marketed through imagery emphasising their spaciousness, highly designed "mixed" Asian/international styled interiors and the quality and comfort of fittings. The accompanying text for The Kubric Suite, for example, states:

> Luxurious, spacious and eclectic is the only description of this wonderful establishment. … Encapsulated in a 1925 traditionally built Singaporean shophouse, this is 1 of 3 newly refurbished suites [in] … this beautiful traditional building… . Located in the Joo Chiat area on Singapore's East Coast … [this building is in an area] which has undergone … rapid gentrification (Rabbit Carrot Gun nd).

This kind of refurbishment, in which the original purposes of buildings are no longer explicitly written into their fabric or, alternatively, one in which their "heritage" structures (shutters, colonial windows, wide eaves sheltering the walkway and decorative trim) are reworked and celebrated, is not unusual, however. According to Teo and Chang (2009: 84):

> [P]layful and whimsical hybridities offered by boutique hotels come in the form of staying in historic shophouses — remnants of the colonial era formerly inhabited by indigenous communities — which have now been refurbished into trendy inns. Past indignities of life in dilapidated shophouses are transformed into present-day heritage and marketed as "one of a kind" experience to the postcolonial visitor.

Politically speaking, we might regard such innovations as perpetuating relations of colonialism whereby the (often) white and wealthy elites are more able to afford the comforts of the "luxurious, spacious and eclectic". From culinary perspectives too, we might assume that nostalgic expatriates and middle-class "local" anglophiles are the most likely customers for the restaurant downstairs, with these attracted by the bucolic Englishness of its menu — "Gamekeeper's Shooting Breakfast" … "Shepherd's Pie" … "Ham Ploughman's Lunch" ("perfect with a pint of our own craft Buckshot Ale") (Rabbit Carrot Gun nd).

Standing at the corner of Ceylon Road, I am feeling decidedly wistful. Where has *my laksa* gone, particularly its distinctive tastes and aroma (and, of course, what right have I, anyway, to claim any such ownership after a brief and casual acquaintance)? Has *laksa* been replaced by pumpkin soup, pork sausages and mash, aged cheddar, as "interesting dining experiences" (*We Love Katong* 2014: 65)? Furthermore, has Rabbit Carrot Gun entered the territory of heritage's "concrete showcase" rather than its "active process"? After all, *We Love Katong*, a locally produced collection of sketches, observations and memories, stresses that: "The conservation of buildings is meaningless if the lifestyles, trades and crafts they house are not preserved" (2014: 5). Alternatively, perhaps the "active process[ses]" of hospitality provision have been restyled for new audiences? A recent review of this hotel's accommodation and restaurant indicates the extent of this makeover:

> If you are looking for a hip and happening place to stay in trendy East Coast Road then this place ticks all the boxes. Individually designed rooms give that feeling of being somewhere totally unique. The choice of traditional furnishings and modern art work blends well with the heritage Chinese building which has wonderful wooden floors. Rabbit Carrot Gun cafe is located directly under the rooms so not far to go for delicious breakfast — poached eggs best I have ever eaten — or if you want to relax in evening after busy day in steamy Singapore (post on Tripadvisor Reviews 2014).

"[H]ip and happening", "trendy", "totally unique", "traditional", "modern", "heritage Chinese building", "delicious [English] breakfast", "relax … [from] steamy Singapore"… It seems that it is possible to have your cake and eat it too — to enjoy, as a guest, the fantasy of "past" times (without any of its inconveniences, or without actually expending the labour needed to sustain this "past"), together with the satisfactions of life in the present (comforted by a familiar breakfast dish, perhaps, or sheltered from an unfamiliar climate). A simultaneous embrace of, and distancing from, the past provides a pleasurable contradiction. And here I am reminded of Lai's acerbic comment in regard to shaping a romanticised "past" through the selective remembrance: "I have never met residents who lament the demise of the village bucket latrine even if they are nostalgic about past kampong days" (2009: 22).

Of course, it is easy to be critical of Rabbit Carrot Gun, as a site of privilege for communities on upmarket holidays or visitors simply looking for "interesting dining experiences"; as a site inscribed with the familiar tropes of colonial power. However, Teo and Chang offer a more sophisticated analysis, claiming degrees of subversiveness for the boutique hotel that muddy such binaries as coloniser-colonised, local-international, past-present:

> [According to Jacobs,] such hotels participate in the "creative remaking of the colonial in the service of a postcolonial present/future;" more than just an innocent recall of the past, these hotels practice a "subversive return to the colonial heart", marketing this stance as a draw to novelty seeking visitors (2009: 84).

Rabbit Carrot Gun then neither represents an erasure of the "past" nor is it concerned with "faithful" reproduction of this. Instead its messages are very "mixed". As "local" Singaporeans themselves either become entrepreneurs in such establishments (though this is not the case here as the owner is, in fact, British) and manage references to this "past" or become "guests" in such establishments and playfully perform multiple "pasts" and "presents" (including, here, perhaps, an ironic nod towards "merrie England" or moments of luxuriating in stylish "Asian-European" eclecticism), colonial relations and identities receive some challenge. Eileen Fong, travel writer, describing alternative holidays for time-poor middle-class "locals", provides a narrative disruption to expatriate dreaming:

> Many Singaporeans complain about their busy schedules and have no time to getaway and relax ... [and are] choosing to have a weekend at a hotel ... in the city, in the island of [S]entosa .... I mean, we haven't got the cottages and castles in the "countryside" so this is our next best option, right? ... The accommodations [above Rabbit Carrot Gun] are in a traditional shophouse which offers you a unique experience having the best blend of both tradition and modern living. ... Head to Mad Nest if you're feeling [like] some fusion Indian-Jap cuisine. Or you can simply settle for some authentic Katong Laksa (2013).

There are several threads that I want to draw out here briefly. The first is that, in the quotation above addressed to "many Singaporeans" with "busy schedules", an obvious shift in the identity of the consumer has taken place (or, in other words, "Asia has moved from "hosts" to "guests"") (Teo and Chang 2009: 96). The second is that the eclectic styling of such hotels (the "best blend of both traditional and modern") signals both the "charm" of "heritage locales" and the energy of a creative, entrepreneurial society, competing on the global stage and able to absorb traditions from elsewhere as well as valuing its own (2009: 85). This is part of the Singapore story (the constant balancing of old and new; traditional and modern; conservative and creative; "grounded" and cosmopolitan); it also signals a certain fluidity of citizen identity and hybridity of performance (Sidaway, cited in Teo and Chang: 95). While Nora might have complained about the restored shophouse, seeing this as a static form of "organiz[ing] the past" and devoid of "real memory", I would argue that its hybrid meanings allows for a different Singaporean identity, and a different space of urban creativity, to emerge. The final point to keep in mind, as we leave Rabbit Carrot Gun for another, very different establishment on East Coast Road, is that we cannot ignore questions of context, of positioning. While sensory pleasures of eating at 49 Katong Laksa are now consigned to memory, other *laksa* stalls are needed to remain in place. Otherwise, how else can one "settle for some *authentic* Katong laksa" (my emphasis) among the plethora of (presumably *inauthentic*) food choices? Is some kind of ghostly *laksa* presence — traces of its corporeality — required to legitimate this "getaway's" olfactory geographies? Are the ambient tastes and smells of Rabbit Carrot Gun borrowed, conveniently, for the moment from the streets nearby?

RUGBY, BEER AND HOKKIEN PRAWN MEE: MARY'S CORNER REINVENTED

My last stop on this brief tour of Katong's eating houses has the curious name of AlibabaR. While Chin Mee Chin provides an example of a "time-defiant" *kopitiam* and Rabbit Carrot Gun an example of an almost complete makeover of a collection of small business and its built fabric, AlibabaR epitomises the philosophy of "old and new" in urban redevelopment. According to a recent guidebook, this is typical of this neighbourhood: "Old and new lifestyles exist side-by-side in Joo Chiat, where street vendors sell traditional fare like roasted chestnuts and rice dumplings against a backdrop of modern bars, cafés and restaurants" (*We Love Katong* 2014: 24–25).

My memories of Mary's Corner from earlier walks through the neighbourhood was of a stall, renowned for its Katong *laksa* and its *tau kwa pau* — a spicy Teochew *Nyonya* dish of bean curd, with a stuffing of fishcakes ("ieatishootipost" 2007). In the same *kopitiam* was a Hokkien prawn *mee* stall, selling a prawn noodle dish of intense prawn flavour, produced by cooking the prawn heads and shells. This stall had been operated by Pang Weng Hong since the early 1970s (Quek 2014). New owners, however, took over the *kopitiam* in 2012, rebadging it as a hawker bar, as a casual eating place with hawker food during the day, and serving a range of drinks (including craft beers) at night: "Alibabar — Kopitiam by Day, Hawker Bar by Night"(Alibabar 2014). Meanwhile, Mary has since moved on to a stall in nearby Dunman Food Centre (post on The Food Collage 2013). Pang Weng Hong, however, after initial doubts about the coffee shop's change in focus, decided to defer retirement and to stay.

> He says in Mandarin: "At first I said no to the changes, when I knew the coffee shop was going to have a bar. But after they did it, I think it is okay." … Indeed, many customers still queue up for his noodle dishes … His stall retains his hawker roots, in contrast to other hipster stalls in Alibabar, such as the French stall Le Petit Paradis, and iCookuEat, which serves homey Eurasian food. Alibabar's bar section, which sells kopi and toast for breakfast, becomes a watering hole in the evening for residents and working professionals winding down for the day, with a wide selection of craft beers. …[The] owner says: "I could have done an Italian restaurant, but at the same time I wanted to retain some of the character of the area. … I wanted it to be a neighbourhood bar, where people can come in their T-shirts and shorts" (Quek 2014).

Nevertheless, the naming of the establishment (originally Alibaba, later Alibabar, now AlibabaR) still seems something of an anomaly, despite the multi-function intentions implied by its "hawker bar" descriptor.[4] Why is there reference to Ali Baba in the name of the establishment, we might wonder? Is this simply another attempt to introduce "new" cuisines to Katong (perhaps, on this occasion, a fashionable "middle eastern" intervention), while still maintaining connection with the coffee shop's hawker history? At the same time, there is a puzzling absence of recognisably middle eastern food on the menu. A respondent to one of Singapore's food blogs, however, offers a more intriguing speculation on the origins of name: "[D]o you know the Ali Baba Eating House has a fascinating Chinese name … (as seen on the sun screen at the side of the shop) which translates phonetically in Mandarin as "Ah Lee Ba Ba Yi Ting Hau!" which sound[s] … close to "Ali Baba Eating House" (post on

---

[4] Note that the variable spellings of this business' name adopted throughout this chapter are a reflection of the different sources' spellings. If referring to the business in the present, and more generally, I have opted for "AlibabaR".

"Chow" 2012). Whether this plausible explanation is true or not, the business' original name is certainly Ali Baba Eating House and has been for some years, and the pun contained in the current rendition of the name (the "baR" in "AlibabaR") intentional. Renovations have been carried out to reflect this re-invention of the eating house as a "bar": internal walls have been removed and areas for seating rearranged to create a lighter, more open effect. "The décor is rustic yet modern with high wooden stools and tables outdoor and tungsten light bulbs hanging off the roof", says "TrisMalis" of Makansutra, a company renowned for its promotion of Singapore and Malaysian street food (2013).

Makansutra also explains the origins of the hawker bar as a hospitality concept:

> For many senior citizens in Singapore, drinking beer in hawker centre is not new. Eating hawker food with beer has been a norm for as long as hawker centre existed. But to attract a younger audience, business owners are repackaging the idea with designer touches. The result: the hawker food gastrobar — kopitiam with hip, cool and sophisticated setting and comfort food ("TrisMalis" 2013).

The combination of sophistication, comfort and value for money in an eating house is a very beguiling prospect. However, for the purposes of this chapter, we might want to ask how does such a "mixed" space (of cuisines, of people, of décor, of temporal and spatial usage) constitute a site of "real" memories and place-making? Is this re-invention as a pastiche of "styles" and uses simply a cynical marketing exercise? Is this the point at which fusion becomes, according to Darra Goldstein (referring to food, in particular), a "murky mélange" (2005: iv)?

To tease out this question, it is worth, firstly, making a quick trawl through the menu on offer via the business' website posts and responses. This would certainly provide some sense of diversity of AlibabaR's offerings of tastes, smells, sounds and sights. The promotional discourse certainly sounds encouraging: "Chicken Ham sub … . So soft it melts easily in the mouth. … Very delicious pizza and buffalo wings done in halal way. … quality gourmet burgers, taco and chilli dog at the most affordable price. … Do come and try [them and watch] World Cup Rugby…". However, in case one feels this represents an unmitigated diet of Western-style fast food, there are also local dishes to sample: prawn noodle soup, of course, and, on occasion, pig's tail and scallop soup, fried *kway teow* [dish of flat noodles, prawns, Chinese sausage, fish cakes, bean sprouts] or fried *mee sua* [fried thread noodles with chicken and seafood], served up with a diet of the latest sport spectacular, such as "EPL Title match — Screening live tonight: Chelsea versus Arsenal". "And not to mention Hei Chor [prawn rolls with water chestnuts] and Kong Ba Pau [braised pork belly in buns] for snack bite … with Craft Beer! Yummy yummy" (Alibabar 2014).

In their responses, reviewers can be quite complimentary, as the following indicates:

> Ali Babar has had a real attempt at bringing food courts into the postmodern hipster age and has actually succeeded. Located on the corner of East Coast Road and Joo Chiat Road …, this little corner food court with just 5 stalls could easily be ignored or dismissed. To do so however would be to ignore one of the most innovative kopitiams in Singapore today. Only one of the 5 stalls serves the usual staples of Hokkien Mee and Prawn Noodles (which it does very well), instead its neighbours include a bar selling beers from all over the world, a Japanese stall, a gourmet burger shack, and — can it be true — a French restaurant! The obvious draw is the French restaurant; where else in Singapore can you sit in a hawker centre and eat Duc l'orange [sic] for just 10 bucks? (Noms 2013).

Where else indeed? Here I must add, nevertheless, that the French stall, Le Petit Paradis (the successor to the earlier Saveur), now has its own restaurant space, further down East Coast Road. In fact, AlibabaR and its antecedents together have provided a jumping off point for several chefs and small food businesses, such as Astons [a steak house] and Casa Bom Vento [a Peranakan/Eurasian café]. While these originally had stalls in the eating house, they now have independent premises nearby. "Though it's early days yet, [the owner, Tan Kay Chuan] …, hopes his new coffeeshop business model will inspire a new generation of hawkers to join the trade, especially 'young chefs who want to try new cuisines without the high overheads of running a proper restaurant', he says" (Yong 2013).

Meanwhile, the "mixed" range of tastes on offer and their mobility — the continuing traditions of *char kway teow* and *tau kwa pau*, together with disappearing but fondly remembered flavours of Le Petit Paradis' pan fried *fois gras*, for example — provide rich resources for sensory remembering: "If you are looking for the most sinful kway teow in Singapore, Yong Huat is the place. Generous portion …, lots of cockles, and their fried pork skin is crispy" (post on AlibabaR 2014) or "The Fried Mee Sua is unreal. The moment you take that first bite you know you're eating something made out of a secret recipe that's been passed down through the generations" (post on HungryGoWhere 2011).

At the same time, some taste memories are better or worse than others: "Forget about the breakfast set of toast and eggs. Use margarine instead of butter"; "The tau kwa bau [tau kwa pau] may look good, but the auntie is unscrupulous and the food is expensive" (post on AlibabaR 2014).

Once again, in the mundane details of these memories, I am reminded of Yeoh and Kong's distinction between "lifeworlds" and "concrete showcases" and of Nora's separation of constructed *lieux de mémoire* and "real environments" of memory. To what extent might AlibabaR be regarded as a somewhat bloodless commercial enterprise, an attempt to ape fashionable foodhalls like Food Republic (with these, in turn, drawing on nostalgic narratives of Singapore in the 1960s), a postcolonial attempt (as with Rabbit Carrot Gun) to draw on contrasting meanings — day and evening, local and "exotic", youth and age — to widen the customer base? This may be the case, but threading through the history of this eating house is not only a sense of its "mixed" provenance but also of its organic growth, and the memories that accrue with such growth. It is not an enterprise "born modern", after all, but one deeply rooted in its own hybrid past in ways that continue to shape the business in the "present":

> Katong is slowly becoming gentrified. Humble coffeeshops are giving way to gastrobars, restaurants, cafes, all-day breakfasts — the eating scene is changing slowly. Interesting new ideas and concepts are starting to evolve. The new AliBabar is one good example of this slow evolution. … Once upon a time, at the corner of East Coast Road and Joo Chiat Rd, was a humble little corner coffeeshop, called AliBaba, famous for selling tau kwa pau. … Over time, it gained a reputation for incubating new restaurants. *Aston's* … *Casa Bon Vento* [sic] … *Saveur* … . As such, one entrepreneur felt that it was timely to do up the place a little and introduce a new concept marrying the tradition of the old coffee shop with its reputation of being a place where one could get good food at hawker prices. Enter AliBabar, coffee shop by day, bar at night! ("Katong Gal" 2013)

The point is that here, the "past" is neither abandoned nor replaced by a stylish "present". The organic growth — the "evolution" — of AlibabaR ensures that historical traces of the "local" remain, joining forces with contemporary meanings of the "cosmopolitan" as locally interpreted tastes of "others". This shifting mix, of past and present, local and cosmopolitan, time and space, ensures diverse memories, stories and sensory mappings are attached to this site. And it is these memories and their "realness" that become critical in creating alternative histories to those enshrined in *lieux de mémoire*. As Lim says:

> In Singapore the creative activities of the non-complying minority and the energy generated in spaces of indeterminacy are essential catalytic substances towards the formation of a distinctive Singaporean culture and urban identity with its own peculiarities. They stand as firm attestations of the persistence of memories of spaces, of instances of people reclaiming the space they live in and of plural alternatives to Singapore's story of nation building that have all but been eradicated by *tabula rasa* (2005: 166).

A final word for this section comes from Serene Goh. Despite her poignant "Katong isn't just a physical space any more, but an emotional yearning", she concludes: "Leaving Katong to decay or replacing it all with high-rise condos would have been disastrous. At least there is enough of the old to trigger the imagination, if you know where to look" (2013). So, while *bibiks* no longer ride trishaws in Katong nor do policemen wear shorts, perhaps in the t-shirts and shorts worn at AlibabaR and its resonant foodscapes of "mixed" tastes and aromas, there are glimpses of "character": uncles who acknowledge you as "regulars" … "grumpy" — even "unscrupulous" — aunties … the lingering tastes of Mary's *tau kwa pau* … "if [only] you know where to look".

RETRO-LICIOUS TASTES AND SMELLS AS "REAL" REMEMBERING

Unlike efforts to reproduce the "real" in exacting detail that underpins many forms of heritage building restoration, we find our walk through Katong peppered simply with sporadic references to its past history and remembered (or reworked) foodscapes. The mélange of old and new landscapes dogs our footsteps. *We Love Katong* captures a sense of this in its urban sketches, as well as in the accompanying texts — fragments of local history and remembrance: "Masjid Khalid … was established … at the suggestion of a group of hawkers who peddled Malay food there. Till today the mosque is known for its delicious food"; "[The] Betel Box Backpackers hostel … is located in a shophouse that was originally built in the 1920s … [and now] boasts a cosy common room where guests … get to know each other over drinks and snacks (2014: 26–29); "Housed in a two-storey shophouse …, local boutique Rumah Bebe strives to preserve Peranakan culture ... beadwork, batik, porcelain, jewellery and embroidery. The café features delicacies such as pineapple tarts, kueh, pastries and curry puffs" (2014: 72).[5] This is the power of the reference — the power of a structural detail of a mosque or shophouse, or even of the "look" of a pineapple tart — to evoke ensembles of memories or possibilities for imaginative place-making.

References, however, need not be simply serendipitous — chance leftovers on the urban landscape from earlier cultural practices and land/building uses. Dawn Mok, discussing the "styling" of "modern" cafes in Singapore refers to the desirability of "soul" — conscious attempts (that might be thought of here as "retro") to draw on meanings and symbols of a not-so-distant past for remembering a generation:

> Sometimes it's a design, it's a visual, it's a colour, it's a smell, it's a flavour, so it could be a restaurant, it could be a shop ... specialising in vintage ... you walk in and you just recognise the pattern, "My Mum had a dress like that" and immediately you like [think] "I love the shop," you know, you just need that one [connecting] hook (Mok, cited in Duruz and Khoo 2015: 59).

As I've argued elsewhere, there is a need to be critical of what might be seen as faux attempts to provide that "hook" of connection: "using sepia tones and curly script in signage as clichéd ways of signifying 'the good old days', or purchasing job lots of 'heritage' chairs to signal (cheaply) a certain [coffee shop] chain's trade in nostalgia" (Duruz and Khoo 2015: 59). On the other hand, even the supposedly "inauthentic" reproduction coffee cups, with their distinctive shapes, colours and brand markings reminiscent of those used in traditional *kopitiams*, might, in fact, have their own claim on meanings of "authenticity", sparking intense memories of everyday cultures of coffee drinking. As Dawn Mok says, "even if the cup is not 'real', the memory is" (Mok, cited in Duruz and Khoo 2015: 59).

However, how "real" are memories themselves? Nora in his pessimistic portrait of 1980s France and French cultural heritage, claims that as our "true" sense of historical memory fades, our ardour for collecting and memorialising its details increases. As a result, these sites of collection —

---

[5] "Kueh" are bite-sized, (mostly) sweet snacks, sold throughout Singapore, Malaysia and Indonesia, as well as parts of China. They are mostly Hokkien or Teochew in origin.

lieux de memoire — represent a form of cultural poverty, a loss of "memory [that] takes root in spaces, gestures, images and objects". So, because "there is no longer ... spontaneous memory ... we must deliberately create archives, maintain anniversaries, organise celebrations, pronounce eulogies, and notarise bills because such activities no longer occur naturally" (Nora 1989: 12). Further, in the fashion of Baudrillard's theorisation of signs, simulation and meanings of the "real" (1994), Nora argues that unlike the reality of historical objects — here, the "real" *kopitiam* cup, for example — "*lieux de mémoire* have no referent in reality, or, rather, they are their own referent: pure, exclusively self-referential signs" (1989: 23). Perhaps a fashionable "retro" style has emerged, after all, cut free from "my Mum's dress" and now reattached to a "new" cosmopolitan vision of Singapore "style", one sign among many in circulation among narratives and imagery of a creative, forward-looking, entrepreneurial generation?

Singapore would seem a particularly suitable place to position this "death" of the "real" and of social, embodied memory. According to Wong, projects in the 1960s and 1970s, directed towards nation building and strengthening national identity, emphasised the erasure of both ethnic difference and of the colonial past:

> Vestiges of the ethnic and colonial past were systematically destroyed during the dramatic urban renewal of the post-independence years. Massive demolition of much of the colonial city centre ... led to the loss of environments of memory, and, correspondingly, a kind of *social amnesia*. The demolition of the physical environment wipes out a significant chapter of the history of a place; even if it does not entirely erase it from social memory, it reduces its possibility to be remembered because memory can no longer be *spontaneously* re-enacted in the place itself (Wong 2007:124, emphases original).

In the 1980s, however, in a climate of the state's embrace of policies of multiculturalism, food as a marker of ethnic difference was now viewed as a social resource: as a means of constructing one's ethnic identity and heritage, and as "exotica for tourist consumption" (Wong 2007: 124).

However, there is another way that food, with all its sensory qualities for place- and memory-making, becomes significant for my argument here. For philosophers like Baudrillard and Nora, an emphasis on constructed screen/ material archives of meaning provides a very fitting backdrop for theories of inhabiting an imaginary, mediatised world — a world of signs without "real" referents. The trail of tastes and smells that I have followed through this chapter, together with their haunting absences, on the other hand, suggest a way of intervening in Nora's somewhat rigid prescription of *lieux de mémoire* ("because there are no longer ... real environments of memory) (1989: 7). Instead, in the "mixed" neighbourhood of Katong, there are occasional "whiffs" and tastes as powerful, visceral reminders of stored memories ("The moment you take that first bite you know you're eating something made out of a secret recipe"), whether these moments are personally nostalgic or constitute a more collective retro-recognition of nostalgic reference, or both (a dress, simultaneously recognisable, as "vintage" and as "My Mum's").

As we recall Wong's arguments about food's corporeality — about our literal ingestion of tastes, aromas, meanings and memories — this corporeality intervenes in the rigid prescription of *lieux de mémoire* as sites of formalised memory-making. "Retro-licious" then becomes not only a descriptor of fashionable commodity style but also a way of acknowledging the recent past through the senses' memory-banks. And even a stranger might partake in the pleasure of the reference, bringing his or her store of memories to bear on this place and at this time. The stranger's story will always be different from those of third generation "Katongites", of course, but a story nevertheless, told through the nose and mouth, as well as ears and eyes. And in moments of "eating together in difference" in "mixed" neighbourhoods like Katong lies the possibility, at least — though not the inevitability — of a profoundly visceral cosmopolitan exchange (Nava 2007).

REFERENCES

Alibabar (2014) Alibabar: kopitiam by day, hawker bar by night. https://www.facebook.com/pages/Alibabar-the-Hawker-Bar/455323781210708, accessed 2 September 2014.

AlibabaR (2014) AlibabaR the hawker bar. https://foursquare.com/v/alibabar-the-hawker-bar/4c3d9f257d00d13a1a703a50, accessed 2 September 2014.

Ang D (2013) Singapore's old school cake shops from the 60s — the traditional and the survivors, 6 June. http://danielfooddiary.com/2013/06/06/oldschoolcakes/, accessed 24 June 2014.

Baudrillard J (1994) *Similacra and Simulation.* Michigan: University of Michigan Press.

Boey KC (2009) *Between Stations.* Artarmon NSW: Giramondo.

Chia J (2002) *Frog under a Coconut Shell.* Singapore: Times Books.

Chin Mee Chin (2014) Chin Mee Chin confectionary. https://foursquare.com/v/chin-mee-chin-confectionary/4b2d8577f964a5204fd824e3, accessed 26 August 2014.

"Chow" (2012) Singapore-Katong laksa wars (March 2012 update), 16 March. http://chowho.com/topics/839207, accessed 19 August 2014.

Chua BH (1995) That imagined space: nostalgia for kampungs. In: BSA Yeoh and L Kong (eds.) *Portraits of Places: History, Community and Identity in Singapore.* Singapore: Times Editions, pp. 222–241.

Duruz J (2011) Tastes of hybrid belonging; following the laksa trail in Katong, Singapore. *Continuum* **25**: 605–618.

Duruz J and Khoo GC (2015) *Eating Together: Food, Space and Identity in Singapore and Malaysia.* Lanham Ml: Rowman and Littlefield.

Edensor T (1998) The culture of the Indian street. In: NR Fyfe (ed.) *Images of the Street: Planning, Identity and Control in Public Space.* London: Routledge, pp. 205–221.

Fong E (2013) Alternative staycations in Singapore, 25 August. http://peregrinatewithme.wordpress.com/2013/08/25/alternative-staycation-in-singapore/, accessed 2 September 2014.

"Gingerbread Mum" (2012) Where did my Katong go? 5 August. http://www.gingerbreadmum.com/2012/08/where-did-my-katong-go_5.html, accessed 19 August 2014.

Goh S (2013) The past is still present: Katong is a doorway to Singapore's past… . *The Straits Times*, 11 August. http://news.asiaone.com/news/singapore/past-still-present, accessed 2 September 2014.

Goldstein D (2005) Fusing culture, fusing cuisine. *Gastronomica* **5**: iii–iv.

Grêlé D (2004) *Discover Singapore on Foot.* Singapore: Select Publishing.

HungryGoWhere (2011) Yong Huat, 5 February. http://www.hungrygowhere.com/singapore/yong_huat/?page=5&neighbourhood=East+Coast&index=92, accessed 28 September 2014.

Hutton W (1999) *The Food of Singapore: Authentic Recipes from the Manhattan of the East.* Singapore: Periplus Editions.

"ieatishootipost" (2007) Mary's Corner: Tau Kwa Pau, 17 January. http://ieatishootipost.sg/marys-corner-tau-kwa-pau/, accessed 2 September 2014.

Imram BT (2007) State constructs of ethnicity in the reinvention of Malay-Indonesian heritage in Singapore. *Traditional Dwellings and Settlements Review* **18**(11): 7–27.

James J (2000) Can Katong's laid-back charm be saved? *The Straits Times*, 1 December. http://eresources.nlb.gov.sg/newspapers/Digitised/Article/straitstimes20001201.2.199.21.aspx, accessed 2 September 2014.

"Katong Gal" (2013) Corner coffeeshop to gourmet gastrobar, 22 March. http://katonglife.blogspot.com.au/2013/03/corner-coffeeshop-to-gourmet-gastrobar.html, accessed 27 November 2014.

Kong L and Chang TC (2001) *Joo Chiat: A Living Legacy*. Joo Chiat Citizens Consultative Committee, National Archives of Singapore.

Kumory (2014) Chin Mee Chin Confectionary at East Coast Road, 7 January. http://kumory.blogspot.com.au/2014/01/chin-mee-chin-confectionary-at-east.html, accessed 2 September 2014.

Lai AE (2009) A neighbourhood in Singapore: ordinary people's lives downstairs. *Asia Research Institute Working Paper Series* 133, National University of Singapore, Singapore.

Lim WSW (2005) *Asian Ethical Urbanism: A Radical Postmodern Perspective*. Singapore: World Scientific.

Loh KF (2013) Let's keep Katong's legacy alive. *The Sunday Times*, 1 December. http://news.asiaone.com/news/singapore/lets-keep-katongs-legacy-alive, accessed 2 September 2014.

Markhsx (2012) The Katong and Joo Chiat trail, 8 February. http://comesingapore.com/travel-guide/article/533/the-katong-and-joo-chiat-trail, accessed 19 August 2014.

Metropolasia (nd) East Singapore and Changi: a sentimental journey — Geylang, Katong and Changi.... http://www.metropolasia.com/East_Singapore_and_Changi, accessed 19 August 2014.

Mok D (2007) *Singapore: CityScoops*. Singapore: CityScoops Media.

Nava M (2007) *Visceral Cosmopolitanism: Gender, Culture and the Normalisation of Difference*. Oxford: Berg.

Noms SG (2013) Ali BaBAR and the 40 European craft beers, 7 July. http://singaporenoms.wordpress.com/2013/07/07/ali-babar-at-katong-review/, accessed 2 September 2014.

Nora P (1989) Between history and memory: les lieux de mémoire. *Representations* **26**: 7–24.

Openrice (2014) Chin Mee Chin Confectionary. http://sg.openrice.com/singapore/restaurant/chin-mee-chin-confectionary/23874/, accessed 2 September 2014.

Phua RYK and Kong L (1995) Exploring local cultures: the construction and evolution of meaning and identity in Katong. In: BSA Yeoh and L Kong (eds.) *Portraits of Places: History, Community and Identity in Singapore*. Singapore: Times Editions, pp. 116–139.

Quek E (2014) Is Katong too cool? New eateries abound in the area, but it may be losing its old-world charm as traditional players are squeezed out. *The Straits Times*, 16 March. http://www.straitstimes.com/the-big-story/my-own-private-places/story/katong-too-cool-20140324, accessed 2 September 2014.

Rabbit Carrot Gun (nd) http://www.rabbit-carrot-gun.com/, accessed 2 September 2014.

Tarulevicz N (2013) *Eating Her Curries and Kway: A Cultural History of Food in Singapore*. Urbana Il: University of Illinois Press.

Teo P and Chang TC (2009) Singapore's postcolonial landscape: boutique hotels as agents. In: T Winter, P Teo and TC Chang (eds.) *Asia on Tour: Exploring the Rise of Asian Tourism*. London: Routledge, pp. 81–96.

The Food Collage (2013) Mary's Corner: Tau Kwa Pau, 22 April. http://thefoodcollage. blogspot.com.au/2012/01/marys-corner-tau-kwa-pau.html, accessed 19 August, 2014.

ThreeHungryCats (2013) Café Hopping: Chin Mee Chin, 12 December. http:// thealternativefoodblog.wordpress.com/2013/12/12/cafe-hopping-chin-mee-chin-confectionery/

Tripadvisor (2014) Rabbit Carrot Gun Reviews. http://www.tripadvisor.com.au/ Restaurant_Review-g294265-d3856447-Reviews-or40-Rabbit_Carrot_Gun-Singapore.html#REVIEWS, accessed 2 September 2014.

"TrisMalis" (2013) The new face of kopitiam, 11 April. https://sg.entertainment. yahoo.com/news/face-kopitiam-145516590.html, accessed 2 September 2014.

Velayutham S (2007) *Responding to Globalization: Nation, Culture and Identity in Singapore*. Singapore: ISEAS.

We Love Katong (2014) Singapore: Epigram Books.

Wilson E (1991) *The Contradictions of Culture: Cities, Culture, Women*. London: Sage.

Wong HS (2007) A taste of the past: historically themed restaurants and social memory in Singapore. In: SCH Cheung and C-B Tan (eds.) *Food and Foodways in Asia: Resource, Tradition and Cooking*. London: Routledge, pp. 115–128.

Yeoh B and Kong L (1999) The notion of place in the construction of history, nostalgia and heritage. In: K-W Kwok, CG Kwa, L Kong and B Yeoh (eds.) *Our Place in Time: Exploring Heritage and Memory in Singapore*. Singapore: Singapore Heritage Society, pp. 132–151.

Yeoh BSA and Lau WP (1995) Historic district, contemporary meanings: urban conservation and the creation and consumption of landscape spectacle in Tanjong Pagar. In: BSA Yeoh and L Kong (eds.) *Portraits of Places: History, Community and Identity in Singapore*. Singapore: Times Editions, pp. 46–67.

Yong D (2013) Alibabar — hawker bar. *The Straits Times*, 19 February. http://www. soshiok.com/content/alibabar-coffeeshop-day-hawker-bar-night, accessed 20 September 2014.

Chapter 7

Mapping Singapore's Culinary Landscape: Is Anyone Cooking?

Vineeta Sinha

SINGAPORE'S FOODSCAPE

Singapore is known as a nation of food lovers and where eating is a national pastime. Singaporeans pride themselves on being connoisseurs of good food and in possession of a discerning palate, not to mention being lavish spenders on food. In any societal context, foodways articulate the complex cultural, social and economic practices that produce particular patterns of food production, distribution and consumption. Scholarly accounts of food have rightly focused on theorising these processes. However, the equally important processes of food provisioning, procurement and preparation, and practices related to these have received less academic scrutiny. These merit attention in all societies, but even more so in developed, affluent urban locales where consumption is a dominant social practice, where production and consumption of food are alienated processes, and both "food" and "eating" have been commodified. In the commercialisation of food and of "cooking" itself, modern day affluent consumers are distanced from food production and preparation processes. How do consumers in Singapore (who are already distanced from the food production processes) procure food on a daily basis? What are the culinary practices that characterise Singapore society?

Since the late 1980s, agriculture has constituted a very small segment of Singapore's economy. In 2010, agricultural activities contributed a mere 0.5% to the country's GDP, and only about 1% of Singapore's population can be labelled farmers (Nexus nd). Currently, the major agricultural products in the country include limited food crops (fruits, vegetables, mushrooms), fishing, poultry and flower crops. The latter include ornamental, decorative plants and orchids and are primarily for export to Japan, parts of Europe, Australia and the USA. In terms of food production, only about 10% of the food consumed by the local population is home grown; 90% of the food consumed is exported into the country — as fresh produce or as processed foods. The primary responsibility of the Agri-Food and Veterinary Authority of Singapore (AVA), the national authority for food safety, supported by the *Control of Plants Act* and the *Wholesome Meat and Fish Act*, is to regulate food imports to ensure safety of fresh and processed foods into the country before they are available in the food retail market. The food retail market here is diverse and comprehensive, ranging from supermarkets, hypermarts, wet markets, specialty food stores and traditional grocery stores — which make both local and imported foods readily available to consumers and throughout the year. In recent years, the market for unprocessed, organic and wholesome foods has been growing locally. Singaporeans are increasingly health conscious and attentive to the nutritional value of foods they consume. Changing eating habits and preferences are reflective of broader concerns about ethical consumerism, eco-friendly lifestyle choices and social responsibility of food consumption practices (Valentine 1999).

The food and beverage (F&B) industry in Singapore is a thriving and dynamic one and has grown exponentially since the late 1960s. According to figures provided by the Singapore Department of Statistics, the hotel, catering and food industry employed 19,100 workers in 1970, a figure which had increased to 30,700 by the year 1977 and to 86,776 in 2009 (DOS 2010). Cooked food has been available to Singapore's residents since the early decades of the 20th century — through mobile street hawkers and home-based food caterers, but the number of food and beverage establishments has registered consistently dramatic increase over the last few decades. Market demands — both domestic and through tourist arrivals — have meant the establishments of more restaurants, fast food outlets, food caterers, cafes, coffee houses, food courts, eating houses and coffee shops on the island: in 2013, there were a total of 6,751 F&B outlets, compared to 6,464 in 2011 (DOS 2014). According to these statistics, all F&B services segments registered an increase in operating receipts in 2013 compared to the previous year. Restaurants recorded the largest year-on-year increase of 8.5%, followed by food caterers (4.8%) (DOS 2014).

This provides further evidence that the market for "eating out" continues to expand in Singapore. These F&B figures do not include the 107 hawker centres (NEA 2013) (for 2013) on the island, each with a range of specialist food stalls which provide "once upon a time street food" but in "almost" open air settings. The demand for affordable food is also satisfied through the provision of more cooked food outlets, undertaken by the Singapore state. A total of 20 more hawker centres have been planned for Singapore between now and 2027. These efforts are driven by the desire to make cooked food available to Singaporeans at affordable prices (Tan 2015). This concern about affordability assumes significance in the notice that Gini co-efficient measures for Singapore have been gradually edging upwards over the last decade, which together with higher costs of living in the city-state, exacerbate the problem. The strategy of providing cheap food in hawker centres not only enables dual income families (especially of those from lower middle class and working class backgrounds) to focus on working (rather than cooking) — essential for Singapore's economy — thus legitimising relatively low wages for this category of citizens.

National and regional surveys note that Singapore (like other developed, consumption-oriented societies) is marked overwhelmingly by the phenomenon of "eating out". This is hardly surprising given the wide range of options for cooked food that is affordable and accessible to Singaporeans, within a price range to suit the size of all pockets. The commodification of cooked food and its easy availability have translated into reduced everyday cooking within the home and, to some extent, marginalised the practice of consuming food that is prepared within the household unit. However, interestingly (and perhaps ironically) this has not meant diminished interest in the practice of cooking amongst Singaporeans. In the last two decades, a variety of culinary institutes and cooking schools have been established in Singapore. Evidence suggests that cooking classes are hugely popular with Singaporeans. This can be attributed to a set of complex factors, including a response to market demand for the acquisition of culinary skills. Culinary schools cater to a range of cooking interests: from the hobbyist to culinary professionals. In addition to an interest in cooking as a hobby and leisure activity, increasing numbers of Singaporeans have been attracted to professional cooking — training as chefs in the numerous culinary schools in Singapore as well as in prestigious culinary institutions internationally. Apart from a vibrant, thriving and burgeoning food industry, Singapore also markets itself as a hub of world culinary/gourmet food events. It is home to a range of national and international food festivals and culinary award shows and often hosts world-class culinary developments, attracting celebrity chefs and Michelin starred restaurants to its shores.[1] Consciously marketing and presenting itself as a culinary hub in the region, the Singapore Tourism Board (STB) has been organising the annual Singapore Food Festival since 1994. This month-long festival affords an opportunity for showcasing local, traditional culinary traditions and draws food lovers, both local and foreign (regional and global). The two-decade-old festival provides a gastronomic experience of local cuisines and culinary tastes, dining experiences and food-related competitions. The other major anchoring STB event on the culinary tourism calendar is the "World Gourmet Summit" (WGS) that has been organised in Singapore since 1997. This idea was developed initially by Singapore-based chefs, hotels and restaurants and has by now been firmly embedded in the STB event calendar. According to a self-description on the event's website,

> WGS is a world renowned epicurean platform that places our little red dot on the international world map as a central focal point for all food bon vivants, artisans and gourmands" (WGS 2014).

The tenor of the annual WGS event pegs eating and cooking as fine art forms and exposes Singaporeans to the world-renowned iconic, culinary professionals in the food and beverage industry. These two signature events ground gastronomic tourism in Singapore and have granted visibility to the island's foodscape internationally. These not only translate into tourism dollars but also have the effect of generating phenomenal interest in culinary tastes and practices amongst Singaporeans, which are themselves also commodified.

Given this scenario, this chapter seeks to document the relationship of Singaporeans with the practice of "cooking", starting with the fundamental question: is anyone cooking in Singapore? Extrapolating, other related queries can be posed: Who is cooking here and why? What is the interest in cooking about and what kinds of cooking are popular? What is the status of

---

[1] According to the latest surveys, 10 high-end Singapore restaurants are listed amongst the top 50 restaurants in Asia. Tan HY (2015b) Asia's 50 Best Restaurants: Why the same old list?

cooking and what meanings does "cooking" connote (Sutton 2013)? I argue that Singaporeans register preference for occasional, event-related, episodic cooking as a recreational activity. In this logic, cooking is viewed as "play", a sensory experience, a hobby, as entertainment and thus as pleasurable. In contrast, Singaporeans are less enthused about "everyday cooking" defined as a set of routinised, laborious, tedious, time-consuming activities, which must be undertaken on a daily basis. The shift towards "cooking" as an activity of choice, as a creative endeavour in contrast to "cooking" as obligatory (and thus an imposition), as everyday mundane "work" (and drudgery) is supported by the large numbers of Singaporeans attending cooking classes across a range of culinary institutes but simultaneously, diminished daily cooking within the home. Eating and cooking processes frame gender roles and gender relations within the household, reproducing the family unit and embedded social relations. How do we theorise the normalisation of "eating out" practices and the highly reduced practice of "everyday cooking" in Singaporean households in the context of an urban, cosmopolitan, consumption-driven, affluent Singapore? What sociological impact do these practices have on reconfiguring domestic and familial landscapes, and on women's roles and gender relations in Singapore's social life?

RESTRUCTURED LABOUR FORCE: RECONFIGURED FAMILIES

The Singapore leadership's careful social planning as well as economic and political strategising has produced the "miracle" of Singapore's success story. Starting as a small trading post pivotal in regional trade in the 19th century, modern Singapore has grown in recent years to become one of the major seaports in the world. After self-government in 1959, the People's Action Party (PAP) took an aggressive lead in promoting socio-economic reforms for Singapore. The need for absolute political stability in the pursuit of economic development for the nation normalised state intervention in societal domains. The attainment of political stability through an efficient, bureaucratic and pragmatic mode of governance (Chua 1985) has facilitated the phenomenal growth of the Singapore economy in the last five decades. To overcome unemployment, labour-intensive industries were encouraged in the 1960s while in the 1970s the focus turned to the manufacturing sector with concomitant emphasis on increasing skills and superior production. Adopting the logic of a free market economy by the 1980s, the city-state aggressively used its geo-strategic location to court foreign capital investment in the manufacturing sector starting with import substitution and then moving to export-oriented industrialisation. Singaporeans from all social backgrounds achieved significant advances in educational levels, income, life expectancy and other social indicators. Singapore's extraordinary economic growth from the 1960s to 1990s has lifted many out of poverty and created a broad middle class.

Singapore leaders have argued that, "lacking" natural resources, its people are its biggest resource; this has included both male and female citizens. Singaporean women have been actively involved in the economic development of the country since the 1970s at least. The proportion of employed female residents has registered upward moves from 23.5% in 1970 to 44.4% in 2013 (MOM 2009), in which year, the resident labour force participation rate for females was 58.1% compared to 75.8% for males (MOM 2014). The Women's Charter of 1961, with the explicit intent to grant legal parity and equality to women, in fact is "mostly concerned with the roles, responsibilities, duties, and rights of women within the family" (Chan 2000). Yet, led by economic, instrumental rationality, in the early 1970s, women were encouraged by the government to join the labour force and to contribute to the economic development of Singapore. In fact the sharpest increase in female employment rates occurred between 1970 and 1980, moving from 28.2% to 44.3%. The state's logic of enhanced educational opportunities for women was led by the instrumentality of the need for efficient utilisation of half of the citizenry as manpower/resource rather than any notion of gender equity or women's emancipation. The state in Singapore constructs the "normal family" as constituted of a heterosexual unit that is biologically and socially productive; where males are household heads and females, even if they are working outside the home, are primarily wives, mothers, daughters and sisters and are responsible for managing the domestic realm. Traditional gender roles and cultural assumptions frame behaviours normatively expected of men and women within the nuclear family unit. The Singapore state has over the decades continued to endorse patriarchal notions of traditional gender roles (Chan 2000; Teo 2011), even as it contradicts its dictum by encouraging women to, at the same time, venture into educational and career opportunities beyond the domestic domain.

Singapore women have heeded this call and responded by joining the labour force in large numbers: between 1980 and 2007, the percentage of females in employment in Singapore increased from 44.3% to 54.3%. This has been linked to record low fertility rates for Singapore (as in Japan, Korea and Taiwan) not to mention that many educated, working women with careers, opt not to get married at all. But this has created a situation where the caring work traditionally performed by wives and mothers in the household has had to be outsourced, not unexpectedly to other women. Indeed the dramatic upward shifts in the participation of married women in Singapore's labour market from 129,300 in 1980 to 337,600 in 1994 (Verma 2009), would remain a puzzle without taking into consideration the inflow of domestic workers into Singapore — coinciding with the rise of the service sector in Singapore's economy.

In the 1990s, Singapore's economic strategy was one of reliance on manufacturing and service sectors "as the twin engines of growth" (MTI 2012). Interestingly, its favourable economic performance continued despite fluctuating and weakened global market conditions. A globalised economic outlook drew international multinational corporations (MNCs) to the island. This created employment opportunities for Singaporeans, as seen in the pervasive presence of electronic, software, banking and financial organisations on the island. Eventually with enhanced educational attainment and qualifications in skills, the local labour force, while highly disciplined began to factor itself out of the local market by becoming unaffordable to employers. Singapore was also losing its edge in the region as an attractive location for MNCs, because of more costly labour and higher infrastructural costs for running businesses and an unwillingness by its people to undertake manual (low paying) work, given the higher costs of living. Consequently, the construction and service sector in Singapore drew on readily available cheap foreign labour from South Asia and Southeast Asia, which eventually resulted in a persisting dependence. Singapore faced regional competition in attracting international multinationals and had to present itself in different terms. Singapore's dependence on foreign labour from the Southeast Asian region and further afield from South Asia — Bangladesh, Sri Lanka and India had grown exponentially since the 1990s. Low cost manual labour was, and is, being recruited from South Asia, especially India, for the construction industry and the cleaning sector. According to figures released by the Ministry of Manpower, the total foreign workforce in Singapore in December 2013 stood at 1,321,600 (up from 900,800 in December 2007), including "skilled" and "unskilled" "foreign workers" (MOM 2013).

Domestic helpers are not new to Singapore. From the turn of the 20th century to the 1970s, traditional domestic workers from China — known as "amahs" worked in Singapore households. There were also local women who worked as domestic helpers on a part-time basis. However, the reliance on foreign domestic workers is a phenomenon that "took off" in Singapore only in the late 1980s. The numbers have seen an exponential increase over the decades and the demand for their labour continues to grow (Wing 1994). Starting from the relatively small figure of 20,000 in 1987, the number of foreign workers had doubled within a year to 40,000; by 2006, 150,000 were employed in Singapore households — working out to one in six families (MOM 2013). According to figures from the Ministry of Manpower, in December 2009, there were 196,000 foreign domestic workers and the latest figures from June 2014 report a staggering total of 218,300 domestic workers — largely from the Philippines and Indonesia, and smaller numbers from South Asian countries such as India, Sri Lanka, Bangladesh and Myanmar (MOM 2013).

The Human Development Report 2013 ranked Singapore 13th (out of 148 countries) in the Gender Inequality Index: in general, women in Singapore fare reasonably well on various social indicators, such as literacy levels, life expectancy, educational attainment, labour force participation and reproductive health. However, women's representation in the boardroom[2] and their presence in public and political life is fairly limited.[3] They also continue to receive lower salaries compared to their male counterparts. Wage differentials by gender, male-dominated industries and absence of women in the top echelons of various societal domains persist, although significant developments have been made in the postcolonial period. Women political leaders and women's groups continue to press for greater gender equality and gender justice amongst Singaporeans.

Women in Singapore, as in other developed economies, have attained high levels of educational attainment, including at tertiary levels. Women now constitute slightly more than half the undergraduate population in local universities and attain excellence in academia; the male advantage in higher education is no longer the norm here as in other developed countries, like South Korea and Japan. Women's presence and participation in the local labour force has risen over the decades, but this is still lower than that in many developed countries. Still, women here continue to be burdened with the dual responsibility of working both in and out of the home. Dual income

---

[2] According to the results of a survey conducted by Board Agender, Singapore women's presence in leadership positions in the corporate world was 7.3% in 2011, which is lower than some other countries in the region.

[3] According to the AWARE CEDAW Shadow Report of May 2011, the percentage of women in Parliament after the 2011 General Elections stood at 10% (Aware 2011).

families in Singapore are not uncommon, with women working outside the home having become normalised. However, many of these women leave the workforce after marriage and childbirth to perform "caring and feeding work" in the household. For example, women's labour force participation rate in the age group 20–29 years edged upwards from 58.7% in 1976 to 72.8% in 1984. In contrast, the percentages of working women in the age cohorts 30–39 years and 40–49 years has been markedly lower during the same period (Yeoh and Huang 1999a). More flexible and supportive work arrangements, structural reconfigurations and government policies are needed to ensure that women and men can balance their careers with family responsibilities. The high levels of female participation rates in the labour force have, not surprisingly, reconfigured families and households in Singapore (Huang and Yeoh 1996; Yeoh et al. 1999; Yeoh and Huang 1999b; Yeoh 2006). Commentators note not only decreasing marriage and fertility rates which are alarming for the state, but also speak of a "care deficit in the domestic sphere" (Tai 2013: 1152).

CARING AND FEEDING WORK

Given shifts in gender demography and women's participation in the formal economic sectors, what has been the emergent Singapore model as far as caring and feeding work are concerned? Is this different from the model in developed economies like the UK and the US where women's participation in the formal workforce has meant a turn to commodified food to satisfy daily family food needs? (Goodman and Redclift 1991; Gottdiener 2000). The latter translates typically to convenience foods secured outside the home in a variety of modes: as processed, ready to eat, almost ready to eat, microwaveable meals. What about in Singapore? If everyday meals cooked by family members (typically women in the household) are not available to family members, is there any caring and feeding work performed in Singapore households and if so, by whom?

A household has been interpreted as a site where consumption occurs, including that of food. It is seen to contain the family unit — an institution that at least in theory, binds individuals into a set of relationships, who perform activities which reproduce the home — both literally and symbolically. The "home" itself has been a critical space in articulating relationships between individuals and the processes of food preparation and consumption. These latter are premised on the social organisation of labour and its performance by household members. The term "housework" is a broad category that encapsulates a variety of essential tasks that need to be performed to sustain both the idea and the "reality" of home. Feminist and Marxist scholars have by now posed critical questions about the nature and politics of housework in insisting that this be recognised as "work" — in fact "unpaid labour" thus acknowledging the exploitation of those who perform this work.

The descriptors "cooking work" and "feeding work" denote activities that enable consumption of food within the home. These refer to food procurement and preparation processes; what is recognised as cooking and feeding work have varied over time and cross-culturally. These variations are determined by cultural notions about how the category "food" is understood, what is meant by "cooking" and how a "proper meal" is conceptualised. Whatever form cooking and feeding work take in any society, this is nonetheless *work* and someone is charged with its performance. Indeed, a great deal of labour is invested in making the home a site for consumption. What activities and processes enable the everyday consumption of food within Singapore households? What makes it possible for consumption to occur within the home unproblematically? Who, if anyone, is actually doing the caring and feeding work in Singapore households?

Just as the home is central in discussions of food preparation and consumption women are "naturally" charged with the responsibility of caring for the health and well-being of family members, including the performance of cooking and feeding work. In most societies, women do the bulk of the work that goes into sourcing, securing and preparing food for not only their own consumption but that of other members in their household unit. This was true for hunting-gathering societies as well as in contemporary industrial societies. As noted by Goodman and Redclift (1991: 2–3):

> Women play a particularly important part in most aspects of food production, processing and consumption, in developed and developing countries ... However, we still lack a body of literature which addresses the central question: what part have changes in gender divisions played in the way food is prepared and consumed.

In urban consumer societies too, the time-consuming, labour-intensive, day-to-day planning of meals, shopping for ingredients, actual preparation of food (cooking), serving food, storing leftovers, clearing up, washing up — are all viewed as "women's work". Gender is strongly associated with housework and cooking in the home for the family is seen to be women's lot. Does this suggest that women are being coerced into performing these tasks? Across many societal contexts, many women report a sense of pride, pleasure, fulfilment and satisfaction in enacting this given role. Within the frames of cultural expectations, caring work is loaded with moral overtones. In fact feeding work is associated strongly with women's love, affection and emotional attachment to their families. In this normative logic, a woman's natural role is to be a wife and mother and to derive enjoyment from performing all the tasks that accompany these identities. But despite this ideology, housework in general and cooking and feeding activities in particular, are tedious, mundane, repetitive, not always pleasant, time-consuming and laborious. But the ideology of the family and women's role within produce a discourse where all these tasks are not defined using the language of labour. Thus much of the cooking and feeding work is not only unrecognised but remains invisible.

Also given that such work is expressed through the language of care and nurture, it prevents articulations of conflict, disharmony, discontentment and frustration. Discussions of division of labour with respect to food preparation in the home, if they are confined at a descriptive level (like who does what work and how much), fail to address the critical question of how these arrangements express and reproduce gendered power relations. It is crucial to also ask how housework gets evaluated on the basis of gender identities. For instance, does cooking work performed by men take on positive connotations? The division of labour in the domestic realm is reflective of broader power differences between men and women, parents and children. Scholars have denoted these as the micro-politics of the home and family life. Such work has emerged especially from feminist and critical perspectives, which have highlighted gendered power relations in the production and preparation of food. Domestic labour, including cooking and feeding work are performed largely by women; but this work is connected to the world beyond the home. It has been argued that the performance of cooking and feeding work, sustains the existing labour force for the capitalist market and also reproduces a labour force for the future. Thus the home may be rightly seen as the site of consumption, but it is also inextricably linked to the world of capitalist production — which is sustained by individuals located in the domestic realm.

In Singapore, with the participation of women in the labour force, the provision of caring and feeding work is apportioned between working women, homemakers as well as foreign domestic workers. With class as a mediating variable, for those who can afford to employ full-time female domestic helpers, housework has been outsourced to this category of women. The reliance on the latter sees caring, cooking and feeding work in Singaporean households being sustained through their labour, which is also commodified. The domestic helpers perform the tasks related to food preparation and cooking of regular meals within the home. Ironically and unsurprisingly, this remains a gendered domain. For those who cannot afford to employ full-time live-in helpers, career women who are wives and mothers continue to multi-task and work multiple shifts — juggling both home and career obligations. It is not just feeding work in the household that career women are expected to perform but also care of children and the elderly. The Singapore scenario suggests that the procurement of daily meals is facilitated in the presence of a diverse range of cooked food outlets as well as some degree of home cooked meals. There is strong evidence that Singapore women struggle to negotiate normative patriarchal expectations about their traditional gender roles as wives and mothers; these are imposed upon even those who seek to make careers outside the home. Many more Singaporean women either leave the workforce upon marriage and childbirth; and if not certainly express the conflicts and challenges they face in managing multiple obligations effectively. The Singapore state too has these dual expectations of women — revealing its internalisation of patriarchal gender roles. Women are expected to reproduce, to maintain/raise societal fertility levels by getting married and having children in a timely manner, even as they are utilised as resource/manpower to sustain the nation's economy. However, the demands made on women are not aligned with appropriate and comprehensive state policies about child care support and flexible work arrangements. To a large extent this policy neglect has to do with the invisibility and depreciation of caring and feeding work that must be performed (by someone) in order to reproduce households, but which remains unacknowledged and factored out of the discussion. While limited effort has been made to socialise men as husbands and fathers to do their share of the caring work in households, these have yet to be translated into equally (or meaningfully) shared gender responsibilities in the home, a task made all the more challenging due to the absence of support from reconfigured institutional frameworks. Few men cook regularly, for example, within the home or share child care duties with their wives. Outside of the couple, much of the caring and feeding work is performed either by full-time domestic workers or by elderly female family members, who may or may not be living with the nuclear family unit.

THE "EATING OUT" OPTION

The dualism of "eating in "/"eating out" has structured discussions in the field of food studies (see Warde and Martens 2000; Finklestein 1989; Bell and Valentine 1997). This binary has been useful for theorising the shift from domestic-based cooking for kin members (as a matter of necessity and obligation) and undertaken as a core household activity, to the widespread and increasingly normalised practice of securing food beyond the domestic realm, from commercial food outlets, where food is commodified and available in the marketplace (Olsen *et al.* 2000). While connoting a clear spatial dimension, the debates transcend the mere notice of *where* eating is taking place. The latter also suggests the relationships that are generated (or not) between individuals as a result of specific eating practices and the all-important question of who is doing the cooking of food and why. Striking contrasts are evident between consuming cooked food as a commodity, secured through a commercial transaction versus having loved ones cook food for family members. Presently, in developed affluent economies there is a strong demand for food as a commodity and the financial capacity to pay for it. Beardsworth and Keil (1997) suggest that the march of industrial, capitalist societies, the creation of cities and the movement of individuals to locales far removed from home, in search of work and livelihood, were important contributory factors which historically produced conditions that separated kin members from their household, creating dependency on non-kin clusters in satisfying food needs. In these foundational historical processes, food as a commodity has become implicated in exchange relations in the marketplace, *in addition* to being embroiled in kinship ties and affective sentiments at the familial and household level (Srinivas 2013).

Sociologists have noted the increasing frequency with which members in urban, industrial societies (both Western and non-Western) are "eating out", that is consuming food cooked outside of their homes by non-kin. In these societies "eating out" has become regular, patterned, routine behaviour whereas still in other settings, this only occurs on special, out of the ordinary moments. Does it matter if the frequency of eating out increases to the extent that individuals are eating fewer and fewer home cooked meals? Some food studies scholars have noted the decline of everyday "family meals" (Murcott 1997). They see the very fate of the family as a coherent and functional unit closely tied to the regular feeding work performed by family members. It has been argued that the production of family meals enables the family itself to be reproduced. But outside the frames of functionalist logic, it has also been asked if the family meal was ever a reality or merely a figment of imagination, or perhaps an ideal to aspire towards? Given the problematic family form, particularly the patriarchal norms and the oppressive and conflicting gendered division of labour that defines household labour, should the passing of the family meal/table be lamented? Approaches that define the nuclear family structure and ideology in normative terms view the increased incidence of "eating out" as destructive to the family and its cohesion? But what if you can eat out with the family? Would this not be good for family interaction and bonding? This trend has been widely reported for Singaporean families. While "eating out" is pervasive in Singapore, it is not isolated individuals who are eating out alone. Rather it is quite common to see families going to restaurants and hawker centres to eat together.

Cooked food retail outlets abound in Singapore offering attractive "eating out" options in the form of hawker centres, food courts, cafes, restaurants, fast food outlets, coffee shops. The easy availability of cooked food, prepared under hygienic conditions, within the frames of rigorous food safety regulations and at highly affordable prices cater to the daily eating needs of large numbers of Singaporeans — from the humble hawker centre option to high-end specialty restaurant. Government bodies, consumer organisations and medical authorities alike have an interest in the changing food/nutritional habits and culinary skills of Singaporeans. Observers of Singapore's eating patterns note that "away from home eating" has by now become part of Singapore food culture (Rebello 2012). Since 2007, the "Electrolux Asia Pacific Food Survey" an online survey which targets a total of 5,000 respondents in 10 countries (Australia, China, Indonesia, India, Malaysia, Philippines, Singapore, Taiwan, Thailand and Vietnam) has generated data about food preparation, cooking and dining habits amongst Asia-Pacific residents (Yasmeen 2013). The data for Singapore suggest that only about 68% of Singaporeans regularly eat home cooked meals within the household even though they register a preference for the same. In this nation of foodies where 93% describe being passionate about food, only less than half (46%) express confidence in their cooking skills. Dining out emerges as the norm even as 85% of the respondents aspire to learn cooking and become more skilled in the kitchen. According to the National Nutrition Survey, 60% of Singaporeans surveyed reported eating at hawker centres at least four times a week in 2010, increasing from 49% in 2004. In terms of where specific daily meals were consumed, the trends show that as compared to 2004, in 2010, more Singaporeans were eating both lunch and dinner outside the home in hawker centres, coffee shop stalls or food courts. This naturally translated into fewer numbers who were eating these meals within the home (HPB 2010). Quite apart from the effects of these eating trends on family relationships, national health and medical authorities have expressed concerns about the relationship between "away from home eating" and its correlations with rising levels of obesity and ill health, trends that have been documented for other developed countries as well. Singaporeans are also big spenders when it comes to food. A Master Card Survey on consumer dining habits reported that in 2014, Singaporeans were willing to spend a great deal on eating out — including at top-end eating establishments. According to the findings of the survey, in 2013 Singaporeans spent an average of SGD 248 a month dining out as compared to the much lower Asia-Pacific average of SGD 175 (*Today*, 6 May 2014). The survey confirms the dominant and normative trend of not just eating out but also an expressed preference for dining out more frequently. In the large undergraduate module "Sociology of Food" which I have been teaching at the National University of Singapore since 2002, I learnt that many students viewed everyday cooking for the family as laborious, difficult, time-consuming and messy and many dismissed it as "impractical and inconvenient". After cooking for the first time in an assigned class project, many students shared that although they found the experience novel and fascinating, they did not want to do this on a daily basis. Many reported that they would either rely on domestic helpers to cook for them or would just eat out regularly. Many of these students, as young adults, who were on the threshold of setting up their own families said that they would turn to the eating out option by choice if not by necessity. For many, buying cooked food rather than preparing food themselves was articulated as a pragmatic choice, a more convenient option as it reduced work, was quicker and hassle-free.

Sociologists have argued that there are important social consequences if the practice of eating out becomes dominant and routinised and if it is normalised (see Burnett 2004; Finklestein 1989; Bell and Valentine 1997; Warde and Martens 2000). The routinisation of eating out is seen to signal shifts in several food-related practices. One clear implication is with respect to food preparation practices in the home: what is the extent of cooking as a routinised activity in the home? Does cooking become a marginal activity? Does it assume negative connotations and is it seen as less desirable? Does this signal a deskilling of society? Is cooking even viewed as a skill or as being necessary for survival? Or does the act of cooking acquire new meanings and connotations? Singaporeans have certainly expressed concerns and even anxieties about the disappearance of cooking skills amongst hawkers. Moved by their palate and passion for sourcing the best foods, Singaporeans hunt down renowned local hawker fare, often being able to articulate a food topography of the island. Many ask if genuine and authentic hawker flavours can be retained for future generations. Members of the public have called for the establishment of hawker training schools to preserve cooking expertise and knowledge by teaching the next generation these vanishing skills. Not surprisingly, few have expressed concerns about the possible disappearance of everyday cooking skills routinely embodied in household units. This has to do with the devaluing of mundane cooking skills as compared to more important public, professional cooking.

Certainly, the routinisation of "eating out" suggests that individuals as consumers are doubly estranged: from food production and food preparation processes. Does it matter if this trend leads to the emergence of "non-food producing", "non-food preparing" individuals and families? The evidence from Singapore reveals that there is certainly less cooking done in many households on a day-to-day basis. With reduced opportunities as well as preference for everyday cooking, are culinary competencies and expertise disappearing amongst Singaporeans? I suggest that the story of cooking in Singapore is much more complicated and it may be premature to signal the death of cooking skills on the island.

COMMODIFYING CULINARY SKILLS

Historically, the commodification of cooking skills in the availability of cooked food outside the home has been documented for many societies. But I turn now to a different variant of this process, in the commodification of teaching and learning cooking skills. Traditionally, everyday cooking skills within domestic settings have been transmitted to the next generation without explicit instruction as part of the socialisation processes that reproduce the family, the household and an ideology of gender roles and relations. The required practical knowledge is learnt first-hand through direct observation and taught by example. Seldom are cooking techniques in the home instilled through codified, explicit and articulate mechanisms. In Singapore society, both in the colonial and postcolonial moments, the value of transmitting cooking skills across generations (especially to women) has seen the involvement of educational institutions; the latter reflect the patriarchal assumptions made about the primary role of women as homemakers, also shared by other state-affiliated institutions. The explicit teaching of cooking within the framework of "domestic science" and "home economics" as subjects in Singapore schools has a long history, going back to colonial times. In 1939, pioneering steps were taken to introduce a policy for teaching domestic science in English girls' schools in Singapore through the training of "domestic science instructresses" in subjects like "diet, cooking and housewifery", as part of the specialist training for this task (*The Straits Times*, 26 Mar 1939). In 1949, "Domestic Science in the form of cooking, household management, handicraft and mothercraft" was extended to Singapore Malay girls' schools (*The Straits Times*, 26 Feb 1949). Eight of these schools were equipped with kitchens and appropriate equipment to facilitate this training. The importance of teaching "domestic science" — which included cooking skills — to girls was repeatedly reinforced in the ideology that these are "future wives" who would be served well with the requisite kitchen management skills. Mrs. Monica Gilks, who supervised domestic science lessons in Singapore schools observed:

> We don't go in for high-class cooking. It is not necessary. A general idea of how to cook is what the girls want and it is what we give them. However, it fits them out for home life, and they will know exactly what to do in the future and how to do it ... we also teach the girls how to serve food nicely, thereby increasing the standards in their own homes (*The Straits Times*, 28 Mar 1949).

In the post-war period, government and government-aided English schools restarted their lessons in domestic science, following disruptions caused by the Japanese Occupation of Singapore. Apart from girls' schools offering domestic science, similar efforts were made at the university level in the founding of a domestic science department in Ngee Ann College, an institution of higher learning in Malaysia in 1964 (*The Straits Times*, 14 Feb 1964). The four-year course the college offered led to a Bachelor of Arts degree. Cookery, together with subjects like dress designing, embroidery, family economics, home nursing and industry and child development were offered to students (*Ibid.*). At this time, the terminology had changed and the descriptor "Domestic Science" was replaced by the term "Home Economics". A unit in its name was also set up in the Ministry of Education as well as in the Home Economics Teachers' Association (*The Straits Times*, 20 Feb 1975).

In the transition to nationhood, the subject remained a part of the curriculum in local schools. Interestingly, as a matter of policy, "Home

Economics" as a subject was made compulsory for all girls in local schools from 1987. Prior to this, four out of ten schoolgirls had the option of studying technical education rather than home economics, like schoolboys. Making this subject compulsory for schoolgirls but not schoolboys generated controversy and was criticised by parents and educationists alike (Hedwig 1984). Responses to this policy were rationalised by policy-makers citing lack of resources and manpower, but these offered a weak justification. The patriarchal nature and logic of the postcolonial Singapore State were strongly expressed here in continuing to read women's and men's societal roles in traditional modes. Over time, instruction in home management skills has become institutionalised in Singapore schools. Presently, the lower secondary school curriculum in Singapore schools includes the subject "Food and consumer education" while "Food and Nutrition" is included in the upper secondary curriculum as an elective subject. Undoubtedly, these are more politically correct, contemporary descriptors. However, such attempts do not dislodge strongly held views about women's roles in Singapore society, supported by a patriarchal state and the policies it formulates. Interestingly, however, it would seem that educated women in Singapore (who have made a career outside the home) have themselves resisted the imposition of these specific gender roles to them. I suggest that it is possible to read the decline of everyday cooking in Singapore as the "refusal" of working wives and mothers to work multiple shifts and slip unreflectively into the role of a homemaker — performing the caring and feeding work expected of them. This does reflect altered thinking about the division of labour relating to household management and child care, in the demand for more egalitarian gender relations. Class is an important factor here providing these women with the option of outsourcing such work to foreign female domestic workers or female members of the extended family network.

What then can be said about the persistence of cooking skills in Singapore? In the last 20 years or so, professional culinary institutes, cooking schools for food hobbyists and enthusiasts, as well as cooking studios catering to local foodies and tourists alike have sprouted across the island. Cooking classes are held in Singapore's hotels, shopping malls, housing estates, Housing and Development Board (HDB) neighbourhoods, private condominiums and community centres. Some of these are local initiatives and function independently on a small scale, teaching laypersons who are interested in learning cooking as a leisure activity. Others are collaborations with international culinary institutions, training culinary professionals for the local and global food and beverage industry. In 2009, there were 18 culinary schools in Singapore, with four that were established in 2008 (Huang 2009). Both professional and non-professional culinary schools have mushroomed. Prominent professional culinary and hospitality schools offer diplomas and degrees, with opportunities for overseas exchange and internship possibilities. Some examples include Shatec (founded in 1983) to produce a skilled workforce for Singapore's hospitality industry; the Institute of Technical Education (ITE) became the member of the French global culinary network called the Institute Paul Bocuse (IPB) Worldwide Alliance; the At-Sunrice Global Chef Academy established a partnership with the Johnson and Wales University, a culinary school from the USA. Graduates of these academies find employment in the F&B industry locally and globally. Some find food-related careers in the realm of popular culture and media sites, setting up television shows, food blogs and writing recipe books. Those with additional entrepreneurial skills establish food related businesses, in manufacturing or processing foods and establishing new food outlets, like restaurants and cafes etc.

Government-run community centres in HDB neighbourhoods have long held highly subsidised cooking lessons (amongst other home-management skills like flower arrangement lessons) on their premises. However, non-professional cooking schools and cooking studios cater to a more affluent set of clients and customers: corporate and business groups, children (*The Straits Times*, 8 Mar 2009), housewives, expatriates, tourists and domestic helpers (Chan 2008). Examples in this category include the following schools: At the Kitchen, Cooking Mantra, The Pantry Cookery School, Culinary Academy At-Sunrice, Palate Sensations, Shermay's Cooking School, Coriander Leaf, Bentfork and Cookery Magic. The Raffles Culinary Academy was established in 1995 and Homechef in 1997; both are upmarket setups tapping an affluent market. On offer are baking classes, demonstrations and hands on lessons in local traditional foods, Western cuisine, Japanese cuisine, Thai cuisine, Italian cuisine and wine appreciation workshops, just to mention a select list. There are options as well for learning specific dishes such as muffins, boeuf bourguignon, tandoori chicken and sushi.

Thus there is a strong demand for cooking skills in Singapore and both their learning and teaching have been commodified. Some of these schools charge high-end prices while others are customised to suit middle-class pockets. Instructors are often professional chefs in restaurants and hotels or food-related celebrities — both local and international. These instructors have strong academic and practical credentials, having been certified in top culinary institutions and with first-hand experience of working in Michelin award food establishments. Very often the draw is precisely to "learn to cook like a chef"' (Tan 2010). The act of codification not only fails to capture the implicit, tacit, condensed dimensions of knowledge but also leads to its inevitable simplification in attempts to articulate. As Michael Polyani rightly notes in his book *The Tacit Dimension* (1967: 4), "we can know more than we can tell". A sceptical reading raises the questions of if, and how comprehensively, cooking skills and competencies can be taught through explicit instruction. It is perhaps more critical to ask what aspects of cooking knowledge *cannot* be imparted in structured lessons. Despite this, there are strong indications that the market for cooking classes is set to grow exponentially (Tan 2010).

This interest in acquiring cooking skills seems to cut across gender, age and class lines. Certainly cooking schools report that their students are both men and women, young and old. Of these social categories, gender assumes a specific significance. Cooking schools report scores of male students in their classes. But this is not really surprising. While women bear the responsibility for routinised domestic food preparation, men are often visible in occasional, situational, episodic, irregular, high status, cooking moments occasionally within the home but especially mostly in public. For most women, cooking, feeding and caring work are obligatory whereas, for men, this is optional and occurs under exceptional rather than routine circumstances. While men can elect to do this work or not, often women do not have the freedom to opt out, without facing some degree of censure. However, I suggest that, in the Singapore context many career women too avail themselves of the option of engaging in episodic, non-routinised, leisure-based cooking. This partly has to do with the structural position that women occupy in Singapore society and in part due to them being "freed" from the obligation of having to perform caring and feeding work, if they have access to the labour of foreign female domestic helpers. Career women who are interested in this kind of recreational cooking see this as an end in itself, rather than to use their acquired skills for routinised everyday home-based cooking. For example, many professional women learn how to prepare specific dishes so they can "repeat" them at a dinner party, admitting that their enthusiasm about learning "some cooking" has to do with the luxury of being able to disengage from obligatory everyday preparation of family meals. They add, unsurprisingly, that if they had to do it every day, cooking would lose its appeal and be far from pleasurable.

A FUTURE FOR COOKING IN SINGAPORE?

According to the "Electrolux Asia Pacific Food Survey 2014", 75% of its Singapore respondents above the age of 50 years had taught their children how to cook, while a much smaller proportion of 28% in those under 30 years prioritised this (Electrolux 2014). On the one hand, there is diminished interest in everyday cooking in Singapore, for men and women, and clearly the practice of cooking at home has declined. In the last two decades, everyday cooking skills have not been reproduced within households. Many Singaporeans rate their skills in the kitchen as dismal and have no confidence in their cooking abilities. On the other hand, recently, there has been a corollary demand for learning specific cooking skills formally and consciously. How can this apparent contradiction be explained? Is this in fact a contradiction? Responses require an unpacking of the categories of "cooking" and "eating". What do these connote? Berger invokes the dichotomy of "everyday eating" practices and "gourmet dining" to theorise daily eating and cooking in America (Berger 1996: 187):

> Gourmet cooking only has meaning because it is the opposite, more or less, of ordinary, plain, everyday cooking. Gourmet cooking, typically, is based on a sense of occasion, uses expensive and unusual foods, often has rich, complex sauces, and is concerned with style and aesthetics.

I suggest that this dichotomy can be used to theorise cooking modalities as well. Cooking as an activity clearly persists and has a firm presence in Singapore's foodscape. But it has acquired a different value for individuals who are motivated to experiment with cooking episodically and occasionally and seek to acquire the requisite skills through explicit instruction. As in many consumption-driven societies, here too the act of "cooking" has been commodified and subjected to market forces[4]: it has moved out from the domestic realm into the space of the market. Of course this is not a new phenomenon for Singapore; the buying and selling of cooked food has deep historical roots and is deeply enmeshed with the colonial migrant history of the island, pushing back the

---

[4] According to Warde, "Food has been singularised for centuries; that is to say, it is purchased as commodities and then transformed by often extensive domestic labour before being finally consumed" (1997: 194).

discussion temporally at least to the mid-nineteenth century. I would argue, however, that in the last two decades, Singapore society has witnessed an *acceleration* of this process, i.e the displacement of cooking skills from the private sphere and its consumption as a commodity in the marketplace. Not only is there firm evidence of limited everyday cooking in the home, the social practice has also been delinked from social relationships that reproduced it in household settings. However, as I have also argued here, cooking as a social practice is very much imprinted on Singapore's foodscape, and expressed in numerous societal locales. While there is limited day-to-day cooking in homes,[5] it certainly survives in the hands of experts and professional cooks in a range of food retail outlets. In addition, now cooking skills also exist in the marketplace as a commodity available to non-professional food enthusiasts, who can learn the art form purely for pleasure and entertainment as a leisure activity. Making over-generalised statements about the practice of cooking in a complex, multi-ethnic, multi-religious society like Singapore is problematic. Here "typicality" of cooking practices are mediated by the dynamics of religion, ethnicity, class, and gender, amongst other socio-cultural markers. In a highly affluent urban context, which is defined predominantly by consumption, both eating and cooking acquire connotations beyond subsistence and functionality. I have suggested that many consumers here have the luxury of bypassing the pragmatics and instrumentality of eating and cooking practices. As affluent consumers, many Singaporeans do have the economic, social and cultural capital and privilege to consume for entertainment, enjoyment, amusement and gratification.

So cooking as a social practice, and now as a reconfigured *consumption practice,* persists in Singapore. In terms of future possibilities, while some cooking skills would still be learnt within the household, this may not be the dominant mode of imparting these capacities to future generations. The acquisition of cooking skills through codified instruction in formal cooking classes conducted by trained instructors in cooking schools is another important institution. Singaporeans today relate to cooking in a multitude of ways: some cook because they have to, others cook as a matter of preference,

---

[5] It is also worth noting that there is enthusiasm for home and family based cooking amongst some clusters of Singaporeans. These individuals and families are motivated by notions of healthy, ethical and sustainable everyday practices, including cooking. Their ideologies and commitments do translate into more conscious everyday cooking within the home.

some cook purely for entertainment, while yet others enjoy reading about cooking or watching others cook. We know of the popularity of local and international cooking shows on television and a growing audience that reads recipe books for pleasure and follows cooking blogs on the Internet, and of the large crowds that turn up to watch cooking demonstrations by celebrity chefs in Singapore's food festivals. Indeed I would argue that apart from *doing* the cooking, *learning* and *teaching* cooking, *reading* about cooking and *watching* others cook are *additional, emergent consumption practices* in the food domain and merit scholarly engagement and scrutiny.

REFERENCES

AWARE (2011) CEDAW Shadow Report. http://www.aware.org.sg/wp-content/uploads/AWARE-CEDAW-Shadow-Report-2011.pdf, accessed 19 November 2014.

Beardsworth A and Keil T (1997) *Sociology on the Menu: An Invitation to the Study of Food and Society.* London and New York: Routledge.

Bell Daniel D and Valentine G (eds.) (1997) *Consuming Geographies: We are Where We Eat.* London and New York: Routledge.

Berger AA (1996) *Manufacturing Desire: Media, Popular Culture and Everyday Life.* New Brunswick and London: Transaction Publishers.

Burnett J (2004) *England Eats Out: A Social History of Eating Out in England from 1830 to the Present.* Harlow, England and New York: Pearson/Longman.

Chan JJ (2000) Status of women in a patriarchal state: the case of Singapore. In: L. P.LP Edwards and M. Roces (eds.), *Women in Asia: Tradition, Modernity and Globalization.* (pp. 39–57). Australia: Allen and Unwin,. pp. 39–57.

Chan R (2008) Singaporeans send maid to pricey cooking classes. *My Paper*, 23 May.

Chua BH (1985) 'Pragmatism of the People's Action Party Government in Singapore: A critical assessment.' *Southeast Asian Journal of Social Science* 13(2): 29–46.

Department of Statistics (DOS) (2014) Services surveys series, food and beverages, reference year 2013. http://www.singstat.gov.sg/docs/default-source/default-document-library/publications/publications_and_papers/services/sssfnb2013.pdf, accessed 22 January 2015.

Department of Statistics (DOS) (2010) Economic surveys series, reference year 2009. Singapore: Department of Statistics, p 2.

Electrolux (2014) Food survey. http://www.electrolux.com.sg/Food-Survey-2014/, accessed 22 November 2014.

Finklestein JJ (1989) *Dining Out: A Sociology of Modern Manners.* New York: New York University Press.

Goodman DD and Redclift M (1991) *Refashioning Nature: Food, Ecology and Culture.* London and New York: Routledge.

Gottdiener M (ed.) (2000) *New Forms of Consumption; Consumers, Culture and Commodification.* Lanham: Rowman and Littlefield Publishers, Inc..

Health Promotion Board (HPB) (2010) National Nutrition Survey. http://www.hpb. gov.sg/HOPPortal/content/conn/HOPUCM/path/Contribution%20Folders/ uploadedFiles/HPB_Online/Publications/NNS-2010.pdf accessed 19 November 2014.

Hedwig A (1984) 428 petition against compulsory homes econs; ministry urged to let pupils choose. *The Straits Times,* 24 November.

Huang L (2009) All fired up over cooking. *The Straits Times,* 8 March.

Huang SS and Yeoh BSA (1996) Ties that bind: state policy and migrant female domestic helpers in Singapore. *Geoforum* **27**(4): 479–493.

Ministry of Manpower (MOM) (2014) Labour force survey highlights. http://stats. mom.gov.sg/iMAS_PdfLibrary/mrsd_2013LabourForce_survey_highlights.pdf, accessed 22 January 2015.

Ministry of Manpower (2013) Foreign Workforce Numbers. http://www.mom.gov. sg/statistics-publications/others/statistics/Pages/ForeignWorkforceNumbers.aspx, accessed 30 July 2014.

Ministry of Manpower (2009) Ministry of Manpower e-News. http://www.mom. gov.sg/statistics-publications/others/publications/Documents/eNews%20 Nov%2009.pdf, accessed 22 August 2014.

Ministry of Trade and Industry (MTI) (2012) Manufacturing and services. http:// www.mti.gov.sg/MTIInsights/Pages/Manufacturing-and-Services.aspx, accessed 22 January 2015.).

Murcott A (1997) Family meals — a thing of the past. In: P Caplan (ed.) *Food, Health and Identity.* London and New York: Routledge, pp. 32–49.

National Environmental Agency (NEA) (2013) Managing Hawker Centres and Markets in Singapore. http://nea.gov.sg/public-health/hawker-centres, 22 January 2015.

Nexus Commonwealth Network. http://www.commonwealthofnations.org/sectors- singapore/business/agriculture/, accessed 27 January 2015.

Olsen WK, Warde A and Martens LL (2000) Social differentiation and the market for eating out in the UK. *International Journal of Hospitality Management* **19**(2): 173–190.

Polyani MM (1967) *The Tacit Dimension.* Cambridge: Cambridge University Press.

Rebello SA (2012) Food environments in Singapore: a focus on hawker centres. Presentation for 1st Singapore International Public Health Conference. http:// phconference.org/yr2012/pdf/PH%20Conference%20-%20Speaker's%20

Presentation%20for%20Website/2%20Oct/Dr%20Salome%20Rebello.pdf, accessed 19 November 2014.

Srinivas T (2013) As mother made it: the the cosmopolitan Indian family, "authentic" food and the construction of cultural utopia. In: C Counihan and P Van esterik (eds.) *Food and Culture: A Reader.* London and New York: Routledge, pp. 355–375.

Sutton D (2013) Cooking skills, the senses and memory: the fate of practical knowledge. In: C Counihan and P Van esterik (eds.) *Food and Culture: A Reader.* London and New York: Routledge, pp. 299–319.

Tai PF (2013) Gender matters in social polarisation: Comparing Singapore, Hong Kong and Taipei. *Urban Studies* 50(6): 1148–1164.

Tan A (2015a) Singapore Budget 2015: 10 more hawker centres to be built by 2027. *The Straits Times,* 11 March. http://www.straitstimes.com/news/singapore/more-singapore-stories/story/singapore-budget-2015-ten-more-hawker-centres-be-built-2, accessed 12 March 2015.

Tan HY (2015b) Asia's 50 Best Restaurants: Why the same old list? *The Straits Times,* 11 March. http://www.straitstimes.com/news/opinion/more-opinion-stories/story/asias-50-best-restaurants-why-the-same-old-list-20150311, accessed 11 March 2015.

Tan RL (2010) Cook like a chef. *The Straits Times,* 4 April.

Teo YY (2011) *Neoliberal Morality in Singapore: How Family Policies Make State and Society.* London and New York: Routledge.

The Straits Times (2009) Kids in the kitchen, 8 March 2009.

The Straits Times (1975) Mattar to open forum on home economics, 20 February, p. 13.

The Straits Times (1964) Domestic science an urgent need for girls, 14 January, p. 10.

The Straits Times (1949) Making school girls better wives; special tuition about homes, 28 March, p. 5.

The Straits Times (1949) Girls to learn cooking, 26 February, p. 7.

The Straits Times (1939) More domestic science to be taught in Singapore schools; selected teachers to be trained, 26 March, p. 12.

Today (2014) Singapore among the top spenders in Asia Pacific for dining: Survey, 6 May. http://www.todayonline.com/singapore/singapore-among-top-spenders-asia-pacific-dining-survey, accessed 19 November 2014.

Valentine G (1999) Eating in: home, consumption and identity. *The Sociological Review* 47(3): 491–524.

Verma A (2008) Unpacking economic necessity: locating the foreign domestic worker in Singapore. Paper presented at the 59th Political Studies Association Conference, Manchester University. http://www.academia.edu/2103482/Unpacking_Economic_Necessity_Locating_the_Foreign_Domestic_Worker_in_Singapore?login=socvs@nus.edu.sg&email_was_taken=true, accessed 22 November 2014.

Warde AA (1997) *Consumption, Food and Taste.* London: Sage.

Warde AA and Martens LL (2000) *Eating Out: Social Differentiation, Consumption and Pleasure.* Cambridge: Cambridge University Press.

Wing SS (1994) Market-procured housework: the demand for domestic servants and female labour supply. *Labour Economics* **1**(3–4): 289–302.

World Gourmet Summit (WGS) (2014) About. http://www.worldgourmetsummit.com/wgs2014/main.php/about, accessed 22 January 2015.

Yasmeen G (2013) Not "from scratch": Thai food systems and "public eating". In: C Counihan and P Van esterik (eds.) *Food and Culture: A Reader.* London and New York: Routledge, pp. 320–329.

Yeoh BSA (2006) 'Bifurcated labour: The unequal incorporation of transmigrants in Singapore' Singapore., *Tijdschrift voor Economische en Sociale Geografie*, 97(1): 26–37.

Yeoh BSA and Huang SS (1999a) Singapore women and foreign domestic workers: negotiating domestic work and motherhood. In: J. H. Momsen (ed.), *Gender, Migration and Domestic Service* (pp. 277-300). . London and New York: Routledge, pp. 277–300.

Yeoh BSA and Huang SS (1999b) Spaces at the margins: Migrant domestic workers and the development of civil society in Singapore,. *Environment and Planning A*, 31(7),: 1149–1167.

Yeoh BSA, Huang SS and Gonzalez J (1999) Migrant female domestic workers: debating the economic, social and political impacts in Singapore. *International Migration Review* **33**(1): 114–136.

Chapter 8

Bloggers, Critics and Photographers in the Mediation of Food Consumption

Tan Xiang Ru, Amy

INTRODUCTION

A profusion of bloggers, critics, and lens men passionately devoted to epicurism erupted on Singapore's food scene following the turn of the millennium (*The Straits Times*, 16 Apr 2005). This explosion kick-started a new development which accrued momentum and this group of food aficionados are arguably in their element today (*The Straits Times*, 24 June 2006), supported by a progressively new-media-savvy local population with "technological capital" (Gilbert 2010). Consumer behaviours and worldviews have been altered in profound ways as a result of their proliferating presence in contemporary Singapore. Practices such as consulting the internet for recipes, visiting food blogs to draw ideas for a *makan* outing with friends, and surveying online crowd-sourced reviews prior to patronising eateries are all examples of increasingly normative behaviours. Likewise, tantalising visuals of food are so readily available on the web and in print (Leong 2013) that a virtual feast may well be an integral part of the everyday lived realities of many Singaporeans. As a collective, the socio-cultural impact that these food enthusiasts have on the city-state's foodscape cannot be overstated. Yet there is surprisingly little attention paid to their influence vis-à-vis food consumption in local scholarship.

This chapter thus contributes to a lean but growing body of literature on how foodways in Singapore are cumulatively mediated by this multi-centred, polyglot community of foodies (Brien 2014; Chan 2014; Soh 2006); it aims to demonstrate and theorise the nascence of new radical paradigms in gustatory appetites, attitudes, behaviours and expectations. The research presented here will also shed light on food consumption as a multi-faceted cultural field. First, I provide a brief overview of the origins of blogging and the inception of food bloggers in genre-specific appropriations of blogs in Singapore before delineating their significance today. I then discuss their increasingly pervasive role in food media by examining how and how often Singaporeans engage food blogs. I further consider how our food blogosphere is taking shape and at the same time question the kinds of potential socio-cultural implications there are for consumers.

Second, I suggest that food bloggers have galvanised a culture of participatory food journalism which is anchored by the interactivity and immediacy of social media platforms. The impact and merits of participatory food journalism are then discussed. Further, the centrality of food bloggers in the formation of (virtual) foodie communities and among a general readership also set in motion new marketing mechanisms in what has been conceptualised as a "prosumer" capitalist economy (Ritzer and Jurgenson: 2010) — the myriad of issues concerning the credibility, ethics and integrity of bloggers brought about by these developments are subsequently explored. As consumers navigate what proves to be an increasingly complex socio-cultural terrain in social media spaces, I propose the emergence of public truism — an ideology based on the sanctity of opinions from the perceived unadulterated populace and that consumers are paradoxically more likely to take confidence in the collective voices of the faceless public.

Third, I scrutinise distinctions between food reviewer and food critic. As the former gains prominence in alternative food media, there have been claims of a democratisation in food criticism. This appears to be a myth as pre-existing conceptions and structural discriminations between critic and non-critic persist. They belie the latent distinctions of taste that Bourdieu (1984) theorises as symptomatic of unequal cultural capital and class disparity. On the other hand, I employ the concept of *habitus* to explain many Singaporeans' partiality for bloggers and lay reviewers. Furthermore, attention is given to the culturally rich and complex field of food consumption as we identify competing and conflating ideologies and (virtual) spaces in consumption.

Fourth and finally, I investigate the subject of food image-making and the reasons for the growth of popular food photography in contemporary

Singapore. The conventional amateur/professional hierarchies have been fragmentised with the onset of amateur (purely for fun or to document special occasions), and serious amateur (invested in creating art forms) photographers. In connection, the fusion of a new aesthetics for everyday objects and the artistic valorisation of local cuisine in media has incited a culture of imagery omnivorousness. I try to make sense of the abundance of food portraits on social media platforms as visual narrations, and consumption-trophies as replicas of the high points of consumption. Additionally, I interpret the predilection for voluntary indulgence in food visual stimuli as binge gazing, owing to their excessive abundance and broad structural implications on consumption today. I borrow the notion of the gaze to connote the visibility and vulnerability of consumers who engage in image-making and the sharing of personal aspects of their everyday lives.

In this chapter, I examine the ethnographic narratives of 12 Singaporeans who, to varying degrees, engage with a melange of food blogs, reviews and photography. Their responses were collected through semi-structured inductive interviews carried out between August and November 2014. All interviews were conducted mainly in English, with a handful of terms used in Mandarin and Malay. I was particularly interested in how, how frequently, and why they engage food blogs; how bloggers compare with food critics and locals' perceptions of both. I was also curious as to the extent to which they influence my informants' consumption choices and philosophies. I also enquired about the frequency with which they encounter images of food and what effect these images have on them; likewise, I was interested to know if they engage in food photography themselves and why. In addition to primary empirical data, I surveyed countless food blogs, social media food groups, mobile applications and newspaper articles to gather secondary data. My informants were aged between 24 to 45 years; nine were female and four were male; they came from all walks of life: students, administrators and homemakers. For the purpose of the thematic inquiry of this chapter, it was necessary to select informants who are familiar with social media and digital technologies. This limited my informants to a certain socio-economic base. Unfortunately, due to space constraints, not all themes that emerged from the data are analysed here. For instance, three informants reported that they regularly consult blogs for recipes and cooking instructions. But due to a greater prevalence of informants who eat out more often than they cook, cooking blogs are not examined here. Nonetheless, this suggests possibilities for further research in related areas.

UNPACKING FOOD IN THE BLOGOSPHERE

> In less than a decade, with the wellsprings of traditional media sputtering, food blogs have begun to spout with restaurant news and reviews, recipes, and mouthwatering photos to the point of becoming an integral part of the food media (Denveater 2009: 43).

The term "blog" is a contraction of "weblog" — first coined by weblog writer Jorn Barger in 1997 (Blood 2002: 7). A blog is generally defined as a frequently updated webpage with dated entries or posts, new ones placed on top, containing links with commentaries to sites of interest on the web. As blog portals such as Livejournal and Wordpress began to create uncomplicated tools and templates accessible to lay-internet users, the blog evolved from a niche concept to a popular self-publishing medium on the internet. As of October 2011, the total count of bloggers worldwide is estimated at 173 million (Statista 2011). When blogs were first conceived, they were most prevalently used as a form of personal online diary with bloggers providing anecdotes of their day-to-day lives for online readership.

As the blogosphere matured, bloggers also began to diversify and specialise according to their interest and passion. The specificity of sub-genres (such as lifestyle, beauty, cooking, parenting, travel, fashion and more) came to be more pronounced and food bloggers too started to mark a unique domain for themselves. Food blogs are considered a niche-interest blog genre where the theme dictates the content of the blog and the blogger charts the directions. In early 2006, the Business Times reported that in addition to corporate and personal bloggers, food bloggers are mushrooming in Singapore (Cheah 2006). Today, they have firmly established themselves as a vital information nucleus.

Some of the earliest Singapore-based food bloggers surfaced around 2005 and their blogs or blogs-turned-sites remain active today. In the last decade, the local food blogging scene has grown tremendously and food bloggers' passion for good food has multiplied their readership among Singaporeans. These pioneering online food journals include: *The Traveling Hungryboy, Chubby Hubby, ieatishootipost, The Skinny Epicurean, Only Slightly Pretentious Food, She Bakes and She Cooks* and many more (*The Straits Times*, 4 Mar 2007). Many of these blogs have now ventured beyond solely reviewing Singapore food. Based on a list retrieved from a meta-blog that consolidates all Singapore-based food blogs, there are at least 224 food blogs/sites maintained by individual bloggers currently (Singapore Food Blogs nd). Yet despite the staggering volume of food blogs available, blog readership in Singapore is, in truth, extremely low. In a survey on Infocomm usage conducted by the Infocomm Development Authority of Singapore in 2012, it is revealed that the statistically significant internet activities registered by residents are communicating (71%), leisure activities (61%), and getting information (49%). Only 3% of all residents surveyed profess to read blogs (IDA). The upshot of the survey parallels the narratives of my informants — all 12 of whom maintain they do not regularly follow any food blog in particular. Ivan, a 26 year-old postgraduate student, shares his typical encounters with food blogs and like most others, he frames his interactions with them in a highly utilitarian fashion:

> Actually for me, I don't really follow a specific blog, what I do is normally I will already have in mind what I feel like eating or what I want to search for, then I will google and then I will just click on the links that show up... and definitely there will be some links to the blogs... usually based on their [bloggers] recommendations, I will see which one is suitable and I will go for it.

Similarly, Yvonne, a 28 year-old assistant manager, explains the functional value of the food blogs for her — she especially appreciates the consolidated listicles where bloggers make informed pre-selections according to the theme they design for each list:

> What I really like about the food blogs is all the lists they have, like Top 10 cafes in Singapore or Top 10 places for dim sum or like Best Buffets, and for some they are sorted by location... all these are really useful and very convenient for us because the bloggers already did the work and narrow it down for you... plus it's easy to read because in blog form, it's more seamless.

The testimonies from a majority of the interviewees clearly convey the role of food blogs as information hubs that are perused for dining-out options and recommendations (particularly for gatherings with family, friends and special functions). It is not surprising that most internet-savvy Singaporeans turn to the web for all kinds of information. However, the reality that food blogs readily appear in online search results and that consumers will knowingly consult them as part of their research signals how food blogs and bloggers have become an integral part of food media today.

We can also firmly establish the structural significance of food bloggers if we consider how often many locals, beyond merely browsing the blogs, will act upon the suggestions of bloggers. Among all my informants, the frequency with which they visit food blogs ranges from daily to once or twice weekly, typically for culinary or dining-out inspirations. The extensive repertoire of reviews and recipes available on food blogs resonates with Cox and Blake's (2011: 204) assertion of food blogging as "serious leisure" — that which hobbyists undertake in attempt to ensure the "central activity in food blogging is the creation of an information source." The shaping of our local food blogosphere and the way consumers are engaging it points to the honing of a culture of gastronomic knowledge production and sharing via social media.

Similar distinct developments have inspired scholars to theorise blogging as the new form of journalism (Domingo and Heinonen 2008) because blogs are also articulating socio-cultural and political ideologies for a mass audience today. Invariably, the socio-cultural implications of food blogging far exceed mere recreational reading. For instance, the highly acclaimed food blog *ieatishootipost* by Dr Leslie Tay advocates the consumption philosophy "never waste your calories on yucky food" (Tay nd); Catherine Ling who authors *Camemberu* upholds the slogan "every meal an adventure" (Ling nd); and Daniel Ang of *DanielFoodDiary* is famed for campaigning the right to bring hawker fare to the posh annual outdoor picnic *Diner en Blanc* in Singapore (*The Straits Times*, 25 Aug 2014). With the growing influence of food bloggers on our food scene, these culturally loaded consumption messages and philosophies also permeate the community and/or individual consciousness with specific connoisseur values, beliefs and practices. Furthermore, it is now more difficult to label consumers as passive agents with the incipient culture of participatory food journalism via social media.

PARTICIPATORY FOOD JOURNALISM AND PUBLIC TRUISM

In comparison to traditional media, blogs are highly interactive platforms that stimulate and simulate social connectivity. In his article published in 2007, Thevenot notes that "blogging is one of the increasingly popular social media, where people are engaged through being part of a conversation" (2007: 287).

I propose that this interactivity between bloggers and readers (subsequently boosted by additional forms of social media) is the overture to a wider culture of citizen/participatory food journalism in Singapore. It is not uncommon for bloggers to respond to the comments, queries and requests of their readers — they often welcome feedback from the public and may reciprocally create posts in response to readers' demands. This dynamism is an impactful change from non-digital media such as print and broadcast — which are intrinsically uni-directional; it has even pushed traditional media to reinvent themselves and many traditional media industry players are progressively adopting social media to expand their influence. Participatory culture is a powerful by-product of new media technologies and it has been identified as one of the key revolutionary changes cum challenges in the 21st century (Jenkins 2009). This section, therefore, discusses some of the benefits, concerns and ideological developments with the rise of participatory food journalism in relation to locals' gastronomical quests.

In the context of Singapore's foodscapes, food bloggers are instrumental in forging a motley community connected by a shared passion for gustatory pleasures. Borrowing Miller and Shepherd (2004)'s theorisation of blogging as social action — blogs are characterised by the social psychology of self-disclosure which serves four main aims: self-clarification, social validation, relationship development, and social control (Calvert 2000). The latter two objectives are externally focused and the desired outcome is essentially community building, to forge as wide a reader base as possible. In the case of local food bloggers, I argue that they first became the focal point around which a (virtual) group of fellow foodie-voices was formed. This engendered an even more extensive milieu of participatory food journalism, contributing to the growth of a myriad of crowd-review sites, groups and mobile applications. Some that are used by my informants include Hungry-Go-Where, Yelp Singapore, OpenRice Singapore, Chope Restaurant Reservations, and various Facebook groups.

For instance, Aishah, a 33 year-old management assistant officer, reads different food blogs and joins Facebook groups to increase her knowledge of Halal-certified dining options in Singapore. She explains how her community also benefits from social media resources:

> For us Muslims, we are always looking for new Halal places to eat because sometimes you get tired of the usual fast food and *nasi padang* [laughs]. So many of these food blogs and online groups like on Facebook, they are really good... they will update you if there are any new theme restaurants or

concept cafes that become Halal certified... it gives us more options so they are really useful for us...

One such platform that Aishah uses is the Facebook page "Dine — Singapore's Halal Dining" (The Cre8tives nd), it is extremely popular with more than 25,000 likes to date. The page highlights recommendations given by followers as well as food establishments that request to be featured. Eileen, on the other hand, has joined a food group on Facebook that is exclusively in the Chinese language and promotes Chinese cuisine recipes and eateries. The 45 year-old administrator reads Chinese well and finds the information shared by members of the group compatible with her dietary preference. Furthermore, 43 year-old Sean who is a vegetarian, goes online to check out reviews of vegetarian restaurants in Singapore, especially prior to patronising them for the first time. He emphasises that the reviews from fellow consumers and the information he gathers from his research will help him determine if there is anything suitable for him at a particular restaurant. This is often done in the spirit of commensalism as it is a good way to ensure he and his non-vegetarian dining companions can all have an enjoyable meal together during large social outings.

Participatory food journalism via social media inherently reflects the polyglot/multilingual and multicultural character of Singapore from the ground. It facilitates the processes through which different groups with varied dietary preferences/needs undertake to expand their dining options beyond home. It further stimulates the cultivation of a local food scene that welcomes diverse foodways and ascribes a greater degree of individual agency to locals. Most respondents agree that due to the pervasiveness and accessibility of public reviews now, doing prior research on a newly opened food outlet or one that they are unfamiliar with has become second nature to them. More importantly, Singaporeans increasingly *prefer* to make independent and informed decisions. Likewise, they relish a newfound sense of "security" in knowing that value for money, time and energy is now pre-determinable, especially when patronising new restaurants. In her account, Jean, a 32 year-old teacher, shares that she has developed the practice of checking reviews as a way to ensure her resources are well spent:

Nowadays I will check for sure, I won't blindly go... they [reviews and photos] will roughly let you know if the place is value for money or not. If the majority say its [sic] not good, then of course I won't waste my money there, I can go somewhere else that I know will give me a good experience... it saves time for you, and you don't make a wasted trip... so basically, it helps me to choose the right place for the right occasion and helps me to know what to expect...

The contingency of experiences with food, particularly for Singapore's constantly morphing culinary scene, is a significant issue. Capitalising on knowledge accumulated through participatory food journalism helps consumers like Jean attain semblances of control over their resources. However, the socially opulent notion of community building via social media is also an opportune method for businesses and advertisers to ascertain the "reach" that a certain platform or blogger commands. Numerous respondents note that they are aware of food bloggers being "paid to review", that is, co-opted as soft marketing avenues for commercialism (*The Straits Times*, 11 May 2014).

Although the inquiry of this chapter is purposefully anchored in food *consumption*, it is important to note that the "prosumer" conceptualisation of the capitalist economy is gaining greater traction in this digital age (Ritzer and Jurgenson 2010). The escalating influence of the internet and social media is reshaping capitalist mechanisms today and some of these dynamics are crystalising in our blogosphere. Local food bloggers potentially epitomise the prosumer model as they inadvertently deconstruct theoretical producer-consumer binaries. More importantly, popular food bloggers are *paid* to consume. This trend, however, appears to provoke readers to be wary of bloggers overselling certain food outlets or products as part of advertorials but without labelling them as such. While the majority of my respondents continue to refer to food blogs in general, questions of authenticity, honesty, transparency and even integrity are increasingly raised as advertisers infiltrate the food blogosphere and crowd-sourced review sites.

Indeed, the issue of bloggers' credibility is hotly debated by scholars in communication studies. It constitutes an ongoing but inconclusive discussion as more layers of issues surrounding ethics, integrity and commercial opportunism are unearthed. In the context of the local food scene, there have been concerns raised with food blogs becoming the machinery of skewed recommendations and hype covertly directed by sponsors. There is also incipient anxiety over bloggers misdirecting the crowd and/or "exploiting" their readership for personal financial gains. Some astute informants emphasise that owing to this development, it is "safer" to scroll down to survey the comments of fellow readers and public figures as a tactic to verify the validity of the blogger's review.

In this way, they actively exercise precaution by reading comments from the masses, in addition to written reviews.

In the context of Singapore's foodscape, there is a subtle negotiation of control exhibited as the bloggers, through their reviews, necessarily direct their readers to patronise or eschew certain establishments. Readers are also learning to respond with some measures of counter-control as new marketing mechanisms via social media gain momentum. End-users are learning to navigate a progressively complex terrain as advertisers target food blogs and borrow the grounded and relatable voices of bloggers to publicise businesses. In a bid towards greater discernment, consumers like my respondents find themselves subconsciously policing the fairness, truthfulness and veracity of food reviews online. Some develop their own yardsticks to calibrate the reliability of specific bloggers; for instance, Yvonne scrutinises the genre of advertisements that appear on the blogs, she maintains that food bloggers should not accept sponsorship from non-food and beverage organisations as it symbolises detraction from pure passion for food and exposes revenue-seeking intentions. As participatory food journalism unfolds in Singapore, consumers are increasingly holding bloggers (especially) to the same journalistic integrity they have come to expect of traditional media.

Beyond the issues of veracity and integrity, as the local food blogosphere matures and bloggers are co-opted as soft marketing spokespeople, it also reveals an emergent (moral) ideology that hinges on public truism — the notion that consumers instinctually assume opinions from the general public (however loosely defined) must also be the most pure, honest, and perhaps believable. Public truism developed negatively, against the background of tacit attitudes that the alloy of unchecked private/capitalist gains with the perceived pristine national passion for good food is heretical and highly suspect. These burgeoning perceptions are compounded by the idea that many star food bloggers originally surfaced from the faceless public and their popularity was founded upon innocent epicurism, resulting in assumptions that they should maintain the purity of their gustatory passion and motivation. The subjectivity of tastes and preferences are largely ignored in the face of public truism; instead, consumers who subscribe to this ideology are often eager to form sententious binaries (of advertising-tainted bloggers and those who are not) — ascribing values like passion, authenticity, integrity and honesty at one end, and labelling the opposing binary as revenue-seeking "sell-outs", unethical or unscrupulous. Public truism also stems from the belief that the (food) blogosphere and social media spaces were once commercially untainted civic spheres; hence, there exists a strong reactionary will to maintain the "sanctity" of these spaces and assail agencies that engage them. The presupposition of bloggers' "moral obligation" to the public is apparent from the former's constant need to justify their intentions and self-regulate associations with advertising bodies.

DEMOCRATISATION OF FOOD CRITICISM? ISSUES OF TASTE AND CLASS

The appeal of alternative food media is easily understandable for many Singaporeans who crave the unadulterated and relatable voices of fellow gourmands in their quest for good food, good value and a good experience. In comparison to food critics, the majority of my respondents profess to identify more closely with food bloggers in terms of shared values, ideals, concerns and taste in gastronomy. Conversely, many also perceive food critics as structurally alienating. With the growing influence and authority of food bloggers in Singapore's foodscape, there arises a need to deconstruct nuances between labels of gourmets and gourmands; this section scrutinises constructed notions of Taste in the Bourdieuian sense to suss out latent issues of class distinctions, inclusivity and exclusivity, as well as social hierarchy. Contrary to mainstream reports of food criticism becoming democratised (Ngo 2012) — which implies that it is now a level playing field for anyone who wishes to give comments and criticisms of food, perceived differences in the cultural weight that varied sources carry suggest that distinctions between a critic and a reviewer have never been more pronounced.

In their article "Taste and Audience in Fashion Blogging", McQuarrie *et al.* use the concept of "the megaphone effect" to explain how, owing to the prevalence of the web today, "a select few ordinary consumers are able to acquire an audience without the institutional mediation historically required" (2013: 137). The same applies to food blogging, and in the local food scene, critics have historically personified the orthodox institutional mediation. This institutional framework under which critics typically operate forms a part of the basis for which many Singaporeans develop a sense of perceived structural alienation. Additionally, when lay reviewers and critics are placed in comparison, assumptions of disparity in cultural capital are made and a nebulous social hierarchy is accordingly drawn. For instance,

Larry, a 27 year-old research assistant, opines that language proficiency and ability to write with flair are normative criteria for food critics:

> There is a difference between criticism and critique... Critics give *critique*, and bloggers just give reviews, I mean critics are supposed to write very well.

As Larry suggests, the term "critic" itself is metonymic of talented penman, elegant narrator, perspicacious judge, and erudite epicurean. Many of these terms imply calibre which is constitutive of the profession and points to the necessity of a high level of cultural capital. On the other hand, Natalie, a 31 year-old real estate agent who is well-acquainted with many of the popular local food blogs, sheds light on why she does not read much from food critics, at the same time offers her impression of them:

> I don't know, somehow I just don't read what they [critics] write... in the first place, I don't subscribe to newspapers... also I don't think we will have the same taste? They usually only review all the very *atas* [high-class] places, which I don't really go to.

Likewise, Emily, a 36 year-old lecturer, professes to consume a variety of videos and blogs for cooking/baking tips and food reviews. She does not, however, connect with food critics because she feels the level of palate sophistication and standards they have for food is beyond her:

> I think their taste is too refined for me already, so I don't really look at what they write. Unless it is in the Sunday Times, if they have a special feature about somewhere interesting, then ok, I will read... But they tend to feature all the very high-end restaurants.

Both Natalie and Emily frequently visit blogs and crowd-sourced sites for food reviews — the former swears by Yelp Singapore because she believes in the authenticity of opinions from fellow consumers, further, she deduces that the taste of the general public resonates with her more than that of food critics. Similarly, Emily is happy to let Google take her to any of the popular local blogs like *ladyironchef, Miss Tam Chiak* and others.

It is crucial to note that in none of the testimonies was the authority of food critics as gourmets ever questioned. Instead, informants tend to reinforce critics' comparatively "superior" connoisseur taste buds and simultaneously allude to their personal and contrasting "inferior" palates. Respondents also imply class distinctions when they profess that they do not frequent high-end restaurants, thus resulting in the incompatibility of information produced by food pundits. Such impressions from the interviewees distinctly demonstrate that food critics are perceived to be unrepresentative of everyday-ness while food bloggers' repertoire of reviews matches the consumption preferences and abilities on more pedestrian levels. Thus, the perceived socio-cultural relatability of most bloggers is the pretext to the belief that they occupy similar dispositions as the masses in the field of consumption; conversely, the perceived socio-cultural inaccessibility of critics stems from the assumption that they possess comparatively far greater cultural capital.

In the classic volume *Distinction*, Bourdieu (1984) interrogates the class-embedded notion of taste and theorises cultural capital as the accumulated stock of knowledge about the products of artistic and intellectual traditions, which is acquired through education and training and social upbringing. Bourdieu postulates that cultural capital, together with other forms of capital (economic, social and symbolic) determines one's *habitus* and disposition in any given field in society. While mastery of language and writing ability can be trained in formal education systems, it is typically the informal acquisition of cultural capital (such as flair, style, refinement in taste and palate) outside of formal education that tends to reinforce disparity in social structures. Exclusion based on cultural capital is immensely subtle and elusive yet it is more powerful (Trigg 2001) — evident from how so many of my informants, despite having received formal education, do not/cannot quite resonate with food critics in terms of "innate" taste and preferences due to the lack of or incompatibility of cultural capital.

The concept of *habitus*, on the other hand, can help us to make sense of inclusivity — the rationale for the "inherent" taste affinity that most Singaporeans share with various food bloggers. *Habitus* is defined as a system of

> principles which generate and organise practices and representations that can be objectively adapted to their outcomes without presupposing a conscious aiming at ends or an express mastery of the operations necessary in order to attain them' (Bourdieu 1990: 53).

The taste practices and representations of food bloggers (such as where they choose to eat and colloquial approaches to knowledge-sharing) concur with the majority of locals as the latter deduce that most bloggers possess similar levels of cultural capital as they do. But individuals are primarily unconscious of the cultural forces that steers them, though they act in accordance to their *habitus* which in itself is adaptable and capable of evolving through different situations. Hence we observe that masses from the non-elite class are drawn to bloggers who share similar *habitus* with them while critics represent a different social status defined by higher cultural capital.

From the tensions between socio-cultural inclusion and exclusion around Taste, we bear witness to the exposure of social hierarchy where critics are commonly perceived to be in a higher position than lay reviewers. Although bloggers essentially write from the vantage point of gourmands and they perform what Watson *et al.* term "skilled consumption" (2008: 289), it is still fairly common for them to circumvent vulnerability of exclusion by disclaiming (self) ascription of the "critic" label and instead, marking out boundaries for themselves to occupy ridicule-free spaces in non-pundit domains. Similarly, one of the pioneering local crowd-sourced review sites HungryGoWhere explicitly distinguishes between the reviews written by their in-house critic (a professional hire) and ordinary crowd-sourced reviews. The in-house critic adopts a strikingly different philosophy and standards (for the practice for critiquing) from bloggers; she asserts to maintain her anonymity (for instance, she avoids having her photo taken so she does not get recognised by restauranteurs) in the name of professionalism and impartiality. These structural distinctions contribute to pre-existing perceptions of differences in the cultural weight that critic and non-critic appraisals carry.

Such displays of differing philosophies, unequal status ascription and (subtle or blunt) dissociation of domains clearly point to socio-cultural inclusion and exclusion around critique and Taste, which are systemically induced. More importantly, they contradict a simplistic scaffolding of an egalitarian, level playing field in food criticism owing to social media in this digital age. To be clear, we are making great strides in accruing diverse, heterogeneous voices from the ground with the burgeoning culture of participatory food journalism — which manifests and encourages greater individual agencies; likewise food bloggers are unmistakably acquiring newfound popularity and authority in gourmet discourses. Nonetheless, consumer perceptions also persist in reflecting embedded structures of class distinctions and social hierarchy between themselves, bloggers and critics in today's foodscape. In this sense, bloggers and critics appear to be operating distinct yet overlapping dimensions, demonstrating both competing and conflating ideologies in consumption — this acutely attests to food consumption as a profoundly convoluted socio-cultural field.

VISUAL CONSUMPTION-TROPHIES AND BINGE GAZING

The job of a food photographer is to elicit the same mouth-watering reaction as the smell of freshly baked bread or the taste of a perfectly grilled steak (Manna 2005: 10).

In pre-digital days, food photography was an exclusive profession, largely commissioned with commercial intent as roll film and post-shoot processing were costly. The range of subject matters in image-making was also highly selective then. Today, however, digital and smartphone technology has made photography infinitely more accessible to lay users. Consequently, there has been a surge in popular/amateur photographers in Singapore. Ivan, for instance, is an hobbyist photographer who owns a DSLR camera. In our discussion of food photographers, he claims that in this part of the world, "so many people are doing it now... especially all the Asians, that's why Caucasians find it strange [laughs]".

This section thus undertakes to make sense of the proliferation of food photographers. This is with a view to enquiring, in the context of food and eating, what could be analytically meaningful about where, and on what, their lenses are focused. To be clear, the discussion here pertains to non-professional photographers who have come into this field of practice in the capacity of amateurs (purely for fun or to document special occasions), serious amateurs (invested in creating art forms) and all shades in between (Zimmerman 1995). I propose that image-making has become a medium that valorises local cuisine as an art form. The confluence of digital/smartphone technologies and social media has also nurtured a new aesthetics of the small and mundane — all of which intensifies the notion of artistic merit in food amongst Singaporeans. Food images have also come to be a vital part of visual narration, in some instances as consumption-trophies. The overwhelming abundance of visual stimuli and their impact on our sensory experiences are consequently coming together to induce what I term "binge gazing".

Ivan's allusion to the notion that consumers in other parts of the world are not as actively engaging food photography suggests that it is a fallacy to assume access to digital technologies compels (interest in) food image-making.

I submit that there are broader socio-cultural undercurrents at play, giving rise to Singaporeans' collective preoccupation with shooting food. First, KF Seetoh's groundbreaking conceptualisation of *Makansutra* in 1997 vernacularised food guides à la Michelin and Zagat for the local audience; more importantly, his training in photography enabled him to wield it as a medium to reconstruct the image of commonplace local food (particularly hawker fare). *Makansutra* the publication and subsequent TV spinoffs marked an significant turning point in the way local food was perceived aesthetically; Seetoh's glamorising representations of local dishes invited Singaporeans to also appreciate local food as objects of everyday art and beauty. It was a paradigm shift as Singaporeans began to move beyond the boundaries of plating, decorations, designs and condiment arrangements that narrowly define nouvelle cuisine as art. This breakthrough, thus, incited budding photographers to venerate and depict the aesthetic value of local cuisine.

Second, in expounding the social use of digital photography, Murray observes a shift in our engagement with everyday images and advocates the genesis of a new aesthetics characterised by the "display and collection of one's discovery and framing of the small and mundane" (2008: 147). I assert that digital food portraits shared via social media epitomises this new aesthetics in the practice of photography. Indeed, there is virtual grub galore on social media today. Both serious amateur and amateur lens men are sharing stills and videos of food on social media such as Instagram, Pinterest and Facebook in the "mediated exhibitionism" (Miller and Shepherd 2004) of their gustatory odysseys. On Instagram alone, there are over one hundred and forty million pictures hash-tagged "food" (see Figure 1). The same trend is true of Facebook as it is not unusual for users to have photo albums specially dedicated to food (see Figures 2 and 3). The inception of a new aesthetics of the small and mundane, compounded by the permeating valorisation of local cuisine as everyday art fortified a culture of imagery omnivorousness and proliferation of food photography locally. These new perspectives are dialectically performed through the instrumentality of digital/smartphone technologies.

What ramifications then do these developments have on food consumption? Food images are now prevalently composites of visual narratives around consumption on social media. There is a tendency for individuals to share moment-to-moment, frame-by-frame visual narratives of their epicurean journeys — these are suspended, distinct episodes in everyday reality, reassembled and introduced in truncation to spectators. This method of pictorial storytelling is often framed to spotlight the high points of consumption which,

Figure 1: Image posted on Instagram by an informant who is an amateur photographer; taken with an iPhone using Instagram's "instant filter".

in turn, produces more deliberate and intentional constructions of picture-worthy moments. Newfound aestheticism in food contributes substantially to the defining of such high points — which in themselves may be socially and/or materially constitutive. In this sense, picture-taking is not an afterthought; rather, it is a simultaneous driver to dine at particular locales, with preferred people and/or engage certain foods. This ripples into an increased propensity for consumers to be conspicuous in dining, as a way of constructing their (virtual) social status. In contrast, however, to Veblen's classic theory of conspicuous consumption which emphasises the leisure class's consolidation of status through social performance and accumulation of property (Veblen 1899), the selective display of visual consumption-trophies on social media amongst Singaporeans points to manifestations of middle class aspirations to move up the social hierarchy.

Figure 2: Posted on Facebook by a serious amateur photographer, in an album titled "Food"; taken with a Canon DSLR.

Figure 3: Posted on Facebook by a serious amateur photographer, in an album titled "Food"; taken with a Canon DSLR.

The sensory experience incited by food images is another prominent theme that emerged from my empirical data. Diction such as "tempting, cravings, guilty, *shiok*, happy, exciting and hungry" were frequently employed to delineate the spectrum of emotional (and physiological) responses food portraits can evoke. In response to Jung and Cisterna's (2014) attempt to expand current understandings of what counts as sensory experience (vis-a-vis food and taste), my findings suggest that food images can also elicit strong visceral reactions from spectators. Nicole's account of her experience with browsing local food images online when she was studying abroad reflects Manna's statement that "a great food photograph can convey feelings of warmth, awaken fond memories, conjure up fantasies, or just plain make you hungry" (2005: 10). Nicole shares her mixed feelings derived from food visuals:

> When I was studying overseas I would look at pictures of local food ... it would make me feel good but sad at the time cause I can't [sic] have them.

Similarly, Eileen candidly expresses, "when you see all these [food] pictures, they can be very tempting you know?" It is unmistakable that quality stills of sumptuous cuisine are visual stimuli for many Singaporeans, often inducing memories of tastes, nostalgia, cravings and gastronomical desires. It is such sensorial reactions from food visuals that ignited the highly contentious concept of "food porn". Food porn is generally defined as "food so sensationally out of bounds of what a food should be that it deserves to be considered pornographic" (McBride 2010: 38). Different camps have debated the validity of the concept and many remain suspicious of such sensationalist neologism. Although my findings do not conclusively support the existence of food porn, there is cogent indication of binge gazing — that which I conceptualise as excessive, voluntary and structurally authenticated visual stimulation in the interest of consumption. The barrage of food images on social media, in the local blogosphere and even non-digital media has concomitantly fostered an excessive feasting by the eye accompanied by sentiments of guilt or over-indulgence. The gaze, in this context, structures consumers' imagery encounters with food particularly around sensory excitement — typically through lenses that focus fragmentarily on aestheticism and the romantic presentation of served dishes (necessarily food post-preparation) in their embellished forms. Binge gazing (especially on social media) has in part reshaped organisation systems and processes toward food aesthetics-focused marketing as it becomes increasingly precursory to actual consumption and by extension, a determinant in forming consumption choices.

CONCLUSION

In "The Virtual Roundtable", Denveater exclaims:

> The passion that so many bloggers exhibit — for their good-old-fashion commitment to cooking from scratch... for the gathering places that restaurants are, and/or for pure grassroots reportage — is not to be denied" (2009: 46).

I believe there is a dialectic relationship between Singapore's "foodie culture" and food bloggers, critics and photographers' collective dedication to their craft. It is this insistence on astutely seeking out the best of gastronomy and culinary experiences that welcomed the growth of participatory food journalism, initiated by food aficionados who proudly display their passion through the brilliant application of social media and digital technologies. While I have shown that participatory food journalism has its challenges, I have also demonstrated the resourcefulness of Singaporeans who are quick to devise tactics to circumvent them. Furthermore, the ground-up illumination of the nation's multicultural character has been immensely beneficial to minority groups and individuals with alternative dietary preferences. It is a "beautiful" passion exhibited by the collective, hence the same, if not more intense, vigour to preserve its sanctity in the virtual spaces where it currently thrives. Although structural distinctions of Taste still has a strong grip on many locals, it is interesting to see that the same passion is shared across groups with varied levels of cultural capital, as clearly, the foodies in some Singaporeans will seek out fellow gourmands who have similar tastes as them. The paradigm shift towards a deeper appreciation of the artistic value of favourite local hawker fare had led citizens to also celebrate everyday food as consumption-trophies in visual representations. Likewise, Singaporeans are collectively binge gazing on food portraits as one way to satisfy their insatiable hunger for good food.

At the recent Singapore Writers Festival 2014, a restaurateur, a food blogger and a food critic sat down at a panel to converse with the audience about the future of Singapore's culinary scene. Through the exchanges, differences in opinions and lively discussions, one salient point shines through conclusively from the speakers — more visibility, more activities, and more representation from various groups would also mean a more vibrant foodscape for Singapore.

REFERENCES

Blood R (2002) Weblogs: a history and perspective. In: J Rodzvilla (ed.) *We've Got Blog: How weblogs are changing our culture.* Cambridge, MA: Perseus Publishing, pp. 7–16.

Bourdieu P (1990) *The Logic of Practice.* Stanford, CA: Stanford University Press.

Bourdieu P (1984) *Distinction: A Social Critique of the Judgement of Taste.* Cambridge, MA: Harvard University Press.

Brien DL (2014) Mission to incite hunger: the contemporary Singaporean food memoir. http://www.arrow.dit.ie/cgi/viewcontent.cgi?article=1054&context=dgs, accessed 14 July 2015.

Calvert C (2000) *Voyeur Nation: Media, Privacy, and Peering in Modern Culture.* Boulder, Colorado: Westview Press.

Chan TH (2014) The Social Phenomenon of Food Blogging. Final Year Project, School of Humanities and Social Sciences, Nanyang Technological University.

Cheah U-H (2006) Blogging explored. *Business Times Singapore,* 13 January.

Cox AM and Blake MK (2011) Information and food blogging as serious leisure. In: *Aslib proceedings* **63** (2–3): 204–220, Emerald Group Publishing Limited.

Denveater (2009) The virtual roundtable: food blogging as citizen journalism. *World Literature Today* **83:** 42–46.

Domingo D and Heinonen A (2008) Weblogs and journalism. *Nordicom Review* **29**(1): 3–15.

Gilbert M (2010) Theorizing digital and urban inequalities: critical geographies of 'race', gender and technological capital. *Information, Communication & Society,* **13**(7): 1000–1018.

Hee R (2003) Out of the box — the makan man. *The Edge Singapore,* 13 January

Infocomm Development Authority (IDA) (2014) Survey Reports. http://www.ida.gov.sg/Infocomm-Landscape/Facts-and-Figures/Survey-Reports, accessed 10 November 2014.

Jenkins H (2009) *Confronting the Challenges of Participatory Culture: Media Education for the 21st Century.* Cambridge, MA: MIT Press.

Jung Y and Sternsdorff Cisterna N (2014) Introduction to crafting senses: circulating the knowledge and experience of taste, Special Issue, June 2014. *Food and Foodways,* **22**(1–2): 1–4.

Leong C (2013) *Images of Singapore Food.* Marshall Cavendish, Singapore.

Ling C (nd) Camemberu. http://www.camemberu.com/, accessed 19 November 2014.

Manna L (2005) *Digital Food Photography.* Cengage Learning.

McBride AE (2010) Food Porn. *Gastronomica: The Journal of Critical Food Studies* **10**(1): 38–46.

McQuarrie EF, Miller J, and Phillips BJ (2013) The megaphone effect: taste and audience in fashion blogging. *Journal of Consumer Research* **40**(1): 136–158.

Miller CR and Shepherd D (2004) Blogging as social action: a genre analysis of the weblog. In: LJ Gurak, S Antonijevic, L Johnson, C Ratliff and J Reyman (eds.) *Into the blogosphere: Rhetoric, community, and culture of weblogs.* http://blog.lib.umn.edu/blogosphere/blogging_as_social_action_a_genre_analysis_of_the_weblog.html, accessed 15 May 2015.

Murray S (2008) Digital images, photo-sharing, and our shifting notions of everyday aesthetics. *Journal of Visual Culture* **7**(2): 147–163.

Ngo T (2012) Turning the tables: the democratisation of food criticism. *The Drum*, 22 November. http://www.abc.net.au/news/2012-11-22/ngo---food-writer/4384074, accessed 20 December 2014.

Ritzer G and Jurgenson N (2010) Production, consumption, presumption, the nature of capitalism in the age of the digital 'prosumer'. *Journal of Consumer Culture* **10**(1): 13–36.

Singapore Food Blogs (nd) http://singapore-food-blogs.blogspot.sg/, accessed 19 November 2014.

Soh STJ (2006) Gastroporn! Food, sex and emotions in the Singapore context. Academic Exercise, Department of Sociology, Faculty of Arts & Social Sciences, National University of Singapore.

Statista (2011) Number of blogs worldwide. http://www.statista.com/statistics/278527/number-of-blogs-worldwide/, accessed 28 November 2014.

Tay L (nd) I eat I shoot I post. http://ieatishootipost.sg/, accessed 19 November 2014.

The Cre8tives (nd) Dine — Singapore's Halal Dining. https://www.facebook.com/halaldinesg?fref=ts, accessed 20 December 2014.

The Straits Times (2014) Is tau hway too low-class for posh picnic? 25 August.

The Straits Times (2014) Getting paid for blogging, 11 May.

The Straits Times (2007) 'Foodies' blogs stir interest, 4 March.

The Straits Times (2006) Eat to tell, 24 June.

The Straits Times (2005) They flog about good food, 16 April.

Thevenot G (2007) Blogging as a social media. *Tourism and Hospitality Research* 7(3–4): 287–289.

Trigg AB (2001) Veblen, Bourdieu, and conspicuous consumption. *Journal of Economic Issues* **35**(1): 99–115.

Veblen T (1994 (1899)) The theory of the leisure class. In: P Cain (ed.) *The Collected Works of Thorstein Veblen*. Vol. 1. Re-print, London: Routledge, pp. 1–404.

Watson P, Morgan M and Hemmington N (2008) Online communities and the sharing of extraordinary restaurant experiences. *Journal of Foodservice* **19**(6): 289–302.

Zimmerman P (1995) Reel families. *A Social History of Amateur Film*. Bloomington: Indiana University Press.

Chapter 9

From Sushi in Singapore to Laksa in London: Globalising Foodways and the Production of Economy and Identity

Lily Kong

INTRODUCTION

The impacts of globalisation are myriad and varied, affecting many aspects of human life and activity. Food production, distribution, and consumption have not been exempted (Mak *et al.* 2012: 173; Lang 1999; Wilhelmina *et al.* 2010). Globalisation has enabled the spread of foods across the world, from the availability of *sushi* in landlocked countries, to the making of French baguette widely accessible and commonplace to households in many parts of the world. Such movements of food have been driven largely by global trade and global empire which had already emerged in the early centuries (Anderson 2005: 249). The exchange of food across regions, nations and continents is therefore not new (Phillips 2006: 38), but it is the scope and speed of this movement that has dramatically increased in recent years (Mak *et al.* 2012: 173). However, the changes not only manifest in the rapidity of movement; the entire system of producing, processing, and marketing is, today, globally organised and controlled by transnational corporations and global trade bodies (Guptill *et al.* 2013: 138).

Over the past decade, an expanding body of research has focused on the nexus between food and globalisation, bringing together scholars from a range of disciplines such as sociology, geography, business, tourism and cultural studies (Bell and Valentine 1997; Goodman and Watts 1997; Grew 1999; Cwiertka and Walraven 2002; Phillips 2006; Nuetzenadel and Trentmann 2008; Inglis and Gimlin 2009). Research that specifically focuses on what may broadly be described as the globalisation of food covers topics like how food offers a way into tracing globalisation processes and world systems, the key drivers of food globalisation, the role of transnational agents/actors in aiding the global spread of cuisines, and the construction and contestations of identity and politics in the globalisation of food.

While these are all significant and interesting issues, not all of them can be addressed in a single chapter. Here, I have chosen to examine the globalisation of food in Singapore as well as the globalisation of Singapore food, and their implications for Singapore's future foodways and foodscapes. In the first part of the chapter, I trace the increasingly diversified foods in Singapore as more and more foreign foods enter the country. I begin with an overview of the various foreign cuisines present in Singapore today, followed by an examination of the factors that have enabled this globalisation of food in Singapore. These include the large expatriate community which introduced and created demand for foreign foods; the desire to build a cosmopolitan identity, for which food offers symbolic status; the history of multi-ethnicity and hybridity that characterises Singapore culture and food that predisposes Singaporeans to difference; the influence of media; and Singapore's strong "foodie" culture. The resistances and defensiveness against globalising forces, of which resistance to "other" foods becomes an articulation, is thus not readily apparent in Singapore.

In the second part of this chapter, I turn to the globalisation of Singapore food, that is, how Singapore foods are spreading to different parts of the world. I also examine the factors which have enabled this, including the role of the Singapore government in actively organising overseas food festivals and food events to give Singapore cuisine international exposure, recognising the value of food as a tourism resource and tool in destination marketing. The government's role in supporting local food manufacturers to export Singapore food products to overseas markets is also significant, generating revenue for the country. Further, the role of enterprising individuals and businesses from Singapore should not be forgotten. Finally, the chapter concludes with an examination of the dynamic nature of foodways and cuisines, and discusses the future of Singapore foods in a globalised world.

GLOBALISING FOOD: TRADE, MIGRATION, TECHNOLOGY AND KEY AGENTS OF CHANGE

Before delving into the specific Singapore context, I set the stage by providing a broader historical and global perspective on the globalisation of food. Hall and Mitchell (2002) highlight three key historical periods in which globalisation has influenced and changed regional cuisines. The first was the period of European mercantilism spanning the late 1400s to 1800s. Driven by the need to secure food supplies, European colonial powers grabbed control of spice trading routes (Turner 2005). Through trade, Asian spices and sugar were brought to Europe (Bryant *et al.* 2013: 38). Chinese flavourings like soy sauce found their way to Europe in the 17th century through Dutch traders. In the United Kingdom, soy sauce was in fact adapted and used in Worcestershire Sauce in 1837 (Cheung and Tan 2007: 203). Ingredients like chilli pepper also spread from the New World to other parts of the globe (Andrews 2000). Cheung and Tan (2007: 2) highlight that the voyages of Columbus during the discovery of the New World greatly facilitated the globalisation of food sources and food ingredients. New World crops like potatoes, maize, beans, papayas, avocados and pineapples were exported to Europe across the Atlantic Ocean. At the same time, crops and foodstuffs from the Old World were introduced to the New World and assimilated into the diet of the local people (Bryant *et al.* 2013: 38).

The second key period in the globalisation of food, following the wave of trade, was the influence of large-scale migrations from the seventeenth to twentieth century (Hall and Mitchell 2002). The movement of masses of people across the world greatly contributed to the shaping of the global culinary landscape (Bell and Valentine 1997: 191). This area of study has attracted much interest, resulting in a rich body of scholarship that explores migration and food diasporas, and theorises how migration affects food and cuisine (Bryant *et al.* 2013: 39; Anderson 2011). Bryant *et al.* (2013) note that the Indian diaspora of the nineteenth century, as well as other waves of migration from Europe, Latin America, Southeast Asia, Africa and the Caribbean, spread millions of people and their cuisines globally.

The third major period in the globalisation of food as identified by Hall and Mitchell (2002) is the late 20th and early 21st centuries in which globalisation has been aided by technological advancements in transport and the food industry. Over the last few centuries, the food system has undergone industrialisation and gained the capabilities to span the globe ever more extensively (Friedmann 1994; Watts and Goodman 1997; Inglis and Gimlin

2009: 13). Rapid growth of urban populations has increased the demand for food, leading the food industry to focus on increasing output and orienting itself towards mass-market production and distribution. New technologies have been developed and utilised to help achieve these; they include new methods of packing and preservation like industrial freezer systems, large-scale canning operations, and the improvement of global freight and cargo systems (Inglis and Gimlin 2009: 14; Shepard 2001; Sorj and Wilkinson 1985; Levinson 2008). Such innovations in food processing and operations have been welcomed and harnessed by food-related transnational corporations (TNCs) seeking to expand into new overseas markets (Phillips 2006). TNCs and the food industry have facilitated the global circulation of food items by building networks using world cities as centres of distribution that act as nodes of the networks. Technological advancements in food production, processing and distribution have thus increased the scale of food trade and diffusion of foods across the globe.

Literature on the globalisation of food also identifies key transnational actors and agents who promote cross-border flows of food. Farrer (2010: 5–6) cites the work of Shoko Imai and Jean Duruz in identifying "celebrity chefs" as social agents who, apart from migrant entrepreneurs, have helped spread and popularise foreign cuisines in other countries. Imai examined how the famous Japanese chef, Matsuhisa Nobuyuki, better known as Nobu, was instrumental in strengthening Japan's culinary influence in the West. Nobu restaurants are located in major world cities like New York, Los Angeles, and London. His restaurants are acclaimed for their culinary works of art and "Nobu-style" nouveau Japanese cuisine that bears North and South American influences. His creative cooking style has attracted many patrons to his highly successful restaurants, and his cookbooks have been well-received in countries like the United States, Britain, Netherlands and South Korea. Duruz (2010) also describes how celebrity chef Cheong Liew has popularised Asian cuisine in Australia and served as an influential agent in aiding the global circulation of food cultures. Originally from Malaysia, Chef Cheong Liew set up his now highly reputable restaurant Neddy's in Adelaide and also taught cooking at Australia's top centre of hospitality training, the Regency Hotel School.

Another category of agents in the globalisation of food is the food critic. Ray (2010:1) identifies food critics according to various degrees of professionalism: professional journalists and restaurant-reviewers, but also ordinary diners who offer their opinions of restaurants (see Tan, chapter 8 in this volume, on food bloggers). Food critics not only shape the popularity and sometimes demise of restaurants, they do the more fundamental work of introducing new foods and cuisines in settings other than their original hearth.

Finally, even governments are actors in the globalisation of food, driven by the desire to promote their national cuisines to achieve "culinary soft power" — "the acknowledged attractiveness and appeal of food culture that adheres to a nation, region or locality" (Farrer 2010: 13). Governments see this as a way to promote tourism, investment and exports and also boost the prestige of their country or region. Farrer (2010) observes that Asian governments in particular are seeking culinary soft power. For example, Malaysia and South Korea have both launched initiatives aimed at raising the status of their national cuisines in other countries (Abu Bakar 2008; Yoshino 2010). South Korea even intends to make Korean cuisine one of the most popular cuisines in the world (Ro 2009). Other governments like those of Thailand and Japan have already been fairly successful in this respect. Thai and Japanese cuisines currently enjoy global popularity, and Japan continues to implement policies to strengthen its culinary soft power. For example, Japanese government groups have developed proposals to promote Japanese culinary culture abroad and have leveraged platforms like international expos to draw attention to Japanese cuisine. Culinary soft power encompasses a "push" element — the exporting of national cuisine as described above — and a "pull" element whereby governments try to attract foreign culinary talent in order to boost the reputation of a city as a global food capital. The latter may see the government engaging in programmes to enhance dining and entertainment districts, develop food media, cultivate the tastes of consumers, and roll out policies to develop resources like restaurant staff and chefs (Farrer 2010).

GLOBALISATION OF FOOD IN SINGAPORE

A Growing Diversification

Beginning in the 1970s, the introduction of new foods and cuisines from overseas dramatically altered Singapore's culinary scene. Leung *et al.* (2001) describe the changes that occurred around this period. Previously, Singapore's food scene consisted mainly of street foods, hawker stalls, *kopitiams* (coffee shops) and "conventional" restaurants. However, the 1970s saw the entry of Western fast food joints into Singapore, and the movement gained momentum in the 1980s and 1990s. Specialty restaurants sprang up during this period, Western fast food chains mushroomed (Leung *et al.* 2001: 51; Omar 2008), a greater range of international cuisines appeared, Japanese food gained popularity (Ng 2001: 8) and ethnic cuisines such as Thai and Indonesian became more widely available. New dining concepts and ways of serving food were also introduced. The now ubiquitous food court which offers an integrated one-stop spread of different food options was one such concept, as was the concept of fast food franchises offering customers speedy and convenient meals. Al-fresco dining caught on and Singapore's nightlife received a boost with the development of Boat Quay and Clarke Quay in 1993 which enabled restaurants, pubs and cafes to be built by the Singapore River. By 1998, close to 40% of restaurants in Singapore served Western or "International" cuisine, while around 56% offered "Oriental" cuisine (Leung *et al.* 2001: 51–52). Since then, a growing smorgasbord of cuisines and foods from all over the world has established a presence in Singapore. This includes food from Europe, Central and Latin America, the United States, East Asia and other parts of Southeast Asia, ranging from convenience food to gourmet food served at high-end restaurants. In what follows, I elaborate in further detail on the foreign foods that have contributed to the globalisation of food in Singapore.

One key evidence of the globalisation of food in Singapore has been the expansion of Western-style fast food and international food franchises into the country. Henderson (2014) notes that the proliferation of international fast food chains and food and beverage franchises are an indication of how the food industry in Singapore is globalising. The very first fast food joint to open in Singapore was A&W in 1966, perhaps best remembered among Singaporeans for its root beer floats and curly fries. Though it subsequently closed down, A&W paved the way for other American fast food chains in Singapore. Kentucky Fried Chicken (KFC) was the next to enter Singapore in 1977, followed by McDonald's in 1979 (Omar 2008). Burger King also commenced operations in Singapore in 1982 and Long John Silver's in 1983. By 2008, McDonald's, KFC and Burger King had become leading players in Singapore's fast food sector (Omar 2008). More recently, Wendy's re-opened in Singapore in 2009, furthering the proliferation and popularity of typical fast food fare like burgers, French fries and milkshakes. Competition in Singapore's fast food industry is intense, which explains the closure of A&W in Singapore in 2003 and why global brands like Taco Bell have come and gone. Yet this has not deterred more recent entrants. Newer players in the Singapore market include Carl's Junior, Mos Burger and Jollibee.

In addition to global fast food conglomerates, international food franchises have also introduced non-traditional foods to Singapore. American-style pizza has become a common food in Singapore, largely due to the promotional efforts of franchises like Pizza Hut, Domino's Pizza and Canadian Pizza. Relatively smaller pizza start-ups like Sarpino's, Oishi Pizza and Pelican Pizza have entered the mix and enabled more choices for consumers. All these pizza chains usually target younger consumers who tend to be fond of Western food (Wang 2006; *Media*, 11 Feb 2010). Similarly, global franchises like Dunkin' Donuts and Krispy Kreme from the United States have heightened the appeal of non-traditional foods like doughnuts among consumers in Singapore.

Another segment of Singapore's food and beverage industry that has witnessed the entry of global players is Western theme restaurants such as Hard Rock Café and Planet Hollywood. MacLaurin and MacLaurin (2000: 76–77) observe that the theme-restaurant industry grew rapidly in Singapore beginning in 1990. Hard Rock Café was the first to open in Singapore that year and was designed around a rock-and-roll theme. The food was mainly Western-style, and customers were able to purchase product merchandise and music memorabilia. Other theme restaurants like Hooters subsequently followed in 1996, and Planet Hollywood also established one of its chains in Singapore in the same year. Consumers thus became acquainted with a new and novel Western/international restaurant concept.

Aside from Western fast foods and global franchises, European foods — particularly Italian, Spanish and French — are also among the most popular cuisines that have played a part in making Singapore a globalised food hub. Italian food and dessert can be found in the many Italian restaurants here from *trattorias* like Pasta Fresca da Salvatore and Da Paolo, to scoop-shops offering *gelato*. Pasta Fresca, which was set up in Singapore in 1988, claims it was one of the pioneering restaurants to introduce fresh pasta to customers here, and that it imports its cheese fresh from Italy and continues to uphold the culinary traditions of the Italian kitchen. Italian fare like pizza, pasta and *tiramisu* is also offered by establishments like Da Paolo which began in 1989 and runs pizza bars, gourmet delis and bistro bars. Even Italian restaurant chains with an international presence chose to expand into Singapore. Jamie's Italian, founded by celebrity chef Jamie Oliver and his Italian mentor Gennaro Contaldo (*The Straits Times*, 9 Oct 2013), picked Singapore as the location of its first restaurant in Asia. Opened in 2013, it offers fresh antipasti and pasta, further adding to the choice and range of Italian foods that can be enjoyed in

Singapore. *Gelato*, the frozen Italian-style ice cream, has also become a familiar and popular food in Singapore with numerous *gelaterias* found all over the city.

Besides Italian food, Spanish cuisine has made headway in Singapore as well. *Tapas* bars became a craze in Singapore in 2010 (CNN Travel, 28 Oct 2010) and well-known favourites like *paella* can be found at Spanish restaurants here. French cuisine can also be savoured in Singapore, whether at high-end award-winning restaurants like Les Amis, or more casual eateries. An interesting concept was introduced when TFS Bistrot — formerly known as The French Stall and started by French chef Xavier Le Henaff — sought to bring affordable French food to Singapore's suburbs/heartlands by opening its eateries in *kopitiams* and food courts. Other European cuisines available in Singapore include Swiss food which, though less common, has been popularised through Marché restaurant outlets in Singapore. Marché in fact chose to establish its flagship Asia-Pacific outlet in Singapore at VivoCity (Marché 2007).

Latin and Central American foods have not quite penetrated Singapore's culinary scene as extensively as European and other cuisines, but can still be found in Singapore. Examples are Mexican and Costa Rican dishes such as *fajitas, quesadillas, salsa, burritos, tortillas and tacos*. These dishes are not only offered at mid- or up-market restaurants in bustling food and beverage districts like Clarke Quay and Duxton Hill, but humble hawker centres as well, such as at Golden Shore Food Centre and Amoy Street Food Centre (*MoneySmart*, 5 Jun 2014; *The Straits Times*, 27 Apr 2014).

Closer to home, East Asian cuisines, like those from Japan and South Korea, as well as those from neighbouring parts of Southeast Asia, such as Indonesia, Vietnam, Laos, Thailand and Myanmar, present among them some of the more popular cuisines that have spread to Singapore. Japanese food is very well-received in Singapore. *Sushi, ramen* (noodles), *teppanyaki* (hot-plate food) and other Japanese dishes are widely consumed in Singapore through a variety of different channels ranging from *ryotei* (formal Japanese restaurants), family restaurants, *kaiten-sushi* (*sushi* on a conveyor belt) restaurants, takeout *sushi* counters to fast food restaurants like Yoshinoya (Tanimura 2006; Ng 2001). The acceptance of Japanese foods by Singaporeans, however, was not immediate and occurred gradually over time. Ng (2001:10) notes that Singaporeans' acceptance of *sushi* was initially tepid in the 1980s as locals were not accustomed to eating cold raw fish. However, *sushi* culture gained a strong following in the 1990s and early 2000s after some localisation of taste and reduction in price. Local entrepreneurs recognised the business potential in bringing Japanese *sushi* chains to Singapore, such as Singaporean businessman

David Ban who opened franchises of the successful Genki *Sushi* in Singapore in 1994 (Matsumoto 2006: 18). Sushi Tei, which debuted in the same year, is owned by a Japanese and imports certain ingredients from Japan, while Sakae Sushi was founded by a Singaporean and also features *kaiten-sushi*. All of them have helped to bring *sushi* to Singapore and popularised it among locals (Ng 2001: 13). Today, *sushi* can even be purchased at counters in supermarkets like Cold Storage, Giant and NTUC Fairprice. *Ryotei* and family restaurants, on the other hand, provide a more extensive menu than *sushi* outlets, with additional dishes such as *bento* (Japanese food served in a lacquered box), *tempura*, *donburi* (Japanese "rice bowl dish") and *teppanyaki*. Prices at *ryotei* are higher as they tend to use higher-quality ingredients and are located in hotels, while Japanese-style family restaurants are less expensive (Tanimura 2006: 43–44).

Korean food is another "well-travelled" cuisine that has made an impact in Singapore. Most Singaporeans have tried spicy *kimchi* (fermented cabbage), hotstone *bibimbap* (Korean "mixed rice") and *bulgogi* (barbecue beef). It is not uncommon to find Korean food stalls in food courts in Singapore, and there is a growing number of Korean restaurants specialising in Korean-style charcoal-grill barbeque or offering other traditional dishes such as ginseng chicken soup or *pa jon* (Korean pancake with eggs, vegetable or meat). The first Korean restaurant in Singapore was set up by Singaporean Lim Siang Hee in 1973 and since then, the Korean food scene has continued to develop. A sort of mini "Korea town" formed in Tanjong Pagar from the cluster of Korean restaurants and Korean supermarkets there, and more Korean restaurants can be found within the Central Business District and hotels. Such development may have been aided by Singaporeans' increased interest in Korean cuisine following the Seoul Olympics in 1988 (*The Straits Times*, 8 May 2005). One of the more recent trends has been the expansion of Korean barbeque chains into Singapore. Three well-known ones — Boss BarBQ, Kkongdon BBQ and Bornga — set up their first outlets in Singapore in 2012, and some have plans to open even more outlets in the country. Two more Korean BBQ restaurants also popped up in Tanjong Pajar in the same year — Supulae and Mini Korea Bistro & Izakaya. As of 2012, there were at least 150 Korean restaurants in Singapore (*The Straits Times*, 2 Oct 2012).

Cuisines from Singapore's Southeast Asian neighbours have also become commonplace in Singapore. Indonesian *nasi padang* (steamed rice with choice of various pre-cooked dishes) is easily found in Singapore. *Nasi padang* originated from Padang, a region in Sumatra, Indonesia, and is particularly common in the area near Masjid Sultan (or Sultan Mosque), a landmark mosque in Singapore around where immigrants set up eateries. Indonesian-style *ayam goreng bumbu* (fried chicken) and *gulai kikil* (beef tendon in curry) are just some of the Indonesian foods that can be enjoyed in Singapore (*The Straits Times*, 26 Nov 2006). Vietnamese and Laotian food, have also entered and become part of Singapore's multicultural culinary market. These ethnic cuisines can be consumed at different places in various settings — from simple stalls at Joo Chiat Road, to more chic and expensive restaurants like the IndoChine chain (Carruthers 2012). Examples of Vietnamese/Laotian dishes available at such eateries are *pho bo* (Vietnamese beef noodles), Sai Kog Laotian sausages, and Laotian *laksa* (spicy noodle soup). Today, most Singaporeans are already very familiar with signature dishes of these ethnic cuisines like Vietnamese rice paper rolls and *pho*. Thai cuisine is popular in Singapore too and the Thai foodscape in Singapore is similarly varied, made up of simple eateries such as those in Thai migrant enclaves like Golden Mile Complex, mid-end restaurants like Sukothai and ThaiExpress situated in more upmarket locations like Boat Quay, Holland Village, the Esplanade or shopping centres (Chua 2003), and restaurants in still more sophisticated settings, like Patara. Though relatively lesser known, Burmese cuisine is nonetheless available in Singapore as well. Most Burmese eateries and supermarkets tend to be concentrated in Peninsula Plaza, with some restaurants even specialising in minority ethnic cuisines of Myanmar. Examples of Burmese dishes found in Singapore are *mee shay* (rice noodles with meat sauce), *lap pat thut* (Burmese tea leaf salad) and *hsanwin makin* (Burmese semolina cake dessert) (*Makansutra*, 21 Jun 2012).

Clearly, many different foods from all over the globe have spread to Singapore and contributed to the vibrancy of the country's foodscape, adding to its already internallly diverse cuisine. As a result of the influence of these foreign cuisines, the presence of fusion food has been growing in Singapore. Lovallo (2013) writes that fusion food is "both a result and indicator of globalisation" and elaborates on various concepts of fusion food. Fusion cuisine can be viewed as a merging of cuisines or culture. Alternatively called "World Cuisine", fusion cuisine has also been described as "a sort of culinary globalisation [sic] generally considered to be 'post-modern'... [a] new international cuisine..." (Clave and Knafou 2012; Lovallo 2013: 3). Both culinary chefs and enterprising restaurateurs have engaged in creative experimentation, mixing elements of different culinary practices, usually based on the similarity of ingredients. For example, some may look for "bridging ingredients" that appeal to the tastebuds of both cultures, upon which global flavours and preparation methods can be layered to result in fusion cuisines (Ganeshram, quoted in Remizowski 2010). Fusion food not only involves a combination of different flavours, but inventive culinary techniques as well. Furthermore, it requires an understanding of the culture and history of component cuisines (Lovallo 2013: 22–24). In 1997, "New Asia Cuisine", a form of fusion cuisine, began to develop in Singapore. New Asia Cuisine may involve combining European culinary techniques with Asian flavours, or fusing Western ingredients with Asian preparation techniques. Singaporean chefs have created interesting fusion dishes that merge local and European foods using modified Asian culinary techniques, and have played with flavours and ingredients to deliver new tastes. Examples are *risotto* with lemongrass, and yam jelly with edamame foam which demonstrates the fusion of Chinese, Japanese and European ingredients (Chaney and Ryan 2012: 312). In an article for the Financial Times, Shoba Narayan similarly noted that "a new cuisine style is transforming Singapore", led by talented Singaporean chefs like Sam Leong, Galvin Lim at Au Jardin, and Yong Bing Ngen of The Majestic. With their vision and imagination, cuisines are being reinvented and redefined. Chef Milind Sovani, for example, comes up with fusion Indian creations by borrowing from different cultures. The result is dishes like *naan* made into mini-pizza, *foie gras* with star anise, and lobster with lemon-chilli marinade made using Kerala *moily* sauce (a coconut-based sauce) (*FT.com*, 22 Aug 2009).

Global City, Cosmopolitan Identity, Multi-Ethnic History: Provocations to the Globalisation of Food

What prompted this globalisation of food in Singapore, and what dynamics have been at play that facilitated the widespread acceptance of foreign cuisines in the country? The ambitions of a global city and the cosmopolitanism that comes with it are deeply implicated. Characteristic of such a city is the existence of a large expatriate community and the presence of unceasing flows of migrants, alongside a population that is well-travelled and open to media flows and influences. While significant, the roots of this openness run deeper, drawing from a historical sense of a diverse society that takes cultural flows and exchanges as a given, borne of the self-definition as a multi-ethnic society and an entrepot port. These conditions have predisposed its people to welcome a range of cuisines and to celebrate the diversity of foods. Finally, the affluence of the country has generated a foodie culture that translates into food business opportunities. I elaborate on these conditions below.

Migrant flows, expatriate communities

The city-state's development over the past four decades making it the commercial hub of Southeast Asia and a thriving financial centre of global repute has attracted expatriates from all over the world who have settled in Singapore to pursue work and business opportunities (MAS 2014). Singapore has a large expatriate community which has introduced foreign cuisines to the island and significantly influenced the food industry to provide food choices to satisfy their palates. Today, the expatriate population in Singapore numbers more than 1 million, with many working as professionals and managers (Henderson 2014: 907). Each nationality naturally introduced its own cuisine, thus expanding Singapore's food scene. Japanese business expansion into the financial sectors and rubber industry during Singapore's early years brought increasing numbers of Japanese workers into Singapore. In the 1910s, large Japanese banks and trading companies sent employees to Singapore. These new arrivals were wealthy immigrants who could afford to live around Orchard Road. There was also another class of Japanese immigrants who came to work as labourers on plantations in Singapore and were therefore poorer. Between 1912 and 1920, Japanese restaurants were set up to cater to these Japanese expatriates and migrant workers. However, the real boom in Japanese cuisine in Singapore only occurred from the 1980s onwards, due to the dramatic increase in the Japanese population in Singapore and interest in Japanese culture. In the 1980s, there were approximately 8,000 Japanese in Singapore; by 1996, this had tripled to 24,000 (Thang 1999; Tanimura 2006: 17–19, 31). Today, the Japanese expatriate community is one of the largest here. As a result, the number of Japanese restaurants in Singapore has risen from around 70 during the 1980s (Ng 2001: 8–9) to over 600 as of 2009 (Yamanaka 2009). Similarly, Korean restaurants mushroomed in Singapore when Korean construction companies sent hundreds of Korean expatriates to the country in the 1990s (*The Straits Times*, 8 May 2005).

Enterprising immigrants also set up their own restaurants in Singapore to cater to fellow expatriates and Singaporeans, thus helping to popularise their home cuisines in Singapore. For example, Italians Salvatore Carecci of Pasta Fresca da Salvatore and Paolo Scarpa of the Da Paolo Group, together with his family, helped widen the appeal of Italian cuisine in Singapore through their long-running restaurants. Michael Ma, the Laotian-Chinese owner of IndoChine, came to Singapore originally as a finance professional, but instead became a culinary entrepreneur by starting his restaurant chain offering Vietnamese/Laotian fare in 1999. His elevation of IndoChinese food into an exotic cuisine presented in classy post-modern settings has proven to be a hit with the expatriate community and locals alike (Carruthers 2012).

However, it is not only the entry of skilled expatriates that has contributed to the globalisation of food in Singapore. The increase in number of low-skilled migrants and labourers into Singapore has also played a critical part. More Thai migrants from northeast Thailand have come to work as construction workers or domestic helpers in Singapore (Chua 2003) and have contributed to the growth of Thai eateries in areas like Golden Mile Complex, which are patronised by more adventurous Singaporeans who value the authenticity and affordability of Thai food there. Similarly, Burmese expatriates and migrants have helped acquaint Singaporeans with their local cuisine. There are around 200,000 Burmese expatriates in Singapore. In addition to Burmese professionals, there is also a community of blue-collar Burmese workers in Singapore (*Makansutra*, 21 Jun 2012). Given the adequate demand, Burmese eateries and minimarts have thus appeared in Singapore, particularly at Peninsula Plaza and Excelsior Shopping Centre.

A well-travelled people

As Singapore has prospered, Singaporeans have become more well-travelled; this has in turn boosted the popularity of foreign cuisines in Singapore. The increase in number of specialty restaurants, offering ethnic cuisines in the late 1980s and early 1990s, can be attributed to the fact that Singaporeans were beginning to enjoy greater affluence and could travel overseas more frequently (MacLaurin and MacLaurin 2000: 76). Increased exposure to the cuisines of other countries in this way has widened the demand and market for foreign foods in Singapore. For example, Chua (2003) noted that the rise in popularity of Thai food in Singapore was related to the growth in the number of Singaporeans visiting Thailand. After becoming familiar with and enjoying Thai food in its native country, returning Singaporeans were glad to be able to continue consuming it at Thai restaurants in Singapore.

Popular culture and media influence

Singaporeans' interest in foreign foods has often also been aroused through exposure to foreign culture via the media and popular culture. For example, Japanese drama series like *Oshin* which was broadcast on television in Singapore in the 1980s was hugely popular and drew a large audience (Chua 2000: 140). Growing interest in Japanese culture through such popular culture motivated Singaporeans to find out more about Japanese cuisine. Other television programmes like Japan Hour, which aired on Channel News Asia, also focused more attention on Japanese food culture. The show introduced viewers in Singapore to regional Japanese specialties from different parts of the country. Even Japanese comic books and cartoons helped generate interest in Japanese food culture among Singaporeans. Tanimura (2006: 89–91) relates personal experiences of how a Singaporean friend came to know of *Doriyaki* (a Japanese confection consisting of red bean paste between two small pancakes) as it is a favourite food of the well-known cartoon character Doraemon; and how another learnt about Japanese food by reading "Oishinbo", a *manga* (comic) about Japanese cooking.

Similarly, Korean culture is very popular in Singapore, with many Singaporeans being fans of Korean dramas, K-Pop entertainment, and Korean fashion. Interest in all things Korean has naturally generated interest in Korean cuisine as well and seen Singaporeans welcome Korean foods. Some Korean restaurants even merge live K-Pop entertainment with dining so customers can enjoy both elements of Korean culture (*The Straits Times*, 2 Oct 2012). Media and popular culture have therefore helped familiarise Singaporeans with foreign cuisines and contributed to advancing the globalisation of food in Singapore.

Multi-ethnic community, cosmopolitan identity

In Singapore, food is used in the construction of a cosmopolitan identity at both the individual and national levels, helping to fuel the acceptance of foreign cuisines and the development of the international food business in Singapore. At the individual level, Singaporeans associate the consumption of foreign foods with cosmopolitan attitudes, and the ability to appreciate foreign cuisines is considered desirable (Duffy and Yang 2012: 69). Consuming foreign foods has therefore become a way for Singaporeans to identify with and construct a modern cosmopolitan identity for themselves. Varying definitions of the term "cosmopolitan" exist. To be cosmopolitan entails an "openness to otherness and difference" (Young *et al.* 2006: 1688) or having an international orientation. A cosmopolitan individual is "someone who can claim to be a 'citizen of the world'" (Robbins 1998: 248). Being cosmopolitan therefore connotes a certain level of sophistication and worldliness (Chua 2003). In seeking to belong to this cosmopolitan class, many Singaporeans seek the consumption of foreign cuisines to demonstrate that they have the sophistication to appreciate other cuisines. It is almost a way for individuals to express or project the superiority of their cultural refinement and knowledge. In particular, the consumption of "exotic" cuisines that are viewed as novel or unusual can especially make people feel cosmopolitan.

The appetite and desire for foreign foods is not only reflected in Singaporeans' patronage of foreign restaurants, but at the retail level as well, in the demand for foreign foodstuffs. With improvements in international distribution and food preservation technologies, supermarkets in Singapore have been able to import a variety of overseas foods which were originally targeting expatriate consumers, but have also found a market among local Singaporeans (Duruz 2006: 103). For example, Japanese supermarkets and grocery shops in Singapore brought in Japanese goods and ingredients for the expatriate Japanese community, but as Ng (2001:9) pointed out, they also enjoy business from Singaporeans. Cold Storage, a chain of supermarkets, began by importing foodstuffs sought after by expatriate Europeans seeking a taste of home, such as Dutch, Swiss, English and Danish cheeses, pickles, jams, custards and fresh produce from many countries. Duruz (2006: 103, 105) writes that Cold Storage offered "meanings of Western cosmopolitanism" to the expatriate community and notes that over the years, the "cosmopolitan eating" that it fosters was not limited to expatriates but attracted Singaporean customers as well.

At the national level, cosmopolitanism has even become part of the government's strategy for developing Singapore and strengthening its global profile and competitive economic position. In the past decade or so, the government has worked towards a vision of Singapore as a cosmopolitan city (Bishop 2011: 642), employing a "two-pronged approach.... The first is to make Singapore a place for cosmopolitans and the second is to create cosmopolitan Singaporeans" (Tan and Yeoh, 2006:148). The latter refers to the development of Singaporeans who possess skills that are marketable worldwide and who have an international outlook, a characterisation forwarded by former Prime Minister Goh Chok Tong (Goh 1999; Chua 2003). But it is the former — creating Singapore into a place for cosmopolitans — in which food has come to play a significant role. The desire to ensure that Singapore is a place for cosmopolitans has led the government to position food as one of the perks of living in Singapore in order to attract the foreign elite. As Bell and Valentine (1997) note, entrepreneurial cities understand that showcasing culinary diversity is a kind of urban boosterism and in doing so, can increase their attractiveness as a place to live and work.

With Singapore's street food scene and mid-end restaurant industry already fairly developed, the country has focused efforts on nurturing culinary cosmopolitanism and developing the finer gourmet segment, with the aim of making Singapore a globalised gourmet hub. In this regard, the development of international fine dining at two new hotel and casino complexes — the Marina Bay Sands (MBS) and Resorts World Sentosa (RWS) — provide an example of the culinary cosmopolitanism that is transforming Singapore in exciting and diverse ways. Eleven internationally renowned chefs have opened restaurants at MBS and RWS. They include legendary Michelin-decorated French chef Joël Robuchon, Guy Savoy from Paris, Kunio Tokuoka from Kyoto, Santi Santamaria from Catalonia, American chef Mario Bartali, Australian chef Scott Webster, and Wolfgang Puck (*The Wall Street Journal*, 14 Oct 2010). Collectively, their restaurants bring cuisines from all over the globe — French gourmet fare, Spanish cuisine, Japanese *kaiseki*, Italian gastronomy, and many others. The Singapore government has aided the development of foreign cuisine restaurants by providing a favourable business environment of low tax rates, low import taxes and stable government. Other factors cited by foreign restaurateurs that encouraged them to set up businesses in Singapore were the presence of a large expatriate population, high levels of disposable income, and the use of English as the main language (*The Wall Street Journal*, 14 Oct 2010; MacLaurin and MacLaurin 2000: 76). In these various ways, Singapore has been able to harness food as "a badge of sophistication, reach and power" (Duffy and Yang 2012: 64) to project a cosmopolitan image of the city, and as a magnet to attract cosmopolitans to Singapore. Food has thus played a notable role in representing Singapore as a vibrant global city in order to attract foreign talent and strengthen its economy.

In one sense, the predisposition to this cosmopolitan identity was already laid in the foundations of the city-state's multi-ethnic and diverse population. Chaney and Ryan (2012) suggest that Singaporeans are accepting of foreign cuisines because their own local foodways have a tradition of sharing. Nyonya cuisine, for instance, relies on ingredients from Malay, Chinese and

Indian cooking. Malay dishes like *nasi briyani* reflect Middle Eastern and Indian influences (Brown and Backenheimer 2006; Chaney and Ryan 2012: 312). This history of openness to other cuisines, and cultural acceptance of "borrowing" or exchanging flavours between different foodways may thus explain why Singaporeans are quick to embrace foreign cuisines and try new fusion foods.

Foodie culture

Another factor that has fuelled the globalisation of food in Singapore and acceptance of foreign cuisines is Singapore's "foodie culture", a characteristic made possible by the overall affluence of society. Duffy and Yang (2012: 59) observe that it has become "axiomatic of the Singaporean identity that they are a nation of foodies", to which Henderson (2014: 904) agrees by pointing out that the keen appreciation of food seems to be a common trait among Singaporeans. Locals are preoccupied with food, and a former Minister for Trade and Industry even remarked at the amount of time Singaporeans spend eating and constantly thinking about food, declaring this fixation with food to be "an inseparable part of our culture" (STB 2004). Singaporeans will queue for hours at stalls and go to great lengths just to procure the foods they desire. Food is almost like a national pastime and locals enjoy looking for new foods and eating places to try out (Wang 2006: 53; Duffy and Yang 2012: 59). So strong is the passion for food that foodies may think nothing of travelling across the island or even to Malaysia to hunt down good food (Wang 2006: 54). Food is also a very popular and frequent topic of conversation among Singaporeans, with people often sharing tips on where to find the best food places. Clearly, food is an important facet of Singaporeans' cultural identity, with Singaporeans united by a common love of food. Theoretical perspectives on the functions of food support these observations made in the context of Singapore of the social-cultural role of food. Chang (2013: 1) writes that food "is more than nourishment, it offers pleasure and entertainment and serves a social purpose". Goode (1992: 234) mentions that food can be used in such a way as to "define inclusion" and encourage "solidarity". Similarly, Mintz and Du Bois (2002: 109) state that "like all culturally defined material substances used in the creation and maintenance of social relationships, food serves…to solidify group membership", though at the same time they note that food may also be used as a divisive force to exclude others.

As a result of Singapore's strong foodie culture, Singaporeans are very receptive to trying out and accepting new cuisines, and they often come to appreciate these new flavours. In one interview, a Brazilian restaurateur commented that Singaporeans' fondness for trying new things translated into good business for her Brazilian restaurant. Singapore was therefore a good place for her restaurant to operate due to the strong demand (Duffy and Yang 2012: 70). The success of many restaurants offering foreign cuisines in Singapore may further attest to this. Singaporeans are also quick to catch on to the latest food fads, such as US-style doughnuts, Taiwanese bubble tea or French macaroons (Duffy and Yang 2012: 59). The national enthusiasm for food is both reflected in and fostered by the plethora of media dedicated to food—from local television programmes that search for the best eateries, newspaper articles featuring new dining places or foods, social media applications that rate restaurants, and online food reviews posted by bloggers (Wang 2006: 53; Henderson 2014: 911; see also, Tan, in this volume). Food is so much a part of the national psyche that it is even used in linguistic expressions; for example, *rojak* — the Malay word for "mixture" which is also the name of a local salad — is used to describe any kind of mix, such as the ethnic mix of Singapore's population (Tarulevicz 2013: 3). Singapore's dining-out culture has also likely helped the globalisation of food in Singapore. Dining out is very common due to higher incomes, increasingly busy lifestyles, the wide variety of dining options available, and the treatment of dining out as a source of pleasure and entertainment (Tarulevicz 2011: 242; Ng 2001: 9; Henderson 2014: 907). To Singaporeans, it is a chance to spend time socialising with friends and family; in this way, food acts as a force that binds the community together (Henderson 2014: 908). Ultimately, the inclination to dine outside the home means that Singaporeans are more likely to be exposed to foreign cuisines and to acquire an appreciation for them.

GLOBALISATION OF SINGAPORE FOOD

The Travel of Singapore Foods: From Toronto to Tokyo, from Seoul to Sydney

Globalisation is not unidirectional. It involves multi-directional flows and influences, though worries about more dominant flows are evident in the concerns expressed over cultural homogenisation, which, in the context of food, has led to fears about the development of a uniform "global palate" and "global cuisine" (Symons 1993; Ritzer 1995; Richards 2002). An examination of the globalisation of Singapore food suggests that, just as foreign cuisines from other parts of the world have spread to Singapore, Singapore food has also been making its way to countries abroad. Though these outward flows do not have the global reach of, say, Western fast food joints, they nevertheless demonstrate the dangers of excessive claims about "an ominous homogenisation of the world — where sameness is ubiquitously imposed, and the difference is steadily suppressed or eliminated" (Cheng 2011: 198, in Kikomr 2012).

Singapore cuisine is enjoying growing popularity beyond its shores and gaining greater awareness overseas. Dishes like *laksa,* chilli crab, *char kway teow*, and chicken rice are turning up in places like London, New York, Toronto, Mumbai, Chennai, Tokyo, Seoul, Shanghai and even Moscow, gradually becoming recognised and associated with Singapore by foreigners. Food products like *kaya, popiah* skin, curry pastes and seasonings from Singapore are also making their way to the shelves of foreign retail outlets and supermarkets overseas. Food festivals featuring Singapore cuisine are being held in various countries abroad, thus helping to introduce Singapore favourites to residents there. This spread of Singapore food overseas has occurred through the efforts of various agents — chiefly the Singapore government which plans and implements various food events, initiatives and policies to promote Singapore foods internationally, Singapore food manufacturers that export Singapore food products, Singapore restaurants opened by entrepreneurial individuals or businesses, and foreign hotels that seasonally promote Singapore food. Below, I elaborate on the initiatives undertaken by each agent in greater detail and the kinds of Singapore foods that they have helped introduce to the world. In the process, the economic and political roles that food plays become apparent.

Government Initiatives: Food as Tourism Resource and Culinary Soft Power

The Singapore government has actively promoted Singapore food overseas through a range of policies, programmes and events. Food is a valuable tourism resource (Hjalager and Richards 2002) that can effectively be used to increase visitorship to a destination (Fox 2007; du Rand *et al.* 2003). As Chang (2013:9) notes, cuisine can serve as a way of differentiating a country from other destinations that compete for tourism arrivals and dollars. Tourism growth in turn contributes to economic growth, and this is significantly so in the case of Singapore. In 2014, the total contribution of tourism and travel to GDP in Singapore amounted to a notable S$39.7 billion (or 10.9% of GDP) (WTTC 2014). Food therefore plays an economic role and contributes to economic development by boosting tourism. It is a critical determinant of tourists' choice of destination, as seen in a 2014 survey in which more than one-third of leisure travellers in the Asia-Pacific region (APAC) said food and drink is the determining factor in where they choose to vacation (*PR Newswire and Hilton Worldwide*, 19 Feb 2014). Singapore government bodies have thus sought to raise the profile of Singapore cuisine overseas to encourage more tourists to visit the country.

Singapore Food Festival and overseas food events

The Singapore Tourism Board (STB) established an internal Food and Beverage Division specially to develop culinary tourism, reflecting the importance that Singapore places on cuisine as a key theme for tourism marketing (Horng and Tsai 2012: 283). In 1994, STB launched the first Singapore Food Festival. The festival is an annual event showcasing Singapore's local cuisine, and it continues to run in various countries across the world, allowing participants to savour the taste of a tantalising spectrum of Singapore foods. In India, where the festival has been held in large cities like Mumbai and Chennai, participants get the opportunity to try chilli crab, *popiah* (Chinese-style fresh spring rolls), Hainanese chicken rice, *mee goreng* (fried noodles with Malay and Indian flavours and Chinese influence) and *tahu goreng* (fried tofu stuffed with vegetables) (*The Hindu*, 14 Sep 1998; *Hindustan Times*, 10 May 2013). In Japan, the festival also featured Hainanese chicken rice and Singapore's signature cocktail, the Singapore Sling (*CNA*, 9 Sep 2006). In London, temporary kitchens were installed at Covent Garden Market for the festival so people could sample fresh *satay*, ice *kacang* (sweetened shaved ice dessert) and the ever-popular Hainanese chicken rice (*CNA*, 22 Mar 2005). Overall, the government's efforts in promoting Singapore food overseas to attract tourist traffic seems to have paid off as Singapore was voted the third favourite culinary destination by leisure travellers in APAC in 2014 (*PR Newswire and Hilton Worldwide*, 19 Feb 2014). Promoting a national cuisine, as Singapore is doing, also helps a country gain "urban soft power" (Farrer 2010: i). As Barthes (1997 [1961]) highlights, food can fulfill a political purpose and "is always bound to the values of power" (Duffy and Yang 2012: 63). Specifically, by building its culinary reputation, Singapore seeks to raise its global profile, using its food as a cultural bridge so foreigners develop positive associations with the country.

In addition to STB, other government agencies have joined in to promote Singapore foods overseas. The main players are International Enterprise (IE) Singapore, SPRING Singapore, and Singapore International Culinary Exchange (SPICE). One interesting initiative borne out of the joint efforts of these four government bodies has been a mobile pop-up kitchen launched in 2011 called Singapore Takeout, which looks like a shipping container and travels the globe showcasing Singapore's culinary offerings. The aim of Singapore Takeout is to promote Singapore cuisine in some of the major cities in the world — London, Paris, New York, Hong Kong, Shanghai, Moscow, Sydney, Delhi and Dubai (*Business Times Singapore*, 26 Feb 2011; *The Asian Age*, 5 Jan 2012) — and market Singapore as a key gastronomic destination. It brings celebrated Singapore chefs like Benjamin Seck to these cities where they prepare dishes like cabbage and carrot *popiah* paired with vinegar and sweet chilli dip, prawn curry, *laksa* and other Nyonya specialties (*Mail Today*, 13 Jan 2012). They also conduct cooking demonstrations. As Ranita Sundra, a Director at STB shared, the Singapore Takeout global tour seeks to establish Singapore as "a must-visit for foodies" and "Asia's most innovative culinary capital" (*Business Times Singapore*, 26 Feb 2011). To further raise the profile of Singapore cuisine overseas, the government has organised the Global Chef Exchange. This initiative is a culinary immersion programme which invites influential chefs from all over the world to Singapore to become familiarised with the local culinary culture. The programme hopes to inspire these chefs to create Singapore-style dishes back home and thus help to spread Singapore cuisine in more countries abroad (*CNA*, 28 Mar 2012). STB has sent delegations to other prominent international culinary events as well to strengthen awareness of Singapore cuisine on the world stage. For example, it sent an entourage of talented Singapore chefs to the World of Flavors conference in the United States, a prestigious professional forum on world cuisines, where they were able to showcase Singapore cuisine to other participants from across the globe (*Business Times Singapore*, 10 Dec 2011).

Supporting Singapore food exports

Singaporean food companies involved in food manufacturing have received much support from IE Singapore in expanding into overseas markets. The

Singapore government recognises the economic potential of its domestic food exports, which nearly doubled from S$2.4 billion in 2006 to S$4.2 billion in 2012 (SingStat 2013), and the value in raising the profile of Singapore food brands and cuisine in markets abroad. IE Singapore aims to help Singapore food products reach the shelves of more foreign supermarkets and restaurants, and for Singapore cuisine to attract mainstream consumers in markets overseas, particularly those beyond Asia and where demand is growing such as the United States, Europe and the Middle East (*Singapore Government News*, 10 Nov 2009). It has done so by building global business networks and inter-country alliances, and providing services to help local enterprises export, develop business capabilities, find overseas partners and penetrate new markets (IE Singapore 2008). Prima Taste is one local food company that has benefitted from IE Singapore's support. The company now sells food mixes such as *laksa*, Hainanese chicken rice and Singapore chilli crab in supermarkets and eateries in around 25 countries, and has seen healthy growth in export sales (*The Straits Times*, 26 Jul 2009). Tee Yih Jia, another Singapore food manufacturer, has managed to distribute its pastry products, like *roti prata* and spring rolls, in major US cities with the help of IE Singapore (*Today*, 19 Jul 2006). Similarly, Singapore convenience foods and sauces from Asian Home Gourmet and Tai Hua are available in the Canadian market. IE Singapore also enabled Singapore foods to enter the mainstream UK market by securing an entire aisle at London department store Selfridges for the sale of Singapore food products, such as pineapple tarts from local bakery Bengawan Solo and Hainanese chicken rice mix by sauce manufacturer Chng Kee (*The Straits Times*, 26 Jul 2009).

Venturing Abroad: Singapore Restaurants Overseas

Another avenue through which Singapore cuisine has spread to other countries is the opening of Singapore restaurants or food franchises in overseas locations. In some cases, these outlets are opened by established food and beverage (F&B) players with the aid of IE Singapore. In other instances, they are initiated by entrepreneurial individuals or businesses of their own accord, without government assistance. An example of the former is when IE Singapore helped Imperial Treasure Restaurant Group, Ya Kun International, and Kriston Food & Beverage open eateries in Tokyo in a prominent retail complex with high customer traffic. IE Singapore managed to ink a deal with the Development Bank of Japan to facilitate the entry of Singapore firms, including Singapore food companies, into the Japanese market. The opening of these eateries helped bring authentic foods found in Singapore like chicken rice, *laksa*, *kaya* toast, and baked *naan* served with *masala* (Indian spices and curry) to Japanese consumers *(Bernama*, 27 Sep 2006; *Business Times Singapore*, 5 Oct 2006). Expansion has been rapid. Ya Kun, for instance, established 26 *kaya* toast outlets in six countries within five years (*The Straits Times*, 26 Jul 2009). Prima Taste has developed its arm of restaurant franchises in eight cities abroad including Colombo, Ho Chi Minh, Beijing, Shanghai, and Surabaya, familiarising locals there with Singapore foods like *bak kut teh* and *satay*.

There are also enterprising Singaporean individuals or businesses who have set up restaurants by themselves overseas. Chef Chris Yeo left Singapore to open four Asian-style restaurants in the United States which offer Singapore dishes like *roti prata* and *laksa* (*The Straits Times*, 26 Jul 2009). Boston's first Singaporean restaurant, called Merlion, was opened by Alfred Chua and serves hawker favourites such as *kway chap* (a mix of pork belly, eggs, tofu and rice noodles in a dark sauce), oyster pancake, *lor mee* and *rojak*. It is not only frequented by Singaporean patrons, but American customers as well (*The Boston Globe*, 4 Oct 1995). In Australia, Dumpling Republic — a Singapore cuisine venture — opened its first restaurant on the Gold Coast in 2013 (*The Gold Coast Bulletin*, 5 Apr 2013), where Singaporean chef Sim Kim Kwee and his team prepare dishes like steamed dumplings and *wonton* soup (dumpling soup). At Ginger & Spice Singapore Restaurant in Sydney, one can find *char kway teow*, *ngoh hiang* (fried pork rolls wrapped with beancurd skin), and *assam* fish (fish in tamarind sauce) (*The Sydney Morning Herald*, 29 Sep 2007). Other eateries in Australia have made Singapore dishes like *laksa* very popular among Australians. Similarly, Singapore cuisine is making its mark in China, where a growing number of restaurants in cities like Shanghai offer favourites like *chai tow kway*, *laksa*, and chilli crab (*Shanghai Daily*, 9 Aug 2011; *CNA*, 12 Aug 2005). In Chengdu, Singaporean company Old Chang Kee has introduced curry puffs and other local Singapore snacks since opening an eatery there in 2008 (*The Straits Times*, 29 Oct 2008). Homegrown restaurant Jumbo Seafood has penetrated the South Korean and Japanese markets through joint partnerships and agreements, thus helping to introduce Singapore's famous chilli crab in these countries. It signed a memorandum of understanding with a key restaurant association in South Korea in 2007 to pave the way for partnership opportunities, and it opened restaurants in Tokyo and Osaka in collaboration with other Singapore business owners (*The Korea Herald*, 10 Feb 2007; *The Straits Times*, 26 Jul 2009).

Marketing Singapore Food: Hotel Promotions

Hotels overseas hold promotions of Singapore food from time to time, and though relatively smaller in scale, these events are another way in which Singapore cuisine is being introduced overseas. Singapore's rich and diverse culinary offerings have a wide appeal that would satisfy a range of consumers. With Singapore's foods becoming better known, hotels likely realise that Singapore food promotions would be well-received and be met with healthy demand. As tourism traffic to Singapore grows, more travellers become familiar with Singapore cuisine and those who enjoy it will probably take advantage of opportunities to taste Singapore food again in their home country. For example, the JW Marriot Hotel Mumbai held a Singaporean food promotion, specially flying in a chef from Singapore to prepare Singapore-Chinese dishes like braised duck and claypot chicken (*Daily News & Analysis*, 16 Aug 2008). Several hotels under the Copthorne Hotel chain in London and Britain offer popular Singapore dishes like *hor fun*, *nasi padang*, and *laksa* (*The Straits Times*, 23 Nov 1998). Even in Dubai, the Park Regis Kris Kin Hotel recreated Singapore delicacies as part of a seasonal promotion. It invited a Singapore celebrity chef to work with its own chef to design a menu featuring dishes like chicken rice and *rojak* (*Islamic Finance News*, 13 Oct 2011). The InterContinental Eros, New Delhi, holds an annual Singapore food promotion that brings many Singapore hawker favourites to guests — oyster omelette, radish cake, *otak otak*, barbeque duck and chicken rice, mutton *rendang*, chicken *satay* and others (*The Pioneer*, 20 Nov 2009). Closer to home, the Regent Kuala Lumpur similarly held a Singapore food fair during which guest Singapore chef Calvin Ow dished up hawker delights like *satay bihun* (rice noodles served with a chilli-based peanut sauce), prawn noodles, fried carrot cake, and seafood *char kway teow* (*Weekend Mail*, 4 Nov 2006). Such hotel promotions have therefore contributed to growing awareness of Singapore cuisine overseas, whether in Europe, the Middle East, South Asia or the closer neighbouring region.

CONCLUSIONS: CHANGING FOODWAYS

Foodways — "what we eat, as well as how and why and under what circumstances we eat" (Edge 2007: 8), or the patterns and practices related to the production and consumption of food – are not static. Cuisines are not fixed things (Cook *et al.* 2000: 113); rather, they are "dynamic phenomena" which "evolve and interact" (Henderson 2014: 904, 906). Indeed, in Singapore, globalisation has changed and continues to alter foodways — foreign foods have become part of the Singaporean foodscape and diet, new forms of cuisine have emerged from the interaction of different cuisines, and culinary practices and technologies continue to evolve. In addition, localisation practices have led to some modifications to foreign cuisines introduced in Singapore. The first wave of migration to early Singapore already demonstrated how foodways can change. It brought the mix of cuisines from different migrant ethnicities that laid the foundation for Singapore's now diverse, varied and hybrid cuisine. In more recent times, Singapore's ambition to be a global city has meant a great openness to flows of people, goods, services and ideas from all over the world. With this has come some Westernisation of tastebuds among Singaporeans (Henderson 2014: 907) and more changes to foodways in Singapore. Western fast food and international food franchises have become very popular in Singapore. Such foods have become ubiquitous and are regularly consumed by many Singaporeans. A 2004 National Nutritional Survey showed that respondents consumed fast food around once every two weeks (Health Promotion Board 2004). Even in hawker centres which are thought to offer a close representation of common local foods that Singaporeans eat regularly, one can usually find a few stalls offering Western cuisine such as fish and chips, steak, pasta and burgers. Towards the gastronomic end of the spectrum, higher-end restaurants and chefs exposed to the influence of Western cuisine have merged Western and Asian culinary elements to create fusion or New Asia Cuisine, or a style that has also been called a "culinary global third culture" (Scarpato and Daniele 2003).

Besides Western-style foods, other foreign cuisines are also becoming less "foreign" to Singaporeans and are being incorporated into local foodways through increased consumption and the localisation of flavours. Evidence of such changes into the traditional foodways of Singaporeans can be seen in everyday food spaces — food courts not only offer the staples of Chinese, Malay and Indian options, but often include Japanese, Thai, Korean and Western cuisines as well. Foreign foods once viewed by locals as alien, exclusive or exotic when first introduced into Singapore have become familiar foods and more easily accessible to the average Singaporean. Japanese food like *sushi*, for example, was initially perceived as an exotic food consumed exclusively by Japanese expatriates, or wealthier and more adventurous locals due to its high price. Over time, however, the price of *sushi* has become more affordable, enabling more of the local masses to consume *sushi* on a more frequent basis

(Ng 2001). In addition, the types and flavours of *sushi* in Singapore have been adjusted to fit the preferences of locals, increasing more Singaporeans' acceptance of the food. As not all Singaporeans are receptive to *sushi* containing raw fish, Japanese eateries in Singapore tend to offer more types of *sushi* made with cooked ingredients. Furthermore, they add a twist to traditional *sushi* by incorporating Singapore-inspired flavours or creating unconventional combinations, such as *otak-otak sushi*, *maki* with *achar* (fruit and vegetable pickle in spiced oil — an appetiser common in Singapore) filling, and *sushi* with corn mayonnaise (Ng 2001: 16). Similarly, Thai food was previously considered a very exotic and special cuisine when it first entered Singapore's food scene, but high tourism levels between Singapore and Thailand and the increased influx of Thai migrant labourers have somewhat diminished its lofty exoticism in Singapore. It is now seen as a commonly available food in Singapore and the increased number of Thai eateries targeting the mid-end market, like ThaiExpress, have enabled more Singaporeans to consume Thai cuisine. Overall, the changes in foodways have therefore involved two aspects — the foodways of Singaporeans have altered to include the consumption of more foreign cuisines, and original traditional cuisines from foreign countries have also undergone some modifications following their introduction into Singapore.

That foodways are fluid and temporal has led sociologist Allison James (1996: 78) to question whether food in a globalised world can still be used as a distinguishing marker of cultural identity. The fact is that cross-cultural consumption frequently occurs as people belonging to one group consume foods from across different cultures. For example, to say that Singaporeans eat mostly Chinese, Malay and Indian foods, or that Singapore food consists of mainly Chinese, Malay and Indian elements, does not capture the fact that the traditional foodways have altered over time to include global influences and that the food scene has been internationalised to include a wealth of culinary and dining options from all over the world which locals themselves often indulge in. Neither does it acknowledge the essentialisation of "Chinese", "Malay" and "Indian", failing to recognise the multiplicities that these categories hide.

On the other hand, proponents of the cultural homogenisation thesis argue that culinary globalisation will lead (indeed, has led) to the standardisation of local food cultures and tastes, ultimately resulting in the erosion of traditional foodways. This frequently debated perspective has invited its own detractors who believe that globalisation does not necessarily produce uniformity among local cultures. Instead, they argue that people adapt global culture to suit their local culture (Metcalf 2002; Allison 2000; Watson 1997; Barber 1992; Tanimura 2006: 75–76). Robertson's notion of "glocalisation" reframes the idea of globalisation as an opposing force of the local. To him, "the local is essentially included within the global" and globalisation involves both homo- and heterogenisation (Robertson 1995; Tanimura 2006: 76). He and other authors have pointed out that food is often modified to fit local cultures and palates. McDonald's, a symbol of globalisation, is a commonly cited example used to illustrate this point. Its localisation strategy sees it regularly feature items that incorporate local flavours and ingredients. In Singapore, for example, McDonald's launched its Shiok Shiok *Satay* Burgers, based on the flavour of the Singaporean dish *satay*, served with peanut sauce. Other Western fast food chains have similarly introduced localised or "Singaporeanised" versions of items on the menu. Burger King came up with a Rendang Burger, and Pizza Hut has promoted *Satay* pizza, Curry Chicken pizza, and Sweet and Sour pizza (*The Straits Times*, 13 Jul 1994).

Still, a key concern is whether the external forces of globalisation will "dilute" Singapore's traditional foodways and cause local foods to become less significant. Henderson (2014: 92–93) argues that this is unlikely, given that traditional foods are "too deeply embedded in Singapore society and culture to disappear", but recognising that they will keep evolving as the country modernises and progresses. While globalisation has indeed led to the proliferation of foreign cuisines in Singapore, she observes that this has not overshadowed the prominence of its local cuisine, and that both international and local foods can "co-exist and coalesce" (Henderson 2014: 904). Global food franchises and restaurants offering cuisines from all over the world may be enriching Singapore's dining scene, but have not yet diminished the relevance and importance of Singapore's traditional local foods. Rather, they co-exist with the local, and have added variety and vibrancy to Singapore's food scene. While foreign foodways have influenced Singapore's food culture, there is a limit to the extent of this influence. Chua (2000: 144) notes that while foreign cuisines are more widely consumed in Singapore especially as a leisure activity, internationalised foreign foods "have seldom, if at all, been incorporated and domesticated into the family kitchens and dining tables of Singaporeans". At home, traditional cuisine and local foods still largely make up the daily meals of Singaporeans. Perhaps because food represents familiarity and continuity (Henderson 2014: 913), Singaporean families usually choose to have local dishes for everyday meals in the home.

While traditional foodways in Singapore look set to stay, there are still real challenges they face. There is concern that the quality of local foods served commercially is declining due to the use of "short cut" strategies of food preparation techniques and lower quality ingredients. The hawker trade, which produces some of the best local favourite dishes, is suffering. Retiring hawkers have no one to pass their skills to as young Singaporeans are not interested in entering a low-paying trade that requires hard work. Migrant workers are taking their places, but there have been complaints that they cannot reproduce Singapore dishes to the same standards of authenticity and quality (Henderson 2011; 2014: 912). Thus, more attention has recently been directed to preserving Singapore's traditional foodways, especially local street food, to ensure its continued longevity and to protect Singapore's food heritage.

At the same time, the globalisation of Singapore food — or spread of Singapore cuisine overseas — is occurring. Local favourites like chicken rice, *satay* and *laksa* have made their way to numerous cities around the world. The international profile of Singapore food is growing through various efforts. Government initiatives play an important part. The government realises that food is a vital tourism resource that can increase visitorship to the country and increase economic revenue in the tourism sector, as well as build its culinary soft power. It also recognises the value of domestic food exports to the country's economy.

Though disappearance of local favourites in local eating outlets does not seem imminent, it would be ironic — not to mention sad — should the day arrive when local foods so commonly available today in hawker centres and coffee shops are largely replaced in such settings by foreign imports, even as they become available mainly on special celebratory occasions in local commemorative and heritage events or as part of overseas "travelling shows" and exports. Amidst the globalisation of food, the commitment to support and retain local foods through continued production and consumption within the home and beyond it signals appreciation of their symbolism and meaning, reminding Singaporeans of "who they are, and where and how they are to be located in the world" (James 1996:92, cited in Lim 2011:89).

REFERENCES

Abu Bakar A (2008) Malaysian cuisine goes global via MyKitchen. *Business Times*. http://www.btimes.com.my/Current_News/BTIMES/articles/mykitchen_xml/ Article/July 31, 2008, accessed 7 August 2009.

Allison A (2000) Sailor Moon: Japanese superheroes for global girls. In: TJ Craig (ed.) *Japan Pop: Inside the World of Japanese Popular Culture*. New York: East Gate, pp. 259–278.

Anderson EN (2011) *Breaking Bread: Recipes and Stories from Immigrant Kitchens*. Berkeley: University of California Press.

Anderson EN (2005) *Everyone Eats: Understanding Food and Culture*. New York: New York University Press.

Andrews J (2000) Chilli Peppers. In: KF Kiple and KC Ornelas (eds.) *The Cambridge World History of Food*. Cambridge: Cambridge University Press, pp. 281–287.

Barber BR (1992) Jihad vs. McWorld. *The Atlantic* **269**(3).

Barthes R (1997 (1961)) 'Towards a psychosociology of contemporary food consumption. In: C Counihan and P Van Esterik (eds.) *Food and Culture: A Reader*. New York and London: Routledge, pp. 20–27.

Bell D and Valentine G (1997) *Consuming Geographies: We are Where We Eat*. London and New York: Routledge.

Bernama Daily Malaysian News (2006) Singapore food breaks into mainstream Japanese consumer market, 27 September.

Bishop P (2011) Eating in the contact zone: Singapore foodscape and cosmopolitan timespace. *Continuum: Journal of Media & Cultural Studies* **25**(5): 637–652.

Brown JD and Backenheimer M (2006) *Berlitz Pocket Guide to Singapore*. Singapore: Berlitz Publishing.

Bryant A, Bush L and Wilk R (2013) History of globalization and food supply. In: A Murcott, W Belasco and P Jackson (eds.) *The Handbook of Food Research*. London and New York: Bloomsbury Publishing, pp. 34–49.

Business Times Singapore (2011) Scintillating showcase, 10 December.

Business Times Singapore (2011) Voila! A pop-up restaurant, 26 February.

Business Times Singapore (2006) Cashing in on S'pore cuisine, 5 October.

Carruthers A (2012) Indochine chic: Why is Vietnamese food so classy in Singapore? *Anthropology Today* **28**(2): 17–20.

Chaney S and Ryan C (2012) Analyzing the evolution of Singapore's world gourmet summit: an example of gastronomic tourism. *International Journal of Hospitality Management* **31**: 309–318.

Chang GMAM (2013) *Gastronomic Tourism: Implications for Singapore*, Unpublished Master of Arts Thesis, University of Pennsylvania, Pennsylvania. http://laudergastronomy.com/wp-content/uploads/2013/05/Gastronomic-Tourism-Implications-for-Singapore_Grace-Chang-Mazza.pdf, accessed 1 May 2015.

Channel News Asia (CNA) (2012) Culinary campaign raises international profile of Singapore food, 28 March.

Channel News Asia (CNA) (2006) Singapore festival Japan, 9 September.

Channel News Asia (CNA) (2005) Singapore cuisine making its mark in China, 12 August.

Channel News Asia (CNA) (2005) Spore food fest — Convent Garden London, 22 March.

Cheung SCH and Tan CB (2007) *Food and Foodways in Asia: Resource, Tradition and Cooking*. London and New York: Routledge.

Chua BH (2000) Where got Japanese influence in Singapore! In: E Ben-Ari and J Clammer (eds.) *Japan in Singapore: Cultural Occurrences and Cultural Flows*. Great Britain: Biddles Ltd, pp. 133–149.

Chua LW (2003) *Consuming Geographies: Gastro-Politics of Thai Food Consumption in Singapore*, Unpublished Masters Thesis, Department of Geography, Faculty of Arts and Social Sciences, National University of Singapore, Singapore.

Clave SA and Knafou R (2012) Gastronomy, Tourism and Globalisation, *Via@ International Interdisciplinary Review of Tourism*. http://www.viatourismreview.net/Appel_a_article1_EN.php, accessed 25 August 2014.

CNN Travel (2010) The best tapas bars in Singapore, 28 October. http://travel.cnn.com/singapore/eat/best-tapas-bars-singapore-263591, accessed 1 May 2015.

Cook I, Crang P and Thorpe M (2000) Regions to be cheerful: culinary authenticity and its geographies. In: I Cook, D Crouch, S Naylor and JR Ryan (eds.) *Cultural Turns/Geographical Turns*. Harlow: Prentice-Hall, pp. 109–139.

Cwiertka K and Walraven B (eds.) (2002) *Asian Food: The Global and the Local*. Richmond, Surrey: Curzon.

Daily News & Analysis (2008) Get in the swing with that Singapore sling, 16 August.

du Rand GE, Heath E and Alberts N (2003) The role of local and regional food in destination marketing: a South African situation analysis. *Journal of Travel and Tourism Marketing* 14(3/4): 97–112.

Duffy A and Yang YA (2012) Bread and circuses: food meets politics in the Singapore media. *Journalism Practice* **6**(1): 59–74.

Duruz J (2010) Four dances of the sea: cooking 'Asian' as embedded cosmopolitanism. In: J Farrer (ed.) *Globalization, Food and Social Identities in the Asia Pacific Region*. Tokyo: Sophia University Institute of Comparative Culture. http://icc.fla.sophia.ac.jp/global%20food%20papers/html/duruz.html, accessed 6 August 2014.

Duruz J (2006) Living in Singapore, travelling to Hong Kong, remembering Australia: intersections of food and place. *Journal of Australian Studies* **30**(87): 101–115.

Edge JT (ed.) (2007) *Foodways*. Chapel Hill, North Carolina: University of North Carolina Press.

Farrer J (2010) Eating the West and beating the rest: culinary occidentalism and urban soft power in Asia's global food cities. In: J Farrer (ed.) *Globalization, Food and Social Identities in the Asia Pacific Region*. Tokyo: Sophia University Institute of Comparative Culture. http://icc.fla.sophia.ac.jp/global%20food%20papers/html/farrer.html, accessed 6 August 2014.

Fox R (2007) Reinventing the gastronomic identity of Croatian tourist destinations. *Hospitality Management* **26**(3): 546–559.

Friedmann H (1994) The international relations of food: the unfolding crisis of national regulation. In: B Harriss-White and R Hoffenberg (eds.) *Food: Multidisciplinary Perspective*. Cambridge: Basil Blackwell, pp. 174–204.

FT.com (2009) A new cuisine style is transforming Singapore, 22 August.

Goh CT (1999) First World Economy, World-Class Home. *National Archives of Singapore*, 23 August. http://stars.nhb.gov.sg/stars/public/, accessed 29 August 2014.

Goode JG (1992) Food. In: R Baumann (ed.) *Folklore, Cultural Performances, and Popular Entertainments: A Communications-centered Handbook*. New York: Oxford University Press, pp. 233–245.

Goodmann D and Watts M (1997) *Globalising Food: Agrarian Questions and Global Restructuring*. London: Routledge.

Grew R (1999) *Food in Global History*. Boulder: Westview Press.

Guptill AE, Copelton DA and Lucal B (2013) *Food & Society: Principles and Paradoxes*. Malden, MA: Polity.

Hall M and Mitchell R (2002) Tourism as a force for gastronomic globalization and localization. In: AM Hjalager and G Richards (eds.) *Tourism and Gastronomy*. London: Routledge, pp. 71–90.

Health Promotion Board (2004) *Report of the National Nutrition Survey 2004*. Singapore: Health Promotion Board.

Henderson JC (2014) Food and culture: in search of a Singapore cuisine. *British Food Journal* **116**(6): 904–917.

Henderson JC (2011) Cooked food hawking and its management: the case of Singapore. *Tourism Review International* **14**(4): 201–213.

Hindustan Times (2013) Today's special — Singapore cuisine Mumbai restaurant, 10 May.

Hjalager A and Richards G (2002) *Tourism and Gastronomy*. London: Routledge.

Horng JS and Tsai C-TS (2012) Exploring marketing strategies for culinary tourism in Hong Kong and Singapore. *Asia Pacific Journal of Tourism Research* **17**(3): 277–300.

Inglis D and Gimlin D (2009) *The Globalization of Food*. Oxford and New York: Berg.

International Enterprise (IE) Singapore (2008) *Canada Gets a Flavour of Tasty Singapore*, Media release, 15 August.

Islamic Finance News (2011) Taste of Singapore at Park Regis Kris Kin Hotel — Dubai, 13 October.

James A (1996) Cooking the books: global or local identities in contemporary British food cultures? In: H David (ed.) *Cross-cultural Consumption: Global Markets, Local Realities*. London and New York: Routledge, pp. 77–92.

Kikomr (2012) Food and Globalization! *Food Communication*, 4 June. http://sites.jmu. edu/foodcomm/2012/06/04/food-and-globalization-2/, accessed 31 July 2014.

Lang T (1999) The complexities of globalization: the UK as a case study of tensions within the food system and the challenge to food policy. *Agriculture and Human Values* **16**: 169–185.

Leung RW, Ahmed ZU and Seshanna S (2001) A study of ethnic restaurants in Singapore. *International Area Review* **4**(1): 51–61.

Levinson M (2008) *The Box: How the Shipping Container made the World Smaller and the World Economy Bigger.* Princeton: Princeton University Press.

Lim CI (2011) A brief introduction to anthropological perspectives on diet: insights into the study of overseas Chinese. *Asian Culture and History* **3**(1): 86–93.

Lovallo LD (2013) *Global Cities, Global Palates: A Look at How Gastronomy and Global Cities are Interrelated and the Role of Fusion Foods*, Unpublished Masters Thesis, Master of Arts, University of Pennsylvania.

MacLaurin DJ and MacLaurin TL (2000) Customer perceptions of Singapore's theme restaurants. *The Cornell Hotel and Restaurant Administration Quarterly* **41**(3): 75–85.

Mail Today (2012) Singapore woos Delhi tastebuds, 13 January.

Mak AHN, Lumbers M and Eves A (2012) Globalisation and food consumption in tourism. *Annals of Tourism Research* **39**(1): 171–196.

Makansutra (2012) Discover and devour: Peninsula Plaza, 21 June.

Marché (2007*) Marché International opens Marché VivoCity, its first wholly owned and managed Marché restaurant outside of Europe*, Media release, 8 February.

Matsumoto H (2006) The world's thriving sushi business: the popularity of sushi overseas — Asia and Oceania. *Food Culture* **13**: 14–19. http://www.kikkoman. co.jp/kiifc/foodculture/pdf_13/e_014_019.pdf, accessed 31 July 2014.

Media (2010) Is Singapore ready for renewed Domino's effect? 11 February.

Metcalf P (2002) Hulk Hogan in the rainforest. In TJ Craig and R King (eds.) *Global goes Local: Popular Culture in Asia.* Hawaii: University of Hawaii Press.

Mintz SW and Du Bois CM (2002) The anthropology of food and eating. *Annual Review of Anthropology* **30**: 99–119.

MoneySmart (2014) Mouthwatering value-for-money Mexican restaurants in Singapore, 5 June.

Monetary Authority of Singapore (MAS) (2014) *Singapore Financial Centre.* http:// www.mas.gov.sg/singapore-financial-centre.aspx, accessed 26 August 2014.

Ng W-M (2001) Popularization and localization of sushi in Singapore: an ethnographic survey. *New Zealand Journal of Asian Studies* **3**(1): 7–19.

Nuetzenadel A and Trentmann F (2008) Introduction: mapping food and globalization. In: A Nuetzenadel and F Trentmann (eds.) *Food and Globalization: Consumption, Markets and Politics in the Modern World.* London: Berg, pp. 1–18.

Omar M (2008) Fast food chains, *Singapore Infopedia*. Singapore: National Library Board. http://eresources.nlb.gov.sg/infopedia/articles/SIP_1037_2008-12-03. html, accessed 25 August 2014.

Phillips L (2006) Food and globalization. *Annual Review of Anthropology* **35**: 37–57.

PR Newswire and Hilton Worldwide (2014) Singapore 3rd top culinary destination among APAC travellers, 19 February.

Ray K (2010) A taste for ethnic difference: American gustatory imagination in a globalizing world. In: J Farrer (ed.) *Globalization, Food and Social Identities in the Asia Pacific Region*. Tokyo: Sophia University Institute of Comparative Culture. http://icc.fla.sophia.ac.jp/global%20food%20papers/html/ray.html, accessed 7 August 2014.

Remizowski L (2010) Flair for fusion: wave of hybrid eateries reflect Boro's diversity. *Daily News* (New York), 21 November.

Richards G (2002) Gastronomy: an essential ingredient in tourism production and consumption? In: AM Hjalager and G Richards (eds.) *Tourism and Gastronomy*. London: Routledge, pp. 3–20.

Ritzer G (1995) *The McDonaldization of Society*. London: Sage.

Ro J (2009) Korean cuisine symposium in Seoul. *Korea Net*. http://www.korea.net/news/News/NewsView.asp?serial_no=20090409007&part=106&SearchDay= April 9, 2009, accessed 7 August 2014.

Robertson R (1995) Glocalization: time-space and homogeneity-heterogeneity. In: M Featherstone, S Lash and R Robertson (eds.) *Global Modernities*. London: Sage Publications, pp. 25–44.

Robbins B (1998) Comparative cosmopolitanisms. In: B Robbins and P Cheah (eds.) *Cosmopolitics: Thinking and Feeling beyond the Nation*. Minneapolis and London: University of Minnesota Press, pp. 246–264.

Scarpato R and Daniele R (2003) New global cuisine: tourism, authenticity and sense of place in postmodern gastronomy. In: CM Hall, L Sharpley, R Mitchell, N Maconis and B Cambourne (eds.) *Food Tourism around the World: Development, Management and Markets*. Oxford: Butterworth-Heinemann, pp. 296–313.

Shanghai Daily (2011) Savor a taste of Singapore cuisine, 9 August.

Shepard S (2001) *Pickled, Potted and Canned: The Story of Food Preserving*. London: Headline.

Singapore Government News (2009) Singapore cuisine enjoys growing popularity around the world, 10 November.

Singapore Tourism Board (STB) (2004) *Makan Delights: An Insider's Guide to Singapore's Unique Flavours*. Singapore: Singapore Tourism Board.

Singstat (2013) *Yearbook of Statistics Singapore*. http://www.singstat.gov.sg/publications/publications_and_papers/reference/yearbook_2013/yos2013.pdf, accessed 4 September 2014.

Sorj B and Wilkinson J (1985) Modern food technology: industrialising nature. *International Social Science Journal* **37**(3): 301–314.

Symons M (1993) *The Shared Table: Ideas for Australian Cuisine.* Canberra: AGPS.

Tan S and Yeoh B (2006) Negotiating cosmopolitanism in Singapore's fictional landscape. In: J Binnie, J Holloway, S Millington and C Young (eds.) *Cosmopolitan Urbanism.* London: Routledge, pp. 146–168.

Tanimura T (2006) *Makan Sushi: Authenticating Japanese Restaurants in Singapore,* Unpublished Masters Thesis, Southeast Asian Program, National University of Singapore, Singapore.

Tarulevicz N (2013) *Eating Her Curries and Kway: A Cultural History of Food in Singapore.* Illinois: University of Illinois Press.

Tarulevicz N (2011) Singapore. In: K Albala (ed.) *Food Cultures of the World Encyclopedia.* Santa Barbara, California: Greenwood Publishing, pp. 235–245.

Thang LL (1999) Consuming 'Things from Japan' in Singapore, Working Paper for Sumitomo Foundation Project 1998/1999: Singapore.

The Asian Age (2012) Singapore express, 5 January.

The Boston Globe (1995) Singapore swing, 4 October.

The Gold Coast Bulletin (2013) Singapore restaurant chain opts for Robina, 5 April.

The Hindu (1998) Showcasing Singapore flavour — S'pore Food Fest Taj Hotel, 14 September.

The Korea Herald (2007) Singapore restaurants offer more than chilli crab, 10 February.

The Pioneer (2009) A mélange of flavours, 20 November.

The Straits Times (2014) New on the hawker menu, 27 April.

The Straits Times (2013) Jamie Oliver to open restaurant at VivoCity next year, 9 October.

The Straits Times (2012) 3 famous Korean chains to launch in Singapore, 2 October.

The Straits Times (2009) Local flavours go global, 26 July.

The Straits Times (2008) Old Chang Kee opens Chengdu eatery, 29 October.

The Straits Times (2006) Nasi padang goes chic, 26 November.

The Straits Times (2005) Seoul food, 8 May.

The Straits Times (1998) Spicing Britain with laksa, 23 November.

The Straits Times (1994) Western food, Singapore flavours, 13 July.

The Sydney Morning Herald (2007) Hawker treats without the heat, 29 September.

The Wall Street Journal (2010) Singapore's hotter tables, 14 October.

Today (2006) Recipe for greater recognition, 19 July.

Turner J (2005) *Spice: The History of a Temptation.* New York: Vintage.

Wang HJ (2006) Food and the Singapore young consumer. *Young Consumers: Insight and Ideas for Responsible Marketers* **7**(4): 53–59.

Watson JL (1997) *Golden Arches East: McDonald's in East Asia.* California: Stanford University Press.

Watts M and Goodman D (1997) Agrarian questions: global appetite, local metabolism. In: D Goodman and M Watts (eds.) *Globalising Food: Agrarian Questions and Global Restructuring.* London: Routledge, pp. 1–34.

Weekend Mail (2006) A touch of Singapore, 4 November.

Wilhelmina Q, Joost J, George E and Guido R (2010) Globalization vs. localization: global food challenges and local solutions. *International Journal of Consumer Studies* **34**(3): 357–366.

World Travel and Tourism Council (WTTC) (2014) *Travel and Tourism Economic Impact 2014: Singapore.* London, UK: WTTC.

Yamanaka M (2009) *ASEAN-Japan Cultural Relations: A Japanese Perspective.* Speech presented at the Forum on ASEAN-Japan Cultural Relations, Orchard Hotel, Singapore, 24 July.

Yoshino K (2010) Malaysian cuisine: a case of neglected culinary globalization. In: J Farrer (ed.) *Globalization, Food and Social Identities in the Asia Pacific Region.* Tokyo: Sophia University Institute of Comparative Culture. http://icc.fla.sophia. ac.jp/global%20food%20papers/html/yoshino.html, accessed 7 August 2014.

Young C, Diep M and Drabble S (2006) Living with difference? The 'cosmopolitan city' and urban reimagining in Manchester, UK. *Urban Studies* **43**(10): 1687–1714.

Index